AF506009

Transnational Economic Cooperation and the Nation State
Volume I

By
Gerhard Kümmel

Translated from the German
by
Carvel de Bussy

SOCIAL SCIENCE MONOGRAPHS, BOULDER
DISTRIBUTED BY COLUMBIA UNIVERSITY PRESS, NEW YORK
2001

CONTENTS

TABLES

ABBREVIATIONS

AA	Auswärtiges Amt
AAC	Alliance Aluminium Compagnie, Basel
ADAP	Akten zur Deutschen und Auswärtigen Politik
ADF	Außenhandelsdifferenzfaktor
AEG	Allgemeine Elektrizitäts-Gesellschaft AG, Berlin
AEI	Associated Electrical Industries
AER	*American Economic Review*
Aganco	Agfa-Ansco Corp., Binghampton
Agfa	Aktiengesellschaft für Anilin-Fabrikation
AHR	*American Historical Review*
AIG	American I.G. Chemical Corp., New York
AJES	*American Journal of Economics and Sociology*
AJS	*American Journal of Sociology*
Alcoa	Aluminum Co. of America
AMC	American Magnesium Corp., Niagara Falls
AmSt	*Amerikastudien - American Studies*
Ansco	Ansco Photoproducts Corp.
Antidolor	Antidolor Manufacturing Co.
AP	*Außenpolitik*
APSR	*American Political Science Review*
Argument	*Das Argument*
Atlas	Atlas Powder Company, Wilmington, Del.
ATT	American Telephone & Telegraph Co.
Autelco	Automatic Electric Co. of Chicago
Babco	Bancamerica Blair Corp.
BAK	Bundesarchiv Koblenz
BAP	Bundesarchiv Potsdam
BASF	Badische Anilin- & Soda-Fabrik AG, Ludwigshafen
Bayer	Farbenfabriken vormals Friedrich Bayer AG, Leverkusen
BFDC	Bureau of Foreign and Domestic Commerce
BHR	*Business History Review*
BIG	Baseler IG
BTGAC	Board of Trade for German-American Commerce
Calco	Calco Chemical Co., Inc.
CAR	Commercial Attaches' Reports
CEH	*Central European History*
Chemnyco	Chemnyco Inc., New York
CIT	Compania Internacional de Teléfonos S.A., Buenos Aires
CMC	Centrale des Matières Colorantes
Cook	Cook Laboratories Inc.
CSSH	*Comparative Studies in Society and History*

CTT	Compania Telegrafico Telefonica del Plata, Buenos Aires
Daedalus	*Daedalus*
DAG	Dynamit AG, vormals Alfred Nobel & Co., Hamburg/Troisdorf
DAPG	Deutsch-Amerikanische Petroleum-Gesellschaft
DCC	Dow Chemical Company, Midland
DDP	Deutsche Demokratische Partei
Degussa	Deutsche Gold- & Silber-Scheideanstalt vorm. Roessler, Frankfurt/M.
DF	Decimal File
DIHT	Deutscher Industrie- und Handelstag
DP	E.I. Du Pont de Nemours & Co., Wilmington, DE
DPL-AHC	Detroit Public Library—Automotive History Collection
DRC	Dillon, Read & Company
EA	*Europa-Archiv*
EDF	Exportdifferenzfaktor
EGC	Ethyl Gasoline Corp.
EHR	*Economic History Review*
Electroclor	Sociedad Anónima Industrial Y Comercial Electroclor
Ericsson	Telefon Aktiebolaget L.M. Ericsson, Stockholm
F&G	Felten & Guilleaume Carlswerk AG, Köln-Mühlheim
FA	*Foreign Affairs*
FAZ	*Frankfurter Allgemeine Zeitung*
FBI	Federal Bureau of Investigations
FDRL	Franklin D. Roosevelt Library, Hyde Park, NY
FMC	Ford Motor Company, Dearborn, Detroit, MI
FMCAG	Ford Motor Company AG, Berlin, Köln
FPR	*Foreign Policy Reports*
GAFC	General Aniline & Film Corp.
GAW	General Aniline Works Inc., New York
GCC	Grasselli Chemical Co., Cleveland
GDC	Grasselli Dyestuffs Corp., Delaware
GE	General Electric Co., Schenectady, NY
GE-GB	General Electric Co., Ltd. (Großbritannien)
Gebechem	Generalbevollmächtigter für Sonderfragen der chemischen Erzeugung
Gesfürel	Gesellschaft für elektrische Unternehmungen—Ludwig Loewe & Co. AG, Berlin
GG	*Geschichte und Gesellschaft*
GM	General Motors Company, Detroit, MI
Goodyear	The Goodyear Tire & Rubber Co.
GR	General Records
GU-SC	Georgetown University, Washington D.C.—Special

	Collections
HBS-SC	Harvard Business School, Baker Library—Special Collections
Hercules	Hercules Powder Co., Wilmington, Del.
HFM&GV	Henry Ford Museum & Greenfield Village. Ford Motor Company Archives, Dearborn, MI
HJWG	*Hamburger Jahrbuch für Wirtschafts- und Gesellschaftspolitik*
HM-DPA	Hagley Museum - Du Pont Archives, Wilmington, Del.
Hoechst	Hoechst AG, Frankfurt am Main
HU-HL	Harvard University, Houghton Library
HZ	*Historische Zeitschrift*
IA	*International Affairs*
IAA	Internationale Automobilausstellung
ICI	Imperial Chemical Industries, Ltd., London
IDF	Importdifferenzfaktor
IEA	International Electrical Association, Ltd., London
IG	IG Farbenindustrie AG
IG Chemie	Internationale Gesellschaft für Chemische Unternehmungen AG
IGE	International General Electric Company
IHP	International Hydrogenation Patents Co., Ltd., Vaduz
IJ	*International Journal*
INACA	International Notification and Compensation Agreement
IO	*International Organization*
IP	*International Peacekeeping*
IPSR	*International Political Science Review*
ISEC	International Standard Electric Corp. of New York
ISQ	*International Studies Quarterly*
ITT	International Telephone & Telegraph Co., Chicago
Iweco	International Western Electric Co. of New York
JAP	*Jahrbuch für Auswärtige Politik*
Jasco	Joint American Study Co.
JBAW	*Jahrbuch der Bayrischen Akademie der Wissenschaften*
JCH	*Journal of Contemporary History*
JCR	*Journal of Conflict Resolution*
JEH	*Journal of Economic History*
JfG	*Jahrbuch für Geschichte von Staat, Wirtschaft und Gesellschaft Lateinamerikas*
JISWA	*Journal of Interamerican Studies and World Affairs*
Kodak	Eastman Kodak Co.
Koppel	Koppel & Co.
liberal	*liberal. Vierteljahreshefte für Politik und Kultur*
LOC-MD	Library of Congress, Washington D.C.—

	Manuscript Division
Lorenz	C. Lorenz AG
MA	*Mid-America*
MDC	Magnesium Development Co.
Metz	H.A. Metz Laboratories Inc.
MGM	*Militärgeschichtliche Mitteilungen*
MWT	Mitteleuropäischer Wirtschaftstag
Nacco	National Aniline & Chemical Co., New York
NARG	National Archives, Washington, Record Group
NH	Norsk Hydro Elektrisk Kvaelstof AS, Oslo
NL	Nachlaß
NPL	*Neue Politische Literatur*
NSDAP	Nationalsozialistische Deutsche Arbeiterpartei
NSDAP-AO	Auslandsorganisation der NSDAP
NYT	*New York Times*
OF	Official Files
OKW	Oberkommando der Wehrmacht
Opel	Adam Opel AG, Rüsselsheim
Osram	Osram GmbH KG, Berlin
PA-AA	Politisches Archiv des Auswärtigen Amtes, Bonn
PAH	*Perspectives in American History*
Philips	N.V. Philips Gloeilampen-Fabrieken, Eindhoven
Phoebus	Phoebus S.A. Compagnie Industrielle pour le Développement de l'Éclairage
polis	*polis*
PPF	President's Personal Files
PSF	President's Secretaries Files
PSQ	*Political Science Quarterly*
PVS	*Politische Vierteljahresschrift*
R&H	Röhm & Haas Co.
RCA	Radio Corporation of America
RDA	Reichsverband der Deutschen Automobilindustrie
RDI	Reichsverband der Deutschen Industrie
RGI	Reichsgruppe Industrie
RESE	*Revue Études Sud-Est Europe*
RLM	Reichsluftfahrtministerium
RM	Reichsmark
Roessler	Roessler & Hasslacher Chemical Co.
RTAA	Reciprocal Trade Agreements Act
RVM	Reichsverkehrsministerium
RWiM	Reichswirtschaftsministerium
RWiMin	Reichswirtschaftsminister
S&H	Siemens & Halske AG, Berlin
SAM	Siemens Apparate & Maschinen GmbH
SaS	*Science and Society*

SB	Siemens Brothers & Co., Ltd., London
Schuchardt	Ferdinand Schuchardt Berliner Fernsprech- und Telegrafenwerke
SEG	Standard Elektrizitäts-Gesellschaft AG
SFr	Schweizer Franken
SIG	Standard-I.G. Co.
SODC	Standard Oil Development Company
SONJ	Standard Oil Company of New Jersey
Sowjetwissenschaft	*Sowjetwissenschaft*
SPI	Sterling Products Inc., New York
SRW	Siemens-Reiniger-Werke
SSW	Siemens-Schuckert-Werke, Berlin
STC	Standard Telephones & Cables Ltd.
Stoewer	Stoewer-Werke, Stettin
SW	*Soziale Welt*
Tea	Technischer Ausschuß der IG
TNK	Transnationaler Konzern
Tradition	*Tradition*
U+F	*Ursachen und Folgen*
Universitas	*Universitas. Zeitschrift für interdisziplinäre Wissenschaft*
Vauxhall	Vauxhall Motors Ltd.
VAW	Vereinigte Aluminiumwerke
VfZ	*Vierteljahreshefte für Zeitgeschichte*
VJP	Vierjahresplan
Vowi:	Volkswirtschaftliche Abteilung der IG
VSWG:	*Vierteljahresschrift für Sozial- und Wirtschaftsgeschichte*
WA-BASF	Werksarchiv der BASF AG, Ludwigshafen
WA-Bayer	Werksarchiv der Bayer AG, Leverkusen
WA-Hoe	Werksarchiv der Hoechst AG, Frankfurt am Main
WCC	Winthrop Chemical Co. Inc., New York
Westinghouse	Westinghouse Electric & Manufacturing Co., Pittsburgh, PA
Wigru	Wirtschaftsgruppe
Winthrop	Winthrop Chemical Co., Delaware
Wipo	Wirtschaftspolitische Abteilung der IG
Wirtschaftsdienst	*Wirtschaftsdienst*
WP	*World Politics*
WPQ	*Western Political Quarterly*
WWA	*Weltwirtschaftliches Archiv*
ZfP	*Zeitschrift für Politik*
ZfS	*Zeitschrift für die gesamte Staatswissenschaft*
ZfU	*Zeitschrift für Unternehmensgeschichte*

PREFACE

Introduction

Modern international relations are characterized by the explosive increase in the mergers of more and more areas of life and of specialties as part of the process of globalization. The creation of a world market and a single, *global* international system by the beginning of the century means that the world is no longer a purely geographical unit, but has obviously become a political, economic, and in Luhmann's sense, socially a global association for interaction. A growing number of actors of the most varied nature are participating in these networks of interaction. Transnational, transregional and global activities are being developed by governmental and private organizations. Along with the contacts of nations at governmental levels come international dealings by institutions, organizations, associations and commercial enterprises down to individuals. They turn international relations into a varied fabric of transactions with reciprocal functions.

The development of these interdependencies leads to the reduction of differences between the agencies involved. Mutual involvement and reciprocal functions can result in positive, i.e., peaceful forms of conflict-solving and thus in the view of the idealists bring about civilizing processes in international relations. According to the hopes of those who believe in progress, in the end there could be a world at peace, in short, "eternal peace." Although this world would not be free of conflict, nevertheless the ways of settling the conflicts would remain reasonable and consensual following rules in any case below the threshold of violent and military attempts at solution.

The end of the East-West conflict and the structural breakdown to which it led in international relations permitted new hope to grow in this respect for a certain time. It was expressed particularly in great expectations regarding a decisive role for the United Nations in the area of world order, as the UN often acquired the characteristics or a world state beyond the rivalries of the super powers. However, in the meantime these hopes have either evaporated or have been reduced to a realistic dimension. But these and similar exaggerated theories appear at irregular intervals on the stage of world politics, as, for example, after the First World War relative to the League of Nations and after the Second World War relative to the United Nations. Realism and skepticism are needed in dealing with this exuberant optimism which returns from time to time.

The option followed in the present study of touching upon the skeptical and realistic view of the world exists in the frame of an historical retrospect of the international system in the years 1919-1939, and more exactly looking back at part of that system, the German-American political and foreign trade relations especially in the 1930s. This look backward will shot that in spite of extensive processes towards globalization and in spite of a sizeable increase in the level of interdependence, during the 1920s the degree of interdependence was drastically reduced and the development of interdependence does not automatically prevent the occurrence of conflicts and their settlement by military means.

Viewed in retrospect, the period from 1918 to 1939 is usually seen from the standpoint of the two world wars. In particular, the Second World War overshadows the events of the period between the wars, although occurring later. This historical era is analyzed from the viewpoint of the disaster of the Second World War in a biased manner—a procedure which often forces analysis into the corset of a restricted framework of interpretation and gives an historical event a one-dimensional, even unavoidable quality. The possibility of another development is neglected because of the reality of the actual event. On the other hand, we shall try here to "win back the openness of a future of which we already know how it is to end."

The epoch-making significance which is accorded the worldwide economic crisis at the end of the 1920s and the beginnings of the 1930s can be used especially as an example of the difficulties and impossibilities of *ex post facto* studies where what was future at that time is overemphasized with respect to its importance for what was the present then. Generally most of the burden for explaining the politico-military disaster is placed on the economic catastrophe through construction of a causal connection between a great depression, the rise of National Socialism and the outbreak of the Second World War. A connection of this type should indeed not be denied, but can also shut out the view to alternatives, since the economic crisis did not necessarily lead to an international political system characterized by unilateralism and confrontation. In view of the unfavorable economic situation, the Western powers actually adopted in the second half of the 1930s a cooperative strategy aimed at preserving peace: one of international understanding at that time of interdependence, which was sequentially followed as well as the route actually taken, which resulted in fragmentation of the international system. Interdependencies must thus be viewed in the framework of politico-economic decisions (and so, in the final analysis, that of the human factor).

Those acting in the international economic arena added other stress points in contrast to the main lines of the worldwide political development. They attempted to maintain and expand the forms of transnational cooperation which had been undertaken in the 1920s. For this reason, in our exposé we shall also include developments from the 1920s, when international cartels were put together and German and American firms either resumed commercial relationships from before the war or set up new ones and entered the German or American market. The disintegration of the world market led finally to increased efforts towards international arrangements in which American and German companies took part. They involved adaptation of existing cartels to the new conditions, creation of new cartels and bilateral agreements for regulation of the markets and thus controlling turbulence.

The concrete area of investigation in this study lies, then, in the amazing parallelism of economic, transnational cooperation and political non-cooperation and even confrontation in German-American relations. This situation, this relationship and this development require explanation. By explaining it, one comes upon the question of the relationship between politics and economy. Views on this relationship, as Franz L. Neumann has shown, "are dominated by stereotypes." Thus, at one end of the debate economy exercises priority, and at the other, politics. In this respect, we have put forward the thesis that in general a clear domination of one area over the other seems to be the exception, instead of which there is an alternating influence in the course of which the importance of each shifts as time passes. For it is only with such an assumption that the (apparent) paradox of economic cooperation and political dissociation can be explained.

This study deals, then, with the effects of continuing commercial relations on the political antagonism between the US and Germany which developed at the beginning of the 1930s and the reactions of the companies to that dualism. It is possible that they contributed to it or the efforts at transnational cooperation had a delaying and softening effect at the politico-diplomatic level. On the other hand, we shall study the consequences for company cooperation of the growing friend-enemy relationship in the political sector and the ways the governments reacted to the continuing cooperation between companies. The governments would eventually allow the transnational relations a free had, perhaps because they did not have the necessary resources to change them. However, they could have influenced the transnational relations in a repressive way and demanded that they adapt to the course of politics. In this case one might expect a difference between the German and American governments, as they presented different political and cultural traditions in governmental intervention and in the worldwide economic crisis followed different, even diametrically opposed policies. Whereas Germany turned its back on parliamentary democracy and changed into an authoritarian and totalitarian state of National Socialist type, the US held fast to the democratic constitutionality of its political system.

The theoretical problem of the present study can be solved by analysis of the role and significance of the national state with respect to the increasing interdependence and advance of globalization and transnational processes in international relations. This relates to the "perennial question of the twentieth century: is the state gaining power or losing it" This includes analysis of the "peace strategy" function of transnational relations and interdependencies which obviously fail (as shown by the Second World War at the close of the period under consideration here).

Dealing with this project starts with a theoretical statement and approach to the problem primarily based on theories of international political economy. Here the point of departure is a (neo)realistic view of international relations. Following are descriptive empirical sections on historical events, at the beginning of which is a chapter on the general evolution and gradual drying up of German-American trade.

Afterwards there is an outline of the German-American political antagonism particularly in the area of foreign economic policy. It sketches the growth and development of the political and commercial conflict and gives a description of trade relations. In this we also deal with the attempted influence of transnational agencies. In contrast to this we have tried to illustrate the forms of economic cooperation on the part of German and American companies. The selection of enterprises was made on the basis of access to historical sources on the one hand, and in view of their significance and effect on the other. This resulted in concentration on the automobile, electrical and chemical industries. In line with Knut Borchhard's warning, a "later black painting in their ideology which points to a political and even more so an ethical-moral failing on the part of the involved concerns vis-à-vis the National Socialist regime which may have had a bearing on their economic marketing practices" was not intended. Recognizing the political power of capitalism, we have adopted a theory that political, and even more so moral, considerations as a matter of principle do not play a decisive role in economic matters, unless they show promise of commercial profit. In this chapter we also deal with the effect of trade relations in the political sphere and influences stemming from politics. It must always be kept in mind that the descriptions in these chapters, which are pre-eminently historical, can only give us "partial truth in retrospect." The concluding section reflects the knowledge we have acquired in the theoretical area, traces the relationship between the state and transnational policy and evaluates the effects of interdependency on peace strategy.

In this framework, Biersteker's thesis appears to be correct, saying that theoretical assertions such as those in this study must take into account the context surrounding them. "Theory is context bounded and emerges either consciously or unconsciously in the service of (or driven by) particular interests." Certainly, where these manifest and latent interests lie is estimated in different ways, but one this is clear: in his research, as indicated above, the author *also* sought the theoretical results of historical observations' relevance to the present situation after the end of the East-West conflict, which has to been seen as an intensified fragmentation and regionalization as a reaction to the advancing processes of globalization. The neo-realistic viewpoint developed in this study thus concurs with others. Indeed, their significance should not be minimized, inasmuch as "theoretical pluralism is the only possible response to the multiple realities of a complex world." However, it is, as no other, of fundamental, irrevocable importance for analysis of international relations.

Source Material

Most of the historical and empirical parts of the present study are based on previously unpublished sources. In the field of the chemical industry, the presentation is primarily based on IG Farben collections, which I was allowed to study through the friendly support of BASF AG in Ludwigshafen, the Bayer AG in Leverkusen and the Hoechst AG in Frankfurt-am-Main, and on collections of the Commercial Archives of the DuPont Co. in Wilmington, Delaware. The few archives of the Standard Oil Co. of New Jersey which are still available, have not been opened for study, according to information from the Exxon Corp. However, a few references were found in the Harvard Business School, Baker Library, in Boston, Massachusetts.

The section on the automobile industry profited from the considerable material in the commercial archives of the Ford Motor Company in Dearborn, Michigan. This was supplemented by the legacy of James D. Mooney, who was for many years head of the Foreign Section of the General Motors Co., at Georgetown University in Washington, D.C., some materials from the Detroit Public Library–Automotive Section, and the Alfred P. Sloan material at the Harvard Business School in Boston. In the regard, thanks must go to Professor Alfred D. Chandler, Jr., who permitted study of the Sloan collection. On the other hand, the archives of the General Motors Co. of Detroit were not opened to the author when he requested them. The archives of Ford AG in Cologne and of Adam Opel AG in Rüsselsheim possess no material for the subject undertaken here due to wartime damage.

The same is true for the historical collections of AEG AG relative to the electrical industry. There could be no access to the archives of Siemens AG in Munich during the research phase of this study, as extensive, time-consuming rebuilding and expansion were being carried out, which did not allow use of the archives. While a request to the General Electric Company was rejected, several informative documents concerning ITT were found in the National Archives in Washington.

In spite of this incomplete availability of sources, the gaps were sufficiently filled by collections in the National Archives and the Library of Congress in Washington, D.C., the Franklin D. Roosevelt Library at Hyde Park, New York, the Federal Archives at Koblenz, with its branch at Potsdam, the Political Archives of the Foreign Office and the volume of references in relevant secondary literature. In this, important materials in the National Archives permitted access to company papers used in antitrust cases.

The section on German-American foreign trade policy is based, beside the archives mentioned above, on published source materials on German and American foreign policy.

I
BASIC THEORETICAL CONSIDERATIONS*

A Model for International Relations

The overall many-sided texture of international relations is characterized by an extraordinarily high and constantly increasing degree of complexity and multidimensionalism. Regarding this phenomenon, Robert Musil said in 1922 that when one looked at the international relations of that time, at first glance one saw "nothing." One can approach this "nothing," or, on the other hand, this almost incomprehensible totality, meanwhile through Ernst-Otto Czempiel's application and expansion of the structural systemic theory of David Easton, who proposed the "grill model" as a thoughtfully constructed image of the international constellation.

It is conceived as an "asymmetrical, three dimensional broken grill." In certain parts of the grill one finds an apparently tight knot, a confusion of facet-like bonds (especially between economically advanced industrial nations like the western democracies), whereas elsewhere the model has a much thinner structure (as in developing countries, and also the socialist countries of the postwar era) and sometimes even presents relatively isolated sections (as, for example, North Korea or occasionally China). Up to now, only nations were named as components of the grill model, but we must now take account of non-national members of international agencies beyond transnational economic enterprises to include private persons. Consequently, the totality of this grill which integrates complex endless interactions and relations without effort is as is inconceivable as its graphic expression can only be incomplete; therefore, simplification and reduction cannot be avoided. It seems sensible to concentrate on sections relating to certain problems, which will be attempted in the present study.

---

* The reader is referred to the original German text for detailed footnotes.

Approaches to the Subject Under Investigation and the Methodology

The section chosen here deals with the inter- and intra-relations of German and American major companies against the background of the development of political and economic relations between the United States of America and Germany in the period between the wars and particularly in the 1930s. Consequently, the central players in this investigation are economic enterprises and nations and their representatives at that time. Their actions, reactions and interactions are the subject of this analysis. The assumption already indicated that the inter- and intra-relations of concerns cannot be considered separately—and this is a fundamental thesis of this study—must be extended to larger areas while dealing with the bilateral relationship between the US and Germany. They must be arranged into a more comprehensive context.

The different facets and ways of looking at the problem and the varying levels of the analysis arise from the fact that the operators, nations and companies work in different subsystems of the international system and international constellation. For the purposes of this study we can separate first the operators' level and the level of the international system or the international constellation. As time passes they all undergo processes of change, requiring differentiation between the changes of single operators and transformations in the structure of the system and the constellation.

In the first rigid approach to the nation as operator and its place in the various levels of analysis, the nation can be considered as a collectivity which exercises sovereignty and monopoly over the legitimate use of force within a particular territory. Nations and their governments and authorized decision-makers, thinking of the common good, strive for the best possible position in the areas of security and prosperity, both at home and abroad. Nations (or quasi-national groups) are the primary actors in the international political system, which is anarchic and unequal in structure and based on the principle of self-help. In this context anarchy does not mean chaos, but only the absence of a supra-national institution of governmental nature. Although there are variations in power in this international system and therefore disparity, it has no formal hierarchical structure. Thus, ignoring power differences between nations, international law stresses the similarity of national actors. From this, Aron concluded there is a "combination of formal democracy and real oligarchy."

Nevertheless, the differences in power do not in fact imply hierarchy in the strict sense, as there is no automatism in form by which the more powerful of the actors has its way in every case. Besides, the international political system and its actor form a "primitive society" which is bound by a precise minimal code of laws and norms, as, for example, international law, the idea of sovereignty and diplomacy. Nations pursue their interests through discussion with other nations. Here, their foreign policy interacts with that of the others and this interaction grows into international policy.

On the other hand, commercial enterprises are non-governmental; they work primarily in the field of prosperity and are bound to a special interest. Their goal is to maximize profits, increasing them for the owner or owners of the enterprise. They operate under rules of competition within a national context, in a national economic system. However, their business activity may extend beyond national borders if they become involved in certain segments of the world market or in the whole world market. They become thereby transnational operators and their transnational "face" does not result from their direct investments abroad or their subsidiary companies. Their participation in international cartels and agreements must be taken into account. Transnational concerns (TNC), that is, "large companies with business activity in several countries," maintain through their transnational business activity relations with natural or legal persons of different countries and in certain cases also with the governments of those countries. These relations are looked upon as transnational policy. With this business activity outside national borders where they originate, the TNCs operate within the international economic system.

If, through interaction within and between the international political and economic systems, certain repetitive processes and structures occur, which can be characterized as regional, geographic or sectional, then we are speaking of international systems where, as with concentric overlapping circles, an operator may belong to several international systems. The sum of these transnational and inter-country contacts, of transnational and international policy reflects the concept of international relations. As, according to the Aristotelian concept of the whole, the whole is more than the sum of its parts, so the totality of these international relations and structures is also referred to as an international constellation.

Thus it has already been indicated that the international political system and the international economic system do not form exclusive worlds, but stand in interrelation to each other. Implicit in this is the assumption that the two spheres of politics and economy or international policy and international economy cannot be clearly separated.

> On the motivational level political and economic factors are frequently so closely intertwined that they cannot be disentangled. In addition, regardless of motivations, politics and economics are almost inevitably linked at the systemic level. An international economic system is affected by the international political system existing at the time, and vice versa.

The three recognizable levels of analysis also do not stand immediately beside or above each other, but partially overlap, influence and limit each other mutually by processes of interpenetration. Interpenetrability may be described as follows: "causes and effects typically move laterally from subsystem to subsystem, but may also move vertically from one level to the next, even leaping over levels." Altogether, the solution of the relations or structural assessment is based on the agent-structure problem in international relations, according to which agents as well as structures constitute one another and thus are "co-determined." Kenneth Waltz expressed this as "the structure of the system and its interacting units mutually affect each other."

Study of these reciprocal relationships may occasionally turn into brinkmanship, for the influence of the international system on the agents may be just as little overestimated as the influence of the agents on the international system is underestimated. The change and transformation of the international system has its origin in the subsystems, i.e., in the agents, especially the more important among them. They come up against processes of change within the system to which other agents reply. This can itself lead to transformation of the system.

The inter- and intra-business relationships of German and American companies must, then, be assigned their place in a national political and economic context, on the one hand, and against the background of developments within the international political and commercial system as well as the international constellation on the other. The question of relations between companies in two countries touches, then, onto a many-sided and complex problem area which may be approached microscopically, as it were, through the use of different "focal distances" and "objectives."

First, attention must be paid to the commercial relations between German and American concerns and the relations within company structure, that is, between company headquarters in one country and a daughter company at any given time in another. This level of transnational relations between commercial enterprises participating in foreign trade and operating abroad is at the micro-level. This raises the question of the factors which entered into business policy, the commercial strategies followed by the firms in their work abroad, the method chosen for the foreign undertaking and the influence of international political economy and its variations on commercial policy.

Thus, company relations must be reflected at the macro level in the light of development of bilateral economic relations relative to changes in the worldwide economic system. This implies logically further differentiation. On the one hand, company relations have to be viewed against the background of development and changes in bilateral foreign trade and the effect of this bilateral trade on the overall foreign trade of the countries. On the other hand, government policies on foreign trade in both countries must be considered, since the trade relations of the nations, i.e., the current governments, will be modeled on the specific form of their foreign trade policies. This is a special area in politics, with specific patterns for negotiation, groups of participants, special legal developments and institutions.

Foreign trade policy is considered to be part of foreign policy, but has less room for operation. It is the point of intersection between foreign trade relations and international policy in the form of interacting foreign policies and a seam between the international economic and the international political systems. It lies in an area of tension between foreign policy and domestic trade policy and reflects a compromise by both. Foreign trade policy is influenced by the views on foreign trade and foreign affairs of the current leaders in the government under discussion, and the interests behind them of concerned economic groups and other social groups and pressure groups. These opinion-building processes, which stem from domestic policies and intra-social sources and affect concrete trade and economic agreements, excise taxes and other like matters, reflect the perception of their participants regarding developments in the world market. Thus, the structure of the world market represents certain framing parameters which must be adhered to in bilateral trade relations. Consequently, foreign trade policy is fundamentally influenced by the restrictions and possibilities of the international economic structure and its reception by the responsible parties of the current political system. Thus, protectionism and free trade are not solely the result of the political pressure of the domestic social and political groups involved, but the "considered response of self-seeking nation-states to varying international structures." On the other side, bilateral trade relations, according to their quantity and quality, affect the overall structure of the world market.

In addition, the inter- and intra-concern relations must be reflected in the light of the political relations between the US and Germany and the orientation of German and American foreign policy. Nations are often, but not always and not necessarily as national states, collective units capable of social activity. They have certain interests—national interests—which are defined within their political system and their society and are brought into the international arena as foreign policy. The nature of the current political system exerts considerable influence over the process of definition of national interests. Larger parts of the population can participate in this process of creating intent in an open, democratic system than in an authoritarian or dictatorial system in which it is restricted exclusively to a small circle of the social elite. So it may be said at the same time that national interests are not fixed conditions, but variable ones. They are modified not only because they are expected from outside, by the international constellation, to make adaptations in the political system, but also because of shifts in domestic social and governmental relations and through processes of change in the political system itself, in case of mutation.

These processes and the new formulation of national interests can significantly affect the area of commercial relations. On the other hand, commercial and business relations can affect the process of mutual understanding. Developments in one area can lead to changes in the other, which may be in conformity with, or in opposition to, each other.

These considerations make it clear that economy and politics, transnational, foreign and international policy, while being separate fields, still influence one another. The question which grows out of this must deal with "How?" and, if possible, the qualitative definition of this reciprocal relationship.

International Political Economy as Theoretical Mental Equipment

In order to answer these questions, we shall deal here with theories of international political economy. The international political and economic systems have been referred to as subsystems of the international constellation and interact with each other on a global basis. International political economy derives from this reciprocity between economy and politics and is defined here, as with Robert Gilpin, as the "reciprocal and dynamic interaction in international relations of the pursuit of wealth and the pursuit of power." According to Susan Strange, it concerns "the social, political and economic arrangements affecting the global systems of production, exchange and distribution, and the mix of values reflected therein." She investigated how "market interdependence affects and is affected by international politics" and how "the interaction of economic and political change" came to be. Additionally, she deals with the effects of the world market on economic development and national efforts resulting from this to influence the rules, which are then used in world trade, the world finance system or direct foreign investments.

Although there exists relative consensus in the different theoretical points of departure, fundamental divergences become apparent in analyzing the nature of the relationship between the international political and the international economic systems. The question of the power relationship is answered in various ways. Economy takes first place for both Marxists and liberals, but the former consider it in a negative way and the latter positive. For the Marxist Krippendorff, the political and governmental power have become, as it were, agents of the economy. On the other hand, just as a struggle must be made against the international system of class relations, it must also be made under the sign of emancipation. Camilleri and Falk also perceive an "increasingly symbiotic relationship between state and corporations" and oppose a world system in which the transnational extent of capital is a basis for definition. The Wallerstein conception of a world system shares this view and is convinced "that the analytical figure of reference is a world system whose definition is based on economic processes and networks." Thus, economy is the point of departure for all studies and possesses an *a priori* value. "There is *a single* world system. This system is world economy and in its form it is capitalistic by definition," read: hierarchical and exploitative.

Liberal scientists support the thesis of economic primacy. Also, in their view, developments in the international economic system, that is, the trend towards internationalization of production and the growth of transnational concerns, have relegated the national state to the status of an evolutionary relic, a dinosaur of the international system. For them, TNCs whose managers bear "the responsibilities of world statesmanship" represent an "unmatched force for peace." In this respect, "sovereignty at bay" and the "nakedness of nations" form no basis for anxiety. On the contrary, they are evaluated in an entirely positive way, as people have confidence in the positive self-regulation of the economy which would in itself lead to overall peace in the world, if freed from national interference and governmental influence.

> Freeing commerce from national interference would inevitably, over time, stimulate mankind to close the gap between the archaic political structure of the world and visions of commerce vaulting beyond confining national boundaries to exploit the full promise of the world economy.

This is based on the assumption that politics will follow the economy: that is, the inter-, or better, de-nationalized "cosmocorporations," the geocentric enterprises would show the way, as true citizens of the world, to politics and nations. Here lies the "true logic of the global economy" and the "full economic promise" of the TNCs. For they constitute "an institutional and supra-national framework which could conceivably make war less likely, on the assumption that bombing customers, suppliers and employees is in nobody's interest." The tendencies towards globalization of economic production and the well-balanced economic dynamic forces might even stimulate the establishment of a world government which would be identified in due time with "eternal peace." "The polis of the future is commensurate with the planet Earth."

On the other hand, conservative observers note the primacy of politics. Adolf A. Berle says that "economic power is subsidiary to political and in many areas is its tool." Exponents of this view stress the dominant place of the nations in the international constellation and estimate their potential for action much higher than that of both previously mentioned paradigms. Countries determine the framing conditions according to their interests within which actors in the international economic system operate. Besides, they point out that up till now there are no denationalized TNCs and that "the complete liberation of enterprises from national ties is still hard to imagine."

Thus the discipline of international political economy is characterized by the coexistence of disparate individual theories. The question of the importance of the nation in international relations is vital in this conflict of paradigms like the controversy in the discipline of international relations overall. We shall here attempt to explain its role through an historical example and in so doing analyze the relationship between it and the field of transnational relations. A simple reference to their complementarity seems inadequate in this connection, as we are seeking to define their relation to each other. In this we shall take up the idea of Reinhard Meyer concerning scientific integration.

The Theoretical Problem of the Relation of Transnational Politics to National State, or: Transnational Politics as a Strategy for Peace?

Transnational politics and transnational relations were not invented in the twentieth century: they are phenomena which have existed at different times in history. Many globalizing processes in politics, economy, society, culture and technology, and the emergence of an international constellation which was worldwide in its breadth both in the international political system and also in the economic one, have led to networks in the international system. Transnational relations, that is, the growth of interaction across borders of non-governmental, social agencies of many types, of international organizations outside of parties, associations, interest groups and concerns operating internationally, as well as private persons with other non-governmental and/or official agencies, have had a prominent part in this. They have deepened international interweaving, so that international relations can no longer be described as a "government world," as they were in the picturesque billiard model of Arnold Wolders. Thus, sociological categories must have a place in the theory of international relations for, in transnational politics, the "hard shell" of the territorial state has become increasingly permeable.

Therefore one must take into account the level of restrictions due to domestic policy and influences on the formulation of foreign policy decisions. The billiard model suppresses this area, since it conceives of the state as a "black box." Thus, foreign policy, when considered apart from domestic events, can often only be inadequately understood; foreign and domestic policy are much more closely related to each other than people for a long time assumed. They form "two distinct levels where a dominant unity materializes in space and time." Finally, the state is threatened by the process of acceleration in technology, the technological revolution in weaponry in the 19th and 20th centuries and change in the nature of military conflict even in its material existence.

Foreign economic relations are among the most important of these transnational relations which render the national "shell" porous. Integration into the worldwide economic exchange and international sharing of labor offer the national economies, their agents, and also the state a benefit which in the long run outweighs a decision for national autarky. It lies in an increase in general welfare. In this, the answer to the question for or against integration into the world market, "national autonomy versus worldwide economic interdependence," is subjective in nature. Inclusion in worldwide economic networks is based almost on logic and prudence, but does not in any way prevent nations from avoiding this solution because of other priorities and seeking their prosperity in national autarky.

Foreign trade is important in a way which lies outside its essential role within the international economic system. It affects the international political system, since it contributes to international understanding and may thus operate in a way to promote peace or peace strategy. Siebert even goes so far as to perceive in it "a basis for a more pacific world." But one must not be misled by such an idealistic view, because international trade can just as well cause conflicts and tensions. The current flow of international products is frequently an uneven exchange whose advantages are asymmetrically divided. Another source of tension is the possible use of foreign trade by countries to apply pressure in their foreign policy. However, theories on foreign trade interpret and deal with it in relative isolation from these political considerations. Thus it is not often mentioned that companies have to take account of government policies and questions of security in planning production and business policy. Consequently, political trends should be noted during analysis of economic relations.

The view, stemming frequently from the growing phenomenon of transnationalization, is expressed that the government in this loses its ability to negotiate. The state is transmuted, as it were, in a transnational way and is restricted in its choices for negotiation. This is interpreted with positive predictions, because, through the processes of globalization and transnationalization, interdependence among the agents in the international system is increasing. In this case, interdependence means:

> reliance on each other within a system, in that two or several partners can only realise a profit jointly, maintaining a certain division of functions, or have to suffer an economic, ecological, strategic or political loss together.

In this, profits and losses are usually not equally shared. Therefore, an ideological identification of interdependence with equivalent reciprocal dependence must be rejected. Instead, interdependencies are also power relations, since the "interdependence vulnerability" and "sensitivity" of the participating agencies varies, and so degrees of power occur, arising from the question of "who needs whom more" and thus one is often faced with asymmetrical interdependencies.

However, many hopes relative to peace strategy are attached to this phenomenon of mutual and sometimes unequal dependency. Richard Rosecrance, a liberal supporter of the theory of international political economy, predicts subconsciously the victory of the "trade world" over the "politico-military world," since interdependence implies lowering trade barriers and an increase in the costs of war and consequently orientation towards world trade is the logical and rational way. On the other hand, this would lead directly to appeasement in the international system. In many places, as already mentioned, people think that the growth of interdependent relations even means a trend in the direction of world government.

Nonetheless, assessments like these, in which premises of the idealistic school are clearly apparent, must be treated with skepticism. The world economic crisis and international political developments in the 1930s and the parallelism of collapse with the disintegration of the international economic and political systems, make it appear that over-optimistic ideas of the coming "victory" of the trade world leading to universal peace in international relations are premature. The progress of globalization and the objectively recognizable trend towards increased international interdependence in no way guarantee *per se* an era of harmony and peace in the international system; there remain imponderables, conflicts and dangers arising from relations of interdependence themselves, and the requirements they place on the agents, and from the answers given by the agents to this series of requirements, with its many levels. This is proven by the German-American relations in the period between the wars, which meshed closely together in the 1920s both economically and politically, were highly interdependent, and dissolved successively in the 1930s and even ended in war. They show that "relapses" running counter to globalization and the growth of interdependencies are not to be excluded, but constantly expected and may have catastrophic results; besides, they show that transnational relations may be shaped by government policy and that their effect on peace strategy is consequently limited. The following chapters intend to document these theses in detail.

II
GERMAN-AMERICAN TRADE RELATIONS BETWEEN THE WARS[*]

Germany, the United States, and their Importance in World Trade

During the First World War, the US rose to be the "dominant economy" in the world and brought pressure against Great Britain's leading position in world trade, which consisted of worldwide export and import. The United Kingdom did indeed defend its position as the greatest nation in world trade (due primarily to its import activity) with the exception of the years 1920, 1929, and 1940, throughout the whole period between the wars. However, regarding the active side of world trade, that is, world *exports*, the United States proved to be the most important export nation at that time. This is documented by the data in Table 1.

Germany's position in the world market, which had worsened dramatically after the war, improved again in the 1920s. Germany increased its competitiveness, but was unable to regain the position it had held before the war and was in third place on the list of large trading countries behind the US and Great Britain. But in the first half of the 1920s, the Reich immensely challenged Great Britain for second place in world export. During the worldwide economic crisis, it succeeded in doing so for a few years, as Germany improved its relative position in world trade and especially in world export, although it must be taken into account that during this phase there was a drastic recession in world trade and also in world export in absolute numbers.

Besides the relative improvement in its position, the export quota, i.e., the part of German industrial production intended for export, also increased. It rose from about 21% (1928) to 31% (1931). However, this was only a temporary situation. Germany only profited for a short time from improving Terms of Trade, since this favorable trend in the

---

[*] The reader is referred to the original German text for detailed footnotes.

TABLE 1

GERMAN, BRITISH, FRENCH AND US SHARE IN WORLD TRADE

(%)	1913	1920	1921	1922	1923	1924	1925	1926	1927	1928	1929
Share in World Imports											
Germany	12.9						9.0	7.5	10.1	9.7	9.1
Great Britain	16.1						17.1	17	15.9	15.2	15.3
France	8.2						6.5	6.1	6.2	6.1	6.5
USA	8.9						12.6	13.6	12.2	11.6	12.3
Share in World Exports											
Germany	13.1						7.1	8.4	8.3	9.1	9.9
Great Britain	14.0						12.1	10.8	11.1	10.9	10.9
France	7.3						7.2	6.5	7.0	6.3	6.1
USA	13.4						15.6	· 16.	15.4	15.6	15.9
World Turnover											
Germany	13.0	2.8	5.8	6.6	5.9	6.8	8.1	7.9	9.2	9.4	9.5
Great Britain	15.1	19.4	17.4	16.1	16.3	15.6	14.7	14.0	13.6	13.2	13.2
France	7.7	8.3	7.5	8.2	7.9	7.8	6.8	6.3	6.6	6.2	6.3
USA	11.1	20.5	16.8	15.3	15.9	14.6	14.0	14.7	13.7	13.6	14.0

TABLE 1, continued

(%)	1930	1931	1932	1933	1934	1935	1936	1937	1938	1939	1940
Share in World Imports											
Germany	8.7	7.8	8.1	8.1	8.9	8.2	7.8	8.1	9.2	8.4	8.3
Great Britain	16.2	17.6	16.6	16.8	17.3	16.9	17.9	17.3	17.6	16.2	17.3
France	7.2	8.0	8.5	9.0	7.6	6.8	7.1	6.3	5.6	n.a.	n.a.
USA	10.5	9.9	9.4	9.3	8.2	9.9	10.9	11.1	8.1	9.8	10.4
Share in World Exports											
Germany	11.1	12.4	11.0	10.2	9.1	9.2	9.4	9.4	9.6	9.5	8.9
Great Britain	10.7	9.6	10.4	10.8	10.9	11.1	10.7	10.2	10.5	8.9	7.5
France	6.5	6.5	6.3	6.4	6.4	5.5	4.6	3.8	4.0	n.a.	n.a.
USA	14.6	12.9	12.8	11.7	11.5	12.0	11.8	13.0	13.9	14.2	18.0
World Turnover											
Germany	9.8	9.9	9.5	9.1	9.0	8.7	8.5	8.7	9.4	8.9	8.6
Great Britain	13.6	13.8	13.7	13.9	14.2	14.1	14.4	13.9	14.2	12.6	12.7
France	6.9	7.3	7.5	7.8	7.0	6.2	5.9	5.1	4.8	n.a.	n.a.
USA	12.4	11.3	11.0	10.5	9.8	10.9	11.3	12.1	10.9	12.0	14.0

Source: Statistische Jahrbücher, 44 Jg., 1924.25 – 59. Jg., 1941/42: passim.
Note: For the years 1920-1924, world trade statistics were not divided into import and export categories.
n.a. = not available

Terms of Trade was due to the fact that in the Depression, prices for raw materials were much stronger than for finished goods. Thus, German imports were cheaper, whereas, at the same time, German exports sank lower in value. But the Depression was soon to catch up with them, too.

In conjunction with the domestic economic program of the National Socialist government, the export quota finally fell by 1934 to 13% and by 1935 as low as 11%. This indicated as well a relative reduction of Germany's role in world trade during this phase, although Germany's portion of world trade, in comparison to the late 1920s only diminished slightly. The Third Reich remained behind Great Britain and the US in third place in world trade. At the same time, the position of the United States in world export crumbled, so that the shares of the three large exporting countries came closer to each other. From the second half of the 1930s the differences again increased. The US built up its position considerably as the strongest exporting country, whereas the Third Reich fell back behind Great Britain to number three of the exporting nations. However, its part in world export was generally greater than in the 1920s.

The two countries which are the subject of this study, the United States and Germany, were, then, in this period of time of prominent importance for world trade. They were significant centres of gravity both for world imports and world exports, which were characterized by an increase in the number of participants involved.

Foreign Trade between Germany and the US Between the Wars

GERMAN-AMERICAN GOODS EXCHANGE

One of the original theses of this study was the assumption that, in the exchange of goods between Germany and the United States, the economic changes in structure in both countries and changes in their positions in the world market reflect political developments and their effects on economic relations. To go into that further, we must first analyze German-American foreign trade, in order to place it properly in the framework of overall foreign trade at that time.

In the period under study here, the US may be considered as a national economy importing raw materials and exporting both finished goods and raw materials; in the 1920s and 30s it had in general a constantly positive trade balance, although it suffered many changes. At this time, raw materials constituted about one third of American imports, while the supporting pillars of American exports—raw materials and more finished goods—in the 1920s together made up far over 60%, and from 1928 about 70% of exports.

On the other hand, Germany may be characterized as a political economy importing foodstuffs and raw materials and exporting partially and fully manufactured goods, for which the trade balance during the world economic crisis was mostly in deficit. Among the exports in the 1930s there was a preponderance of manufactured goods which, together with those partially finished, counted for well over 80% of German exports; as for imports, the portion filled by the principal sectors of foodstuffs and raw materials came to about 65%. In the 1930s this valued increased by a few percentage points due to larger imports of raw materials.

TABLE 2:
THE GEOGRAPHIC DISTRIBUTION OF GERMAN FOREIGN TRADE

	Exports to (in %)						Imports from (in %)					
Year	I	II	III	IV	V	VI	I	II	III	IV	V	VI
1913	7.7	7.4	76.1	2.1	5.4	1.0	16.5	11.3	54.7	4.7	9.7	3.0
1923	8.1	7.8	74.3	1.9	7.6	0.2	19.3	8.8	55.0	4.3	9.2	3.4
1924	7.8	9.0	72.7	2.2	7.8	0.4	19.2	8.9	55.4	4.2	9.4	2.9
1925	6.9	8.4	74.1	2.2	7.9	0.4	19.1	9.2	52.8	4.2	12.1	2.6
1926	7.8	7.6	72.2	2.4	8.9	0.7	18.7	11.4	51.0	4.4	11.2	3.2
1927	7.8	7.4	73.9	2.4	7.6	0.8	17.3	12.6	53.2	4.3	9.9	2.6
1928	7.2	7.4	74.8	2.3	7.7	0.6	17.1	12.3	51.0	5.1	11.8	2.6
1929	8.0	7.4	73.7	2.4	7.7	0.7	15.6	12.0	52.6	5.1	11.9	2.6
1930	6.3	6.3	77.9	2.2	6.7	0.5	13.9	10.6	56.0	5.1	11.7	2.2
1931	5.6	4.3	81.0	1.9	6.7	0.4	13.3	10.5	55.9	5.1	12.4	2.2
1932	5.5	4.3	81.0	1.9	6.9	0.5	14.1	11.1	53.6	5.5	12.6	2.4
1933	5.7	5.9	78.0	2.2	7.6	0.5	13.4	10.5	54.3	5.8	12.7	3.1
1934	4.3	6.5	77.7	2.6	8.2	0.6	9.8	10.8	59.0	5.8	11.0	3.3
1935	4.5	9.3	73.2	2.9	9.3	0.7	6.1	14.3	61.6	6.3	10.4	1.0
1936	4.3	10.9	70.7	3.3	9.8	0.9	5.9	14.0	59.8	6.9	11.8	1.3
1937	4.1	11.2	69.3	3.6	10.9	0.8	6.1	17.0	55.6	7.5	11.7	1.7
1938	3.3	11.5	70.6	3.7	9.8	0.9	8.8	15.9	56.2	6.7	10.8	1.3
1939	2.7	9.6	75.9	2.6	8.5	0.6	5.1	13.7	62.9	6.4	10.9	0.9

Source: Daten aus und berechnet nach den Statistischen Jahrbüchern, 44. Jg., 1924/25 - 59. Jg., 1941/42: passim.

I = North America; II = Latin America; III = Europe; IV = Africa; V = Asia; VI = Australia/Polynesia

Table 2 on the previous page documents the geographic distribution of German foreign trade. The data show that German foreign trade was oriented mainly towards Europe: more than half of German imports in the 1930s came increasingly from the "Old World." Approximately three quarters of the exports went to European countries, whereas this portion was somewhat reduced in the later 30s. During the world economic crisis, Europe became increasingly important as distributor and customer from which the American continent suffered almost exclusively. However, later on Latin America became more important as a trade partner for the Third Reich. At the same time there was a significant shift among the European foreign trade partners towards southeastern Europe, where National Socialist Germany became clearly the most important trade partner of most countries in that region. Table 3 below gives an impression of this shift.

TABLE 3
THE SHIFT OF GERMAN FOREIGN TRADE

| Region/Country | Share in German | | | | | |
| | Imports (in %) | | | Exports (in %) | | |
	1913	1929	1938	1913	1939	1938
Southeastern Europe	1.0	3.8	9.8	2.1	4.3	10.3
Russia/Soviet Union	13.2	6.9	4.4	8.7	6.5	4.2
Egypt, Turkey, Near East	1.8	1.4	3.8	1.4	1.4	5.4
Latin America	11.0	11.4	14.9	7.4	7.4	11.7
Northern Europe	5.1	7.3	11.4	6.7	10.2	12.9
Western Europe	13.7	15.7	11.9	25.5	26.2	20.8
Great Britain	8.1	6.4	5.2	14.2	9.7	6.7
USA	15.9	13.3	7.5	7.1	7.4	2.8
Other	43.4	40.7	35.8	35.6	33.5	29.4

Source: Petzina/Ableshauser/Faust (1978). Die Werte für die USA wurden mit Tabelle 5* abgeglichen und gegebenenfalls angepaßt.

---

* Table 4 in the English-language edition.

These data prove that Europe's surpassing importance as foreign trade partner of the US prior to the war had considerably weakened in favor of a more balanced distribution. To begin with, Europe recovered portions of the market after the war—an indication of greater resistance to crisis by economic relations between industrialized countries—and developed its position in the crisis, particularly as a supply area for American products. However, Europe lost this position especially from 1934 on. In this phase following 1934, the western hemisphere, but also Asia, Africa and Oceania, became more important as trade partners. Their value increased due to the retrogression of the West in American foreign trade.

DEVELOPMENT

Changes in German-American trade relations are shown in Table 4* below.

This overview shows that American exports to Germany in 1920 almost reached the prewar level; however, its portion of total American exports only came to 3.8% as compared with 14.2% in 1913. Nevertheless this must be considered together with the unusually large total American exports in 1919/1920. The German part increased as soon as the following year, reaching a normal percentage of 8.3. With hyperinflation, it declined in value and percentage, increasing continually through the stabilization of the Dawes Plan and of the German currency—with exception of the crash of 1926, resulting from the German recession. It culminated in 1927, when it reached close to 10%. Then it sand after the Depression constantly until 1931 to 6.6%, which is to be taken as a the qualitative turning point in 1929.

US exports reached their highest value in the second half of the 1920s, whereas the German share fell to 7.7%. In 1930 American exports to Germany fell in value by 20-25% and in 1931 again by an additional 30%. For a short period, i.e., from 1932 to 1933, the German share again improved, while at that time American exportation reached its lowest point. Finally, 1934 marked a new turning point when 5% represented the lowest point since 1921. In the second half of the 1930s the German share fluctuated at about 4%, while

---

* Table 5 in the original German edition.

TABLE 4

SYNOPSIS OF CHANGES IN GERMAN-AMERICAN TRADE RELATIONS

Year	I World imports (mil. RM)	II World exports (mil. RM)	III Total German exports (mil. RM)	IV German exports to USA (mil. RM)	V German share of total exports (%)	VI Total German imports (mil. RM)	VII German imports from USA (mil. RM)
1913	83400	76800	10097	713.7	7.1	10770	1711.1
1919							
1920	153700	136400	69421.2	4418.3	6.4	99077	28194.3
1921	100400	88500					
1922	103700	97300					
1923	109900	103200	6102.3	474.9	7.8	6149.8	1171.1
1924	122300	116700	6534.8	491.3	7.5	9135.5	1706.5
1925	138000	130000	9290	603.5	6.5	12362	2199.5
1926	134100	123600	10415	744.1	7.1	10001	1603.1
1927	140800	130200	10801	776.2	7.2	14228	2072.9
1928	143900	135000	12276	795.9	6.5	14001	2062.2
1929	147900	136200	13483	991.1	7.4	13447	1790.4
1930	120100	108700	12036	685.2	5.7	10393	1306.8
1931	86600	77500	9599	487.5	5.1	6727	791.4
1932	57800	52000	5739	281.2	4.9	4667	591.8
1933	52000	47700	4871	245.9	5.0	4204	482.8
1934	49900	46100	4117	157.8	3.8	4451	372.7
1935	50500	46600	4270	169.5	4.0	4158	240.7
1936	54500	51300	4768	172.0	3.6	4218	232.2
1937	67800	63000	5911	208.8	3.5	5468	281.9
1938	59300	54900	5619	156.9	2.8	6052	454.5
1939	57400	54800	5653	125.1	2.2	5207	197.8
1940	60700	54700	4868	11.2	0.2	5012	15.8

TABLE 4, continued

Year	VIII German share of total imports (in %)	IX USA-German total exports (mil. RM)	X USA exports to Germany (mil. RM)	XI USA share of total exports (in %)	XII USA total imports (mil. RM)	XIII USA Imports from Germany (mil. RM)	XIV USA share in total imports (in %)
1913	15.9	10314.1	1464.6	14.2	7507.8	773.3	10.3
1919				1.2			0.3
1920	28.5			3.8			1.7
1921		18837	1562.4	8.3	10538	336.0	3.2
1922		16094	1327.2	8.2	13075	491.4	3.8
1923	19.1	17501	1331.4	7.6	15926	676.2	4.2
1924	18.7	19282	1848	9.6	15162	582.8	3.9
1925	17.8	20622	1951.5	9.5	17753	689.9	3.9
1926	16.0	20198	1499.6	7.4	18610	833.7	4.5
1927	14.6	20433	1994.0	9.8	17577	843.7	4.8
1928	14.5	21538	1928.5	9.0	17182	930.3	5.4
1929	13.3	22012	1687.1	7.7	18476	1069.6	5.8
1930	12.6	16141	1139.7	7.1	12856	741.8	5.8
1931	11.8	10181	676.4	6.6	8782	534.9	6.1
1932	12.7	6766	549.9	8.1	5557	309.7	5.6
1933	11.5	7035	469.0	6.7	6090	265.8	4.4
1934	8.4	5333	268.2	5.0	4138	172.9	4.2
1935	5.8	5708	224.6	3.9	5118	193.4	3.8
1936	5.5	6140	246.6	4.0	6058	197.7	3.3
1937	5.2	8373	300.9	3.6	7710	230.7	3.0
1938	7.5	7735	267.5	3.5	4900	162.5	3.3
1939	3.8	7943	115	1.4	5795	130.0	2.2
1940	0.3	10053	<1.25	<0.01	6563	12.5	0.2

Sources: see the original German text for detailed information on data sources.

meanwhile there was a definite tendency downwards and a clearly absolute increase in American exports. In 1939, exports to Germany came to just 1.4% of total American exports and one year later they were entirely irrelevant.

In the entire period between the wars, the German share in American imports did not reach the prewar level by far. In the first half of the 1920s, after early difficulties, it varied between 3 and 4%. In the second half of the 1920s it rose continually until it reached its highest level at 6.1% in 1931. Also, the two following years showed high percentages for Germany above the average, so that, during the crisis, Germany became more important for the United States as an importer. However, this share was retrogressive because of an uneven trend in American imports overall. In 1934 and 1935 it tended to decrease to 4%, in the next years to 3%, until, in 1939 and 1940, at 2.2 and 0.2% it became practically meaningless.

The American share in German exports oscillated in the second half of the 1920s, after normalization of Germany's economy, around 7% and in 1929, at 7.4%, reached its highest point in that period. During the worldwide economic crisis, when the absolute figures fell between 1929 and 1932 by more than 70%, it barely reached 5% (in 1932). It even rose in the following year to 5%, but fell during the rest of the 1930s—except 1935—to values below 4%, while the overall movement of German exports was irregular. There was a qualitative reduction in 1938 and 1939, when the American share slipped down to less than 3% and in 1939 to only 2.2%, losing much of its importance.

A glance at the American share of German imports shows almost everywhere a decline. In 1923 it came to something over 19%. From 1925 until 1927 there was a significant decrease, when the value fell by three percentage points. Under pressure from the world economic crisis, when German imports from the US fell by two thirds, it declined by 1931 to 11.8%, rising the following year again by one percentage point and falling again in 1933 to 11.5%. Then came the more important qualitative breakthrough. From 1933 to 1934 the American share declined with further diminishing results by about 3%, from 1934 to 1935 by another 2.5% to 5.8%. Afterwards, it moved to around 5%, but in 1938 it experienced a sudden, relative, but temporary increase to 7.5%. In the year of the outbreak of war it came to its lowest level at a little over 4% with a massive fall at the same time. In comparison with 1923, this meant a decrease of about 80%; in comparison with 1929/32, a decrease of more than two thirds. Finally, in 1940, the American share of German imports was only 0.3%.

As for the balance of trade, it was continually active for the United States until 1938. The immense surpluses which the US achieved at the beginning of the 1920s, when it exported double to three times as much to Germany as it received, diminished during the following years. After 1929, the surpluses in the American balance of trade shrank; imports from Germany did not decrease as rapidly as American exports to the Weimar Republic. As the 1930s progressed, American surpluses again increased, but fell in the second half of the 1930s, with the exception of 1938, to more moderate levels. From 1939 on, the German balance of trade which had remained passive up to then, became slightly more active. During the war, deliveries to Germany were more than orders.

COMPOSITION

Table 5* shows raw materials and partly finished materials and the largest separate areas of German imports from the US. In the 1920s they accounted for 60% and rose at the end of the decade to nearly 70%, especially in the branches of food and beverages, but fell to somewhat over 64% until 1932. But even in the years of crisis, when German imports from the US fell by over two-thirds, their share was clearly greater than in the years 1923-1938. In 1933 this sector reached a record, as food and beverages continued to fall: in that year raw materials and partly finished materials did not decrease much less than 3/4 of German imports from the US. By 1937 this share grew to about 90%, decreasing significantly in the following years. At the same time food and beverages became less important and even finished goods lost by half after a brief recovery. In 1938 food and beverages rose by leaps and bounds to over 24% and later on finished goods improved again.

Food, beverages, and animals were not important for German exports to the US during nearly all of the period under study here

---

* Table 6 in the original German text.

TABLE 5:
GERMAN TRADE WITH THE USA BY PRODUCT GROUP

Year	Proportion of Exports to the USA (in %)				Proportion of Imports from the USA (in %)			
	Live animals	Food & beverages	Raw materials & semi-finished goods	Finished goods	Live animals	Food & beverages	Raw materials & semi-finished goods	Finished goods
1923	0.3	0.5	15.6	83.6	0.00	37.9	60.0	2.1
1924	0.5	1.3	18.8	79.3	0.04	37.6	58.9	3.4
1925	0.4	1.7	23.9	73.9	0.06	34.8	59.9	5.3
1926	0.5	1.8	24.9	72.8	0.03	33.5	57.4	9.1
1927	0.5	1.6	27.0	70.9	0.05	26.7	62.2	11.0
1928	0.4	2.4	27.9	69.3	0.10	24.3	61.8	13.8
1929	0.4	3.6	25.5	70.4	0.06	18.8	67.1	14.1
1930	0.4	2.8	26.0	70.8	0.05	16.5	69.5	13.9
1931	0.4	2.8	25.7	71.5	0.04	20.4	65.6	14.0
1932	0.7	1.8	21.9	75.6	0.02	24.8	64.3	10.9
1933	0.4	2.7	24.4	72.4	0.01	17.4	72.6	10.0
1934	0.4	6.4	27.0	66.2	0.03	13.1	74.9	12.0
1935	0.6	4.8	23.2	71.4	0.20	6.9	80.9	12.0
1936	0.5	5.9	23.3	70.3	0.10	7.6	86.9	5.4
1937	0.5	10.2	23.6	65.7	0.30	4.2	89.7	5.4
1938	0.5	3.6	18.3	77.6	0.10	27.2	68.0	4.6
1939								
1940		6.3	4.6	89.3		28.6	50.6	20.8

Source: Berechnet nach den Statistischen Jahrbüchern, 43 Jg., 1923-59. Jg., 1941/42: passim.

except for the years 1934-1937 and more fell into the sectors of raw materials, partly finished and finished goods; in that area, their proportion was about 3:1 in favor of finished goods. The percentages of raw versus partly finished goods varied usually between 23 and 28%, mostly in the area of partly finished goods. Thus they represented about a quarter of German exports to the United States. Compared with this, the area of finished goods reached 70% from time to time. Here there was a noteworthy tendency towards slight increase from 192829 until 1932, when finished goods attained their highest value in the 1930s. Consequently, during the Depression, when German exports to the United States diminished to less than a third of what they had been before the crisis, it became more important. In an intermittent manner, its share reached its lowest point by 1937 at barely 66%, after an absolute gain between 1934 and 1937. At the same time, its share increased again significantly as absolute values persistently fell.

Thus, German-American exchange of goods consisted in general in the delivery of finished and partly finished good from Germany against American raw materials, partly finished goods and foodstuffs. Finally, to complete the picture, there remains a glance at the development of individual products, as shown in Table 6* on the following page.

The most important outcome for imports was a significant shift towards strategically important groups of products (like copper and petrochemical items) instead of traditionally important items (like lard and wheat). As for exports, chemical, pharmaceutical, precision tools and optical products were particularly important.

---

* Table 7 in the original German text.

TABLE 6
SHARE OF CERTAIN GOODS IN GERMAN FOREIGN TRADE WITH THE US ACCORDING TO VALUE

Exports to the US (in %)	1927	1930	1933	1934	1936	1937	1939	1940
Hides and furs	5.7	5.5	4.1	1.9	0.7	1.3	n.a.	n.a.
Chemical raw materials and semi-finished goods	5.2	6.2	3.9	5.2	9.3	11.8	6.8	2.7
Chemicals and pharmaceuticals	10.5	12.5	17.5	20.2	17.4	14.8	21.4	33.0
Iron products	6.6	6.7	7.1	7.8	6.7	4.8	4.9	1.8
Machinery (excluding electrical)	4.0	4.2	3.0	3.8	6.1	6.9	6.5	2.7
Precision tools and optical products	1.2	1.4	1.1	1.5	5.7	6.8	9.3	20.5
Textiles	16.6	11.7	11.2	7.6	3.1	2.1	1.6	0
Leather goods	5.8	8.7	7.3	3.9	0.9	0.7	n.a.	n.a.
Musical instruments	1.4	1.3	1.0	1.9	2.3	2.1	2.6	0
Toys	3.5	2.5	2.5	2.3	2.7	2.4	2.5	0
Imports from the US (in %)								
Wheat	8.9	2.6	0.4	0.4	n.a.	0.7	n.a.	n.a.
Lard	6.0	6.2	7.0	2.4	1.0	n.a.	n.a.	n.a.
Cotton	32.3	32.7	46.2	39.2	33.5	27.8	21.1	27.2
Metals	12.1	6.6	4.5	10.1	n.a.	18.7	n.a.	n.a.
of which: Copper	11.0	6.0	3.0	8.0	4.2	12.6	12.4	3.2
Fuels, petroleum, lubricating and mineral oils	6.2	16.0	7.2	8.3	19.3	21.1	28.8	6.3
Chemical raw materials	0.4	0.7	.05	0.7	8.7	4.4	6.8	0
Ores and minerals	0.3	0.2	1.2	1.2	5.0	5.0	4.4	0.6
Chemicals and pharmaceuticals	1.4	1.8	2.9	2.9	2.9	2.9	2.8	3.8
Machinery (excluding electrical)	2.1	2.0	0.8	1.4	n.a.	n.a.	2.2	2.5
Tobacco	0.8	1.1	1.0	1.1	2.2	1.6	1.7	20.3

Source: Eigene Berechnungen anhand des Datenmaterials aus den Statistischen Jahrbüchern, 47. Jg., 1928-59. Jg. 1941/42: passim.
n.a. = not available

IMPORTANCE

In addition, it is necessary to study how important exchange relations were for the two national economies. In so doing, one must take into account that percentage-wise a reduction or increase in the bilateral exchange relationships does not always explain changes in quantity or value, as they only refer to volume of foreign trade due to all the shifts which occurred. Regarding the development of world trade with respect to value, price, and volume, it should be notes that the volume of world trade from 1929 to 1933 only fell by 25%, but feel by more than half in price and even more in value.

The data in Table 4 show that world imports and exports shrank by two-thirds between 1929 and 1934. On the other hand, German exports to the US diminished by 84% and German imports from the US by more than 79%. American exports to Germany diminished by 84%, as well as imports from Germany. The decline in Germany's share towards the US in foreign trade between the partners reflected not only reduction in the volume of foreign trade worldwide, but more besides. This means that involvement of the United States and the German Reich in foreign trade diminished during the world economic crisis. This development continued later on because exchange relations did not run parallel to the moderate recovery of world trade, but sank towards the end of the 1930s and finally became insignificant when the war began.

In addition, the following facts are helpful in making an evaluation: until 1912, the German Empire was the second, and in 1913 the third most important country for American exports; for US imports, Germany held second place on the list of countries of origin. At the same time, the United States was the third most important country of destination for German exports. In 1927 the Weimar Republic was the third most important export market for the United States, whereas Germany only held seventh place for American imports. In contrast, in 1925, the US was the most important country for imports and the third most important for exports from Germany. Thus the United States had been able to retain their relevance for German foreign trade from prewar days, while Germany lost its position regarding exports in foreign trade with America. Thus the economic significance of bilateral trade relations, the essences of these exports, was far greater for the Weimar Republic than for the US. This was shown by the fact that, until 1927 the growth of German-American trade was still less than that of American foreign trade overall. During the crisis, the United States maintained its position as the most important German import country; for German exports, on the other hand, they lost their place as the third largest country of destination and by 1932-33 sank as a result of the larger concentration of German foreign trade in Europe down to seventh place. In 1935 the US lost its place as the most important country of supply for Germany to Great Britain and two years later, it lost the second place to Argentina. However, in 1938 the US won back the first place. But as early as the following year it fell behind Italy, Sweden, Hungary and Romania to fifth place, and one year later it slipped down to 33rd place. As a destination for German exports, the US slipped in 1935 to eighth place, in 1936-37 to ninth, in 1938 to eleventh, 1939 to thirteenth and finally, in 1940 down to 32nd place.

Similar results derive from a more strongly quantitative consideration of foreign trade relations. For this, a more exact view of trade data is required. It has long been assumed that the share of a nation in its partner's foreign trade was an indicator for the absolute position of that country on the other country's scale of priorities in foreign policy. However, this factor appears to be too coarse-grained to allow the drawing of well-founded conclusions about the bilateral economic involvement and political relations, for these shares in trade are influenced primarily by the partner's volume of trade. If one wants to evaluate the noncommercial sectors of foreign policy, the more appropriate indicators are the factors of difference in trade (ADF), i.e., difference in imports (IDF) and especially difference in exports (EDF), which are their active side. According to Andreas Birken, the latter are particularly helpful when analyzing

> the evolution of relations between states. The development of trade share corresponds first of all to change in the share of world trade of the trade partners. Therefore, theories based on a narrow reciprocal action between foreign trade and foreign policy must be used with caution. There are only marginal possibilities for mutual influence. Economic action is generally based on economic factors. By contrast, change in export difference factors runs largely parallel to foreign policy and so is an indicator for the development of relations between states.

The EDF shows "to what extent foreign trade value differs from the value resulting from the share of the trading partner in world trade." It identifies the factor "by which the actual trading share varies from the share in worldwide imports." Thus, bilateral exchange relations are viewed in relation to shares in world trade. Roughly, this means that the EDF is positive or negative according to whether the exchange of goods lies over or under the current shares in world trade. The share of country B in the total exports of country A is viewed, then, in relation to country B's share in worldwide imports. If the share of country B in the total exports of country A is larger than the share of country B in worldwide imports (here, the total imports of country A must be subtracted from world imports), then the EDF for country A is positive; if it is smaller, the EDF is negative. The lowest value possible is −1; altogether the sum of all EDFs of a country has the is equal to 0.

The following values are necessary in calculating the ADFs, in this case for the German-American situation.

$$
\begin{aligned}
e &= \text{US exports to Germany} \\
i &= \text{US imports from Germany} \\
USE &= \text{total US exports} \\
USI &= \text{total US imports} \\
e/USE &= \text{German share of total US exports} \\
i/USE &= \text{German share of total US imports} \\
E &= \text{German exports to US} \\
I &= \text{German imports from US} \\
DTE &= \text{total German exports} \\
DTI &= \text{total German imports} \\
E/DTE &= \text{US share of total German exports} \\
I/DTI &= \text{US share of total German imports} \\
WE &= \text{world exports} \\
WI &= \text{world imports}
\end{aligned}
$$

For the US the EDF is calculated according to Birken's method by this formula:

$$
EDFUS = \frac{e/USE - DTI/(WI - USI)}{DTI/(WI - DTI)} = \frac{e \times (WI - USI)}{USE \times DTI} - 1
$$

The formula for calculating the EDF for Germany is analogous:

$$\text{EDFD} = \frac{\text{E} / \text{DTE} - \text{USI} / (\text{WI} - \text{DTI})}{\text{USI} / (\text{WI} - \text{DTI})} = \frac{\text{E} \times (\text{WI} - \text{DTI})}{\text{DTE} \times \text{USI}} - 1$$

According, these are the formulae for calculating the IDS:

$$\text{IDFUS} = \frac{\text{i} \times (\text{WE} - \text{USE})}{\text{USI} \times \text{DTE}} - 1$$

and

$$\text{IDFD} = \frac{\text{I} \times (\text{WE} - \text{DTE})}{\text{DTI} \times \text{USE}} - 1$$

Calculation of the ADFs on the basis of the data in Table 4* gives us Table 7† on the following page.

First of all, it is surprising in this context that the EDFs in the entire period between the wars—stronger for Germany, weaker for the United States—were negative. The IDFs were likewise negative with one exception, where the US showed negative values to a much greater extent. These data must not be interpreted as a proof for an economic interdependence which was limited. For, on the one hand, account must be taken of geographical distances, i.e., the intercontinental nature of German-American trade under problematic conditions of traffic and transportation routes. In the case of Germany, the greater negative value may be explained by the larger number of trading partners in its regional European area. On the other hand, the size of the national economy of both countries must be noted, as this led to a larger number of trade relationships than had by smaller national economies. According, high ADF values seldom occur for small national economies.

---

* Table 5 in original German text.

† Table 8 in original German text.

TABLE 7
FACTORS OF DIFFERENCE IN TRADE

	Export Difference Factor for Germany	Export Difference Factor for US	Import Difference Factor for Germany	Import Difference Factor for US
Year	**EDFD**	**EDFUS**	**IDFD**	**IDFUS**
1913	-0.32	0	0.03	-0.32
1925	-0.54	-0.08	0.04	-0.54
1926	-0.52	-0.14	-0.10	-0.56
1927	-0.48	-0.15	-0.15	-0.51
1928	-0.51	-0.19	-0.18	-0.50
1929	-0.47	-0.26	-0.26	-0.51
1930	-0.51	-0.27	-0.25	-0.56
1931	-0.54	-0.23	-0.22	-0.57
1932	-0.53	-0.09	-0.13	-0.56
1933	-0.60	-0.27	-0.30	-0.64
1934	-0.58	-0.48	-0.34	-0.59
1935	-0.64	-0.57	-0.57	-0.64
1936	-0.70	-0.54	-0.58	-0.69
1937	-0.71	-0.61	-0.65	-0.72
1938	-0.70	-0.69	-0.52	-0.72
1939	-0.80	-0.86	-0.76	-0.81
1940	-0.98	-1.00	-0.98	-0.98

Source: Calculations based on data from Table 4.

Besides, the size of both national economies causes us to record the data with two digits behind the decimal, as changes in the ADFs which appear to be insignificant may include absolute shifts which are not irrelevant. Although analysis of the ADFs does not immediately support the thesis of high-grade interdependent economic relations and even less that of a special political relationship in the 1920s, the ADFs and particularly the EDFs which were becoming more negative and were moving towards an absolute low point in the 1930s impressively reflected both the economic and the incipient political disengagement and dissolution of interdependent relationships between the US and National Socialist Germany.

III
FROM COOPERATION TO CONFRONTATION: THE DEVELOPMENT OF GERMAN-AMERICAN OPPOSITION*

Compatibility of German-American Interests in the 1920s and Loosening of the German-American Relationship during the World Economic Crisis

In the decade after the First World War German-American relations developed from the wartime military antagonism to a "special relationship." In particular, the Stresemann foreign policy made an effort to synchronize with Washington's foreign policy, as it was in Germany's interest, after overcoming international isolation and returning to the world market to be congenial to the American Open Door policy. The aims of the Weimar policy of understanding could be used by Washington as a lever in realizing an "indivisible world market," that is, an open and freer world economy combined with unconditional preferential treatment. Here, especially in the area of foreign economic policy, lay the value of expanding the German-American relationship. On the other hand, this required Washington's active cooperation in dealing with the question of reparations and comprehensive economic and financial aid for Germany. In this way, the Weimar Republic became the junior partner of the US in Europe and looked forward to the prospect of recognition as an economic, political, and finally also as a military member in the circle of great powers with equal rights. The interdependency created by the economic relations, increasingly interwoven with political concerns, had a positive effect on the reparation and revision policies of the Weimar Republic. However, here there lay an essential potential for conflict, because the interests were in no way identical.

---

* The reader is referred to the original German text for detailed footnotes.

Stresemann's concept for revising the Treaty of Versailles, breaking it primarily by *peaceful* means, i.e., economic ones, reached its limits by 1929-1930. The foreign policy of Heinrich Brüning and his successors veered gradually away from the Stresemann policy of negotiation and used other methods for attaining its objectives, so that the foreign policy of Weimar in its real meaning ended in the early 1930s. In its place, the direction followed was strongly unilateral and independent, less oriented towards interdependence. The change in the style of foreign policy appeared somewhat in the project for a customs union with Austria and in the attitude of the German delegates to the disarmament conference in Geneva, which met with rigid disapproval in the United States. However, Berlin did not develop a new kind of overall foreign policy, because considerations concerning reparations and finance required a certain regard for international interdependencies. German foreign policy in the era of presidential cabinets had, logically, a transitory character: it had the face of Janus. Following the *de facto* annulment of reparations at the Lausanne Conference in June/July 1932, there appeared a confrontational element, directed towards the development of an independent great power, which was to be perceived in the German policy on the question of disarmament. The Hitler regime continued this policy and made it more serious. When the world economic conference failed and Germany withdrew from disarmament negotiations (14 October 1933), Germany announced its decision not to take part in multilateral activities of the international system and with its non-aggression pact with Poland it turned towards a foreign policy which was bilateral in emphasis. In this, Hitler showed himself to be an active power. Foreign policy became Hitler's "private domain."

The government in Washington had very little influence on these events, as American strategy in foreign policy, which, since the war, had looked upon trade policy as the real, better foreign policy, had turned out to be deficient. The hopes engendered by the principle of a trade policy without a parallel political alliance, with the motto of "Creating Peace through Trade," had not been fulfilled. While the worldwide economic crisis which seemed to bring the American model into question showed that the belief of American diplomats that the political problems of Europe and the world could be solved by economic means was an illusion. The American "unofficial economic

confusion in areas of responsibility made Hitler's position all the more secure. Besides, the polycratic elements did not oppose Hitler's policies. Thus, Hitler was not a "weak dictator," for his ability to wage a war down to catastrophe, contrary to all prudence and all criticism, shows that he was the highest person to make decisions, set on his program.

The phases of Hitler's program may be described as follows. First, he sought to regain freedom in foreign policy by withdrawing from multilateral situations. In this phase conflicts in foreign affairs were to be avoided until Germany's military potential was sufficiently consolidated (the screening phase). Along with this, a free German state, with the view that "war is the final goal of politics" was to establish the German-Germanic people after a struggle over several generations as the dominant race. Hitler's three-phase plan provided first for the subjugation of continental Europe and the Soviet Union in order to create a base of worldwide power in Europe. After that, there would be expansion overseas and discussion with the US about worldwide superpower status. Finally, in the distant future, German triumph would mean the end of the dynamics of power politics and German domination of the globe, i.e., the racial domination of the German nation. Thus, world history would have reached the end of its racial outline and the dynamics of the historical process would congeal in a biologically static Utopia.

Under his program, Hitler originally wanted to create the German-Germanic continental empire in Europe during his lifetime. He believed as late as the autumn of 1941 that a confrontation with the United States would not take place till a future generation. Therefore, the building and consolidation of Germany's hegemony in continental Europe had to be accomplished in such a way as to avoid intervention by the US, the main rival in sight. This prominent place for the United States in Hitler's view was already apparent in the 1920s. In Hitler's *Second Book*, in 1928, he perceived in the US a first-rate factor in world politics capable of changing the power relationships in international affairs to its advantage and of placing it at the head of nations. The resources, the economy of the United States and its racial superiority due to Nordic immigration from Europe gave advance indication of this development. One could only stand up to the US if a nation (in his view, the German nation) paid attention to its racial purity, perfected it and provided an adequate government. Until his death, Hitler held firmly to this perception of America which, like the other elements of his program, grew out of the 1920s when he saw the strongest rival in the US (despite his neglect of the American factor in his policy until 1940, which may be partially explained by American legislation on neutrality). At the time of the world economic crisis, America appeared to him in a more negative light. The economic problems were secondary. Rather, the most important element for him was the mixture of races which could lead to racial inferiority. For Hitler, this had the pleasant side-effect that Washington initially moved towards the edge of the power monopoly. He believed until 1938 that the United States would not enter a European war and for this reason, the first months of war awakened new hopes. However, Hitler continued to hold the view that world domination would finally be decided by a German-American struggle, that is, after extermination of the Jewish people. "A later generation would have to face the problem of Europe-America." Then would begin

> the greatest undertaking in history. With English and French property in America as a base, we shall then deal with the "dollar Jews" of the United States. We shall destroy this Jewish democracy.

However, Washington must first be mollified and kept out of the European war and to do this the idea of a Monroe Doctrine for Germany and Europe was taken up. In this two currents may be identified: a national one and one dealing with international law; these currents are associated with the names of Werner Daitz and Carl Schmitt. Whereas for Daitz the "new principle of world order" was racial, consisting of "a Monroe Doctrine with a biological base," Carl Schmitt developed an order for a large region based on science and international law, prohibiting the intervention by powers outside the area. Both versions represented a reactionary Utopian formula for a world conceived as anti-West, rejecting the principle of equality between states. Despite the zeal and vehemence of their authors, Hitler only used them as tactical means giving him freedom of action in the daily political and military activities and keeping the US out of the struggle for Europe. In the long run, Hitler did not consider them valid formulae for international organization.

The hope of bringing Washington into a world organization by superficial and pretended synchronization and parallelism in concepts for world order proved deceptive. The United States were unwilling to let Hitler act as he wanted, because the German attitude constituted a worldwide challenge for the US. The Third Reich had become a universal threat of political, ideological, military, economic, and social nature. It touched security, the political system, the economy, society and the "American way of life." Not to have sufficiently reflected on this and above all to have underrated the potential political power of the United States was Hitler's historical mistake.

2. American Foreign Policy Towards the Third Reich

As early as 1933 Roosevelt perceived the threat posed by National Socialist Germany and its rearmament policy for the community of nations. However, when he came to power he had no effective economic or political means which could be used to influence the policy of the Third Reich. In foreign policy Roosevelt's hands were tied by the isolationism of the time which culminated in rejection of membership in the World Court, in the American legislation on neutrality and the priority required by the domestic reform of the "New Deal." At the same time there grew in American society a feeling of rejection against the measures of the National Socialist government. Anti-Semitic decrees, book burning, bringing social organizations and institutions into line, lack of freedom in cultural, political and social matters, the brutal suppression of opponents and the growing intrusion of the government into more areas of society aroused suspicion of the Hitler regime. However, Hitler's lip service towards international cooperation in the beginning, which accompanied the screening phase of National Socialist foreign policy, limited this suspicion at first to domestic conditions in Germany.

Because of the domestic policy limitations, Washington reacted with restraint to German initiatives such as reintroduction of military conscription (16 March 1935) and the reoccupation of the Rhineland (7 March 1936). Until 1936 Roosevelt followed a strategy of "peaceful multilateralism," which turned out to be an "impractical, idealistic concept predicated upon the return of Germany, Italy and Japan to liberal political principles." His initiatives for convoking a peace conference or summit meeting with Hitler and Mussolini were based on principles which were unacceptable for Berlin, Rome and Tokyo (disarmament and free access to international markets and raw materials) and were consequently refused. The failure of this strategy was accompanied by a growing realization that coexistence of the western democracies with National Socialist Germany and its allies was impossible. Encouraged by stronger international cooperation (a fiscal agreement between the US, Great Britain and France) and his impressive electoral victory in the autumn of 1936, made Roosevelt appear "as a kind of savior of the Western democracies."

The intensification of the Japanese-Chinese war in the middle of 1937 moved him in his quarterly speech on 5 October 1937 to call for joint action by the community of nations against the "sick" countries. However, it only had a cosmetic effect on American foreign policy, since Roosevelt lacked the domestic political resources for a more active foreign policy; its actual effect was more rhetorical and symbolic in nature. It emphasized that Washington had decisively taken sides with democracy. Moreover, it can be considered as a "test balloon" to evaluate the strength of isolationist opposition in the United States and as an additional "pedagogical" measure by Roosevelt, in order to create in the US a greater consciousness of America's responsibility in world politics. In any case, the picture of Germany in America was further troubled. Dieckhoff reasoned a few days before Christmas in 1937 that one was gaining more and more the impression that Germany, Japan and Italy were forming a closed phalanx of aggressor countries. Besides, the ideological antagonism was increasingly penetrating public consciousness and people were becoming more and more convinced that National Socialism was to be exported throughout the world.

The events of 1938 made clear the need for a change in the course of American foreign policy regarding increased activity in international politics. At the beginning of the year Roosevelt reacted to the turbulence in international politics by a call for increased efforts towards armament in the US and the rest of the year confirmed that step. The annexation of Austria was met with disapproval in the American press and in the government; Germany policy in Czechoslovakia strengthened this growing anti-German attitude and the German-Americans organized by the German-American Volksbund (National Federation), supported by the National Socialist Party, were increasingly looked upon by 1938 as a "Trojan Horse." American foreign policy received new impetus in November 1938 from the anti-Semitic pogroms of the "*Kristallnacht*" and in March, 1939, from the invasion of Czechoslovakia. All efforts at restraining Germany from war were fruitless, as Hitler's determination to fight was irreversible.

In the United States, the beginning of military operations in Europe was greeted by internationalists as a threat to the US. They defined security in a much broader way than the isolationists and saw the war as a global struggle between systems in which the US would be inescapably involved. In consequence, Washington had to place itself actively on the side of democracy. Roosevelt shared this view, which was finally confirmed by the Japanese attack on Pearl Harbor.

Thus Hitler's attempt at world domination brought in the United States, which became the "arsenal of democracy." Against Hitler's "story" of the racial world order, which went beyond the theory of a national state, was the radical counterpoint of the humanitarian and liberal view of world civilization held by the US. Therefore, the military manifestation of this structural conflict approached the intensity of civil and religious wars. It became

> a life-and-death struggle of constitutional democracy in its Western form against intolerant totalitarianism, indeed a "crusade" against the destroyer of Christianity and morality, the tyrant, waged like an ideological war.

The Beginning of Controversy in Foreign Trade Policy

1. The Seizure of Power and First Economic Disputes

A. *The Question of Debts and Obligations*

The German-American dualism manifested itself tangibly especially in the area of foreign economic policy and the international financial market. The withdrawal of Germany from international interdependency was demonstrated in 1933 in the payment of international debts. In view of its precarious fiscal situation, Berlin stopped its debt payments, which the president of the Reichsbank Hjalmar Schacht (who became Reich Minister of Economics in 1934) referred to as an "invisible occupation." Prior to the world economic conference of May, 1933, he visited the US to explore the situation. Besides problems in trade policy, the question of German debt payments was discussed. From these talks, among others also with Roosevelt, Schacht gained the false impression that there were no objections against a moratorium on transfers. Up to 1 July 1933 Germany still met 50% of its debts as they fell due, because, in foreign trade, it relied on export surpluses with the West and in foreign policy it did not yet feel able to face severe confrontation with creditor nations. For the time being, they were forced to follow a policy of minimal co-operation in international affairs and reached an understanding on this with the creditor nations to hold a conference on this problem at the end of the year. But shortly thereafter Berlin shattered this consensus by making an agreement in October, 1933, with Switzerland and the Netherlands on special payments and clearing. The Foreign Office expected considerable complaints because of these offenses against custom in international trade and payments, but these objections were put aside. In this way the equality of rights among creditors was abolished, resulting in corresponding protests from London and Washington.

The American government was brought under pressure by the owners of German bonds who were understandably afraid of losing their money. They accused Washington, saying that "this country has taken no steps for the protection of the investment of its citizens." On 19 January 1934, the United States finally made an official protest against the detriment and discrimination of its citizens in favor of Swiss and Dutch bond holders. It was announced that the American government could not avoid pressure by the American public to enact practical countermeasures, although it was still undecided what they would be. The German ambassador in Washington, Hans Luther, who transmitted the Washington protests, requested advice to avoid a "serious economic conflict." Schacht explained to the American ambassador in Berlin, William E. Dodd, the German viewpoint, stressing German willingness to negotiate on 22 January 1934, and suggested two solutions to the transfer problem: either German exports should be facilitated or there should be milder requirements for the German debt. A provisional compromise was reached by the end of January. However, it was conceivable that it would only allay the situation temporarily, since the German foreign trade balance and fiscal situation were growing worse. German Foreign Minister von Neurath therefore urged in February 1934 a conference with the United States in order to increase bilateral trade, that is, to encourage the US to import more from Germany. The American Secretary of State Cordell Hull welcomed the German proposal, but pointed out at the same time that, from the standpoint of domestic politics, this was an unfavorable time for an agreement. To this, Luther noted that it was "pointless to oppose this attitude, because in general arguments bring no results."

In April it was again clear that Berlin was using the bond to put pressure on the US for concessions. In a conversation with the temporary chargé d'affaires in Berlin, J.C. White, Schacht combined the repayment of the outstanding bonds with the demand for increased imports by the US from Germany. White saw through this cheap trick, saying "the scheme looks entirely in Germany's favor." However, Schacht tried to lure the American with the prospect of a blossoming German market, saying that "one cannot sell so much to Malay coolies as to highly qualified German factory workers." Even a good half a year later Schacht tried "to impress the outside world that it cannot do without the market of 66 million Germans, hungry for all kinds of products which the world produces."

In mid-June 1934, Dodd, in a conversation with von Bülow, State Secretary in the Foreign Office, again protested against the one-sided German debt payment and requested a transfer of the agreements made with Switzerland and the Netherlands to the United States. Von Bülow rejected the American complaints, in view of the dilatory policy of the US concerning an agreement on trade policy. When it became known that a unilateral German moratorium on transfers would take effect on 1 July 1934, Hull not only referred to the losses by American investors, but he put this move into a larger context. He interpreted it as "a further dislocation of the process of international finance on which the international trade of the world has developed and a discouragement to international cooperation." Von Bülow naturally rejected these accusations. Luther continued to seek understanding for the German moves, saying that they had arisen from a clear emergency and were temporary and at the end of September, in a note to the American government, von Neurath defended the unilateral transfer arrangement. At the same time he renewed criticism of the US concerning agreement on trade policy.

However, the German protestations were unable to convince the State Department. At the end of October 1934, Rudolf E. Schoenfeld of the Division of Western European Affairs prepared a memorandum on discrimination against American investors and bond holders in favor of citizens of several European countries with which Berlin had signed payment agreements. Altogether Schoenfeld saw in the partly contradictory German measures a "conscious discrimination against American trade in Germany." He reached the conclusion "that there has been a willful and conscious policy of pressure and discrimination designed to force it into unjustified concessions." The accuracy of this analysis was proven when Germany resumed its debt payments to Great Britain. Earlier, London had recognized the foreign trade policy of the "New Plan" specifically in the Agreement on Payments of 1 November 1934. Because the United States were not ready to make similar concessions in foreign trade policy, Washington was not included in the resumption of payments. From the German side there was undoubtedly an attempt to use the question of debt in discussion with the US on trade policy. Because of this, the American government transmitted another note of protest on 23 November 1934, which likewise effected no change in German policy. The debt problem was finally solved by a moratorium which was extended annually until 1939.

B. American Insecurity in Trade and Politics
after the Seizure of Power

In spite of the drastic decline in German-American foreign trade relations, there were many who, at the apogee of the Depression, expected in the future similar exchanges in trade as there had been in the 1920s. The Assistant Commercial Attaché in Berlin, Douglas Miller, believed that Germany was an "attractive market for a very large variety of American goods and a market which seems likely to grow in the future." This hope proved to be a fallacy, for when the National Socialists seized power the process of alienation which was already felt in both countries gained new strength.

Members of the American Embassy in Germany felt considerable cause for apprehension in the Nazi seizure of power. If only half of the National Socialist rhetoric was to take effect in practice, enormous complications could be expected. Consul General George S. Messer-smith sent a cable to Hull saying that it was now more necessary for American commercial interests in Germany to have diplomatic protection. The Commercial Attaché in Berlin, H. Lawrence Groves, advised American commercial interests in Germany in April, 1933, "to reef the sails as much as possible, reduce outstanding commitments to the lowest feasible limit without disrupting existing business connections." Germany would increasingly become a difficult area for American business interests. He said that one would probably have to expect more closures of American representations in Germany, inasmuch as in the National Socialist view of an organic economic body there was no place for foreigners. "It is like the presence of a hostile bacterium in the human system which must be eliminated before the body can be restored to health."

Against this background, American companies which operated branches in Germany would have to think seriously whether, after 1933, they still wanted to carry on their business in Germany. Such was the case for the American Radiator Co., the Gillette Safety Razor Co., or the Toledo Sale Co. In fact, American firms were liquidating their installations in Germany, because the restrictive measures of the German government agencies discouraged many of them in 1933 and 1934. For example, the Sun Oil Co. was able in 1934 to divest itself of its 50% share in Mineral Öl Albrecht & Co., valued at about US $250,000 with a relatively small loss by turning to a few intermediaries. Others even had to make allowance for losses of up to 60%. Even the American automobile manufacturers, as Dodd reported in November, 1934, expected to "abandon Germany." This report was based on Schacht's decision to stop setting aside foreign exchange for the importation of American automobiles. So, General Motors, Chrysler, Nash, Packard and Hudson-Essex either had to give up their business in Germany or try to make some barter arrangements if they wanted to continue exporting to Germany. Miller commented on this, saying that "it looks very much as if we have come to the end of the trail in Germany for most American automobiles." He said that Berlin was engaged "in what amounts to a trade war with the United States."

In addition, the elimination of opposing economic organizations such as the *Reichsverband der Deutschen Industrie*, was followed by American diplomats with a feeling of anxiety. Hull himself feared moves by the new government which would make the situation exceptionally difficult for American investors in Germany and lead to deterioration in trade and fiscal relations. On the other hand, others, like Dodd, a Jeffersonian Democrat and a follower of Wilson, wrote that

> Hitler realizes that any further attempts at Nazification of business and industry might throw the German economy completely out of joint and thus imperil the existence of his regime. Inexorable economic laws have proved stronger than the Nazi monster known as *Gleichschaltung*.

At this time the field of foreign economic policy was actually undergoing a creeping process of regression. In the second half of 1933, Hull warned on the subject of the American quota for plum exports to Germany against the catastrophic effects on trade relations which would occur if the quota system became the rule. Since von Bülow had refused to become involved in this matter, an official American note of protest was delivered in Berlin. It noted a lack of willingness in Berlin to discuss this question "which involves principles of such vital importance to the continuance of their cordial and friendly commercial relations." On the other hand, Berlin complained of a liquor control law in New York state.

Added to these first conflicts in foreign trade policy was the political development in Germany, which was incompatible with American concepts of a democratic-parliamentary system. In particular, the anti-Semitic measures were greeted here with indignation. This clearly obvious mood of criticism against Germany in the United States impressed Schacht during his visit to America in May, 1933. German rearmament, combined with the burning of books on 10 May 1933 and Berlin's anti-Jewish policy had aroused suspicion among Americans who admonished restraint in German policy. As protests against these actions, a boycott movement was formed in the US against the importation of German products. On the other hand, American social circles which were interested in continuing trade with Germany, such as the Steuben Society and the Board of Trade for German-American Commerce (BTGAC) voiced opposition, in their correspondence with the State Department, to the requested boycott. Thus it became obvious that the form of foreign trade policy between Germany and the US had become a bone of contention between the two governments as well as within the respective societies.

2. Bilateralism versus Multilateralism

A. Schacht's "New Plan" in August, 1934

During the worldwide economic crisis there was a fundamental change in foreign trade and fiscal policy in all industrialized countries. As the Depression grew more intense, Germany adopted a policy of financial control to which the presidential cabinets saw no alternatives for economic and political reasons. Regarding foreign trade policy, the Brüning, von Papen and von Schleicher cabinets moved away from most-favored-nation and multilateralism and approached a trade policy which was strongly bilateral in orientation. The disintegration of the international trade and monetary system lent this policy entirely a certain rationale, however power politics relative to southern Europe also played a considerable part in this.

After coming to office, the Hitler government at first made no arrangements to change monetary and foreign trade policy, but left things as they were. The domestic business program of the National Socialists which was directed from the beginning towards a war economy, followed political-military considerations which, however, created conditions requiring increased activity in the areas of foreign trade and monetary policy. After 1933 there was pressure on the German balance of trade through the absorption of imports, deriving from the domestic expansionary economic policies. Besides increased importation there was stagnation in export activity because profits assured by domestic business and German rearmament led to a "non-typical fatigue" in exports, which threatened the base of imports. However, importation of raw materials and other products was unavoidable for execution of the rearmament program. Consequently, exports had to be stimulated also. In this context it was now important which countries were prepared to accept German products.

Thereupon Reich Minister of Economy Schacht thought up the so-called "New Plan" in order to deal with these problems in foreign policy and trade. The plan was to supply raw materials and foodstuffs in ways safe from crises and blockades and gave clear priority to national economic interests over presumptive or actual world economic interests. All German foreign trade under the New Plan was subject to overall planning and regimentation through the establishment of foreign trade agencies and the adoption of bilateral clearing systems. In this way, the conduct of German enterprises in foreign trade could be controlled and opened to government intervention. The central idea of this accounting was: "A clearing agreements means that what you sell me I record and what I sell you, you record and then we must see that both accounts come out even." Consequently, imports and exports were to be balanced bilaterally. However, the kernel of the concept was the intentional shift of German foreign trade and the primary position of imports moved to those countries from which certain products like raw materials were desired and which, on the other hand, were willing to accept increased German exports. Besides this, domestic production of raw materials and substitutes was accelerated. Bilateral policy in trade was not a genuine creation of National Socialism: the Hitler government picked up the threads of the former presidential cabinets but it combined them with concerns of a political and military-economic nature.

The inauguration of the New Plan was legitimized by economic necessity. It was touted as a defensive weapon "forced upon us by the monetary crisis, which is to guarantee for us the imports necessary for life" and as an answer to the fact that, at the beginning of the 1930s, multilateral strategies for dealing with the crisis had "completely failed." This move from multilateral relations to bilateralism had great significance for international trade. A bilateral clearing system leads, through the coupling of imports and exports which are to be balanced bilaterally, necessarily to an inflexible trade policy and has an effect of multiplication and contractuality on world trade.

Still more important were its political consequences. The New Plan made it possible for the National Socialist leaders to continue military rearmament and degraded foreign trade "to a pure instrument in Germany's economic preparation for war." The New Plan gave the National Socialist leaders the means to steer imports, i.e., to give priority to imports relating to rearmament and to decisively influence domestic production through the system for distribution of imported materials. The conclusion of bilateral contracts could be placed better in the service of power politics by the Reich than the multilateral system, for in this way the costs of interdependencies were lessened and short-term economic (and also political) agreements could be made which were considerably easier to revise and modify than is the case with collective, multilateral systems.

B. The Reciprocal Trade Agreement Act of June, 1934

In the United States there was also discussion of foreign trade policy. With the Hawley-Smoot Tariff Act of 1930, the US made a decision with serious consequences, as it implied turning away from the Open Door Policy, which at that time it was no longer considered "vital to the nation's economic well-being or its national security." The enactment of this customs law led to strong stimulation of protectionist movements in other countries, curtailing exports from the US. In view of the size of the domestic market, it was indeed "conceivable that the United States could be a world to itself" but there arose many considerable disadvantages for the progress of the American economy and the American people. Progress in economic technology would also suffer from it. Therefore, a return to free trade was proposed, because turning to political and economic nationalism was a risky business. At first, Franklin D. Roosevelt placed himself in this debate over economic and foreign policy in the camp of the free traders. During the electoral campaign in 1932, he criticized the protectionist tariff law. However, after the election Roosevelt changed sides for reasons of domestic policy and supported protection for American industry and opposed reduction of excise taxes on agricultural imports. However, beneath the surface he knew that he was a supporter of internationalism and the idea of interdependence and that the economic prosperity of the US depended on a worldwide economic recovery and that this required American initiatives. His statements on important questions of international policy such as disarmament and the world trade conference gave rise to hopes that Roosevelt would be a leader in international cooperation. Hull put it this way:

> ...the destiny of history points to the United States for leadership in the existing grave crisis. [...] The present world state of economic war not only strikes at the very vitals of international commerce, but it may also gradually infect the whole fabric of international relations.

When Hull arrived at the World Trade Conference in London in 1933, he called for a "spirit of cooperation" which he said was essential for solving the "Herculean task of promoting and establishing economic peace which is the fundamental basis of all peace."

However, Roosevelt disappointed these expectations in his "Bombshell Message" in which he expressed refusal of international economic cooperation. True to his inaugural speech in which he had formulated his priorities as "first things first," for him, in the immediate future, domestic economic measures took precedence. Not until one's own house was in order could one set about doing something on an international scale. With this decision of Roosevelt's, the cooperative way of solving the crisis was nearly shut down, because an extremely important participant had withdrawn.

Reverses in implementing the New Deal made it increasingly clear in the Roosevelt Administration that the domestic economic crisis could not be overcome without a revival of foreign trade. This led the American government to review Hull's proposal for foreign trade policy and in June, 1934, it passed the Reciprocal Trade Agreements Act (RTAA), which was praised by some as a way to reduce excise taxes and lower the barriers to international trade, and was decried by others as a self-serving instrument of Washington. The trade law laid the basis for the conclusion of bilateral reciprocal trade agreements in which the US would reduce excise taxes on its imports if its trade partner likewise reduced its taxes on American exports. Although at first this was only a purely bilateral matter, the law went beyond bilateralism and stressed the aspect of multilateralism. It also looked ahead towards a reciprocal adoption of unconditional most-favored-nation status, i.e., bilateral customs agreements were expanded on a multilateral basis. Despite its entirely self-serving motivation, the RTAA was a very important step towards a more open and *freer* world trade.

After the enactment of the law, an intensive controversy arose between George N. Peek, who had been appointed as Special Advisor to the President on Foreign Trade, and Secretary of State Cordell Hull over the formulation of American policy on foreign trade, interpretation of the law and control of foreign trade policy. On 23 May 1934, Peek wrote a letter to Roosevelt, explaining to him the negative evolution of American foreign trade, concluding that it was necessary to attain a more balanced relationship between imports and exports. In addition, he suggested setting up bilateral trading accounts with current trading partners. Thus, Peek sued for more flexibility and creativity in trade policy, which expressly implied acceptance of bilateralism in trade policy and also barter. Hull viewed this as an attack on multilateralism and naturally saw the foundations of his program being threatened. This impression was strengthened when, in the middle of November 1934, Peek sought departure from unconditional most-favored-nation policy, namely, a "return to the traditional realistic policy of conditional most-favored-nation treatment" and wanted to postpone the conclusion of reciprocity contracts for the time being. He justified this by saying that "the general national interest, particularly the demands of our internal economy, must determine our foreign policy whether it be in its commercial and financial or in its diplomatic and political aspects." At the end of December he even requested the establishment of a central agency for foreign trade. Hull strongly opposed this intrusion into governmental management. He confirmed his assumption that the United States would gain materially from the most-favored-nation policy and more open world trade. At the same time, he expressed his "unshakable faith in the power of free trade to bring about prosperity and peace."

The argument with Hull finally wound up in a cul-de-sac. Indirectly, Roosevelt was being invited to make a fundamental decision. He was not ill-disposed towards Peek's ideas and a barter system. In fact, he even encouraged Peek to work out a plan for exchanging cotton with Germany. However, Hull finally won out over Peek. Roosevelt identified himself visibly with Hull's trade policy, but was not as "rigidly doctrinaire" as he Hull. On 16 July 1935 Peek submitted his resignation, which Roosevelt at first refused. In November he retired for good. With this, the Hull interpretation of the RTAA on the basis of multilateralism won an important victory and gave a sharper tone to American foreign trade policy.

The Development of German-American Dualism in Foreign Trade Policy from 1934 to 1939

THE DE FACTO END OF THE CONTRACTUAL TRADE RELATIONSHIP BY OCTOBER, 1935

Arguments concerning the course of American foreign trade policy were of great importance for German-American foreign trade. Whereas Peek and his supporters tended from a pragmatic standpoint to meet the Germans halfway on trade policy, the group around Hull clung almost dogmatically to their principles on foreign trade policy; this in turn implied a more rigid attitude towards Germany's desires. Significant differences appeared in the valuation ascribed to trade with Germany. Herbert Feis, Economic Advisor at the State Department, did not consider foreign trade with the Third Reich of great importance at the end of June, 1934. Cancellation of the interdependence relationship could be coped with because it was asymmetrical in nature, i.e., more important for the Germans. "Roughly, it may be said that in a conflict carried out to the most bitter limits, this country could dispense with almost everything now procured from Germany, and Germany could dispense with almost everything procured from this country except cotton." For the US itself he was saw no need for commerce and thus tended towards Hull's view which opposed German desires to enter into concrete negotiations on commercial policy. A special commission studying German-American trade relations also came to this conclusion. The outlook for improvement in these relations was thought to be dim because of German checks on foreign trade. Concessions to the German clearing system were rejected as well as a commercial treaty because "by and large, our major exports to Germany are of far more vital significance to her economy than are German exports to the American economy." The American minister in Vienna, George S. Messersmith, was pessimistic about German-American trade relations in early September, 1934:

> If this Government [Hitler's] continues in power we cannot look forward to Germany as a market. [...] The only hope for Europe, and in a way for us all, lies in the elimination of the present German Government.

American policy officially rejected commercial concessions to the German Reich. At the end of June, 1934, Ambassador Leitner of the Economic Section of the State Department, announced that the US "could never agree with the theory of a bilateral settlement of trade accounts" as proposed to Washington by Berlin. However, as already indicated, this position was not universally accepted within the American administration. Vice Consul Alan Steyne, of the American Consulate General in Hamburg, who saw in the German system of barter trading "a retrogression to an antique form of trading," warned that

> once new trade channels are opened and become the accustomed purchasing centers [...] it will be very much more difficult for American products [...] to regain a foothold in this market when trading conditions become less chaotic.

John Donaldson of Peek's office, said "the only means of maintaining a two-way trade between the countries" was barter. If this were done in the case of American cotton, 50% of American export trade to Germany would be guaranteed. This allowed Germany more weight as a trade partner, a view shared by American companies having trade relations with Germany. Peek was strongly supported by American cotton and tobacco producers, who were especially hurt by sinking trade with Germany. In the case of cotton, half of its export losses were caused by unfulfilled contracts from Germany. So they turned to the State Department and proposed barter exchanges with Germany (and other nations), for "we are in desperate need about foreign markets for our cotton." For James D. Mooney, head of the foreign section at GM, who had held talks with Schacht and Hitler in mid-1934 on foreign economic relations, a barter exchange system was likewise an entirely acceptable solution and he supported Schacht's suggestion of exchanging German wines and beers for American grain and lard.

In this controversy, Assistant Secretary of State Francis B. Sayre tried to take a compromise position. By the end of 1934 he adopted the most-favored-nation method and equal treatment of all commercial partners as a basis for American foreign trade policy. The most-favored-nation situation was to be applied to all countries that operated on that principle. An economic program which placed bilateral settlement at its center would be "suicidal" for the United States, since American foreign trade was triangular. Although this was largely an acceptance of Hull's position, Sayre made qualified this by adding: "In pursuit of these policies, however, doctrinaire action must be avoided." The German government cleverly joined in such statements, pointing out that most-favored-nation status was compatible with the German system of directed foreign trade.

The wriggling through of the American government was struck down by the inconsistency of the position of the American administration regarding the export of American armament business to Germany. A few measures were taken as early as 1933 against the exporting of military airplanes to Germany, since an approximate rough view of the German rearmament program became apparent from the German requisitions. However, these measures were only half-hearted. Miller reported this in April 1934 concerning the support of the expanding *Luftwaffe* by American firms. In this connection he named the United Aircraft Company and its daughter Pratt & Whitney Company, which had received an order for the armament of 2,000 planes, as well as the Sperry Gyroscope Company, which delivered autopilots, compasses and navigation instruments. He also mentioned the Curtis-Wright Company and the Douglas Company. All orders were paid for in cash by Germany, which indicated the importance of the air program in Germany. On 18 September 1934 the State Department finally issued a press communiqué criticizing armament exports to Germany. The Foreign Office looked upon them "with grave disapproval." But no concrete measures were taken. The shipment of products for military use continued undisturbed by governmental influence, frequently through Krupp. With some bitterness, Dodd pointed in dealing with German rearmament to "the assistance of our great corporations: Du Pont, Standard Oil, U.S. Steel, and others."

To clarify the trade relationship and the different interpretations of the most-favored-nation situation, the German government finally gave notice in October 1934 of terminating the friendship and trade treaty with the United States running from 1923 to 15 October 1935. There was no intent to challenge the American foreign trade policy in principle, as Germany wanted to continue to import American raw materials and agricultural products. In stead, the remaining time of about one year was to be used for intensive negotiations with the Roosevelt administration to work out a satisfactory *modus vivendi* in trade policy. The American side did not share this confidence. Thus, after notice was given on the trade agreement, Dodd expressed skepticism about the chances for success in such conversations. As reasons for this, he mentioned for one unemployment in the US, domestic political priorities and Hitler's draconian action relative to the so-called Röhm putsch at the end of June, 1934.

In trade talks with the US, what the Germans wanted above all was an increase in American imports from Germany. For example, at the close of 1934, Schacht pressed for a reduction in American excise taxes on German products. The head of the section on trade policy in the Foreign Office (AA – *Auswärtiges Amt*), Karl Ritter, pointed in this connection to America's favorable trade balance with Germany. If the United States was not prepared to consider meeting Germany halfway, then Germany would have to live with continuing alienation in trade relations and, if necessary, consider appropriate counter-measures. However, for the time being, at an in-house conference on 20 February 1935 on the subject of German-American trade relations, it was agreed not to threaten the Americans yet with retaliation, but first to seek a solution through negotiation.

But the chances for such an agreement were visibly fading, as the State Department made this contingent on a debit position in German trade diplomacy, which was unacceptable to the Germans. Sayre and the head of the West European Division in the State Department, J.P. Moffat, made it quite clear to Ambassador Leitner at the end of April, 1935, that the solution to the problems in trade policy lay in a German initiative alone. Berlin had to find a way

> ...of reconciling our commercial philosophies, but that he [Sayre] did not mean trying to find a half-way compromise. He really meant a fundamental acceptance by Germany of our trade philosophy and a thorough-going partnership with us along the road of equality of treatment and the reduction of trade barriers.

An official German note of May, 1935, requesting resumption of trade talks was consequently refused.

In this critical juncture in international affairs, the American Government does not believe that it would contribute to the progress of foreign trade, promote stability of international relations, or stimulate in any constructive way the economic recovery in our two countries, to conclude a pact with Germany along the lines indicated in Your Excellency's note. This would only tend to strengthen throughout the world the system of discriminatory practices.

It was made clear to the German diplomats also that, although the US was interested in a trade agreement with the Third Reich, this could only occur under Washington's conditions. Leitner summarized the American position in these words: "Instead of infringing on their principle, they prefer to give up signing a trade pact with Germany." Schacht replied, while misunderstanding the economic significance of German-American exchange in raw materials the closing of this trade threatened for the American economy, Germany had changed its mind in the past months. One was ready for cooperation with the US, but one could live very well without it, since one is not dependent on US exports at all.

In practice, Germany was actively destroying what remained of willingness to cooperate from the American side. Thus, in several cases, the German authorities wanted, as with the Standard Oil branches and the German daughter of American Express, to involve the American mother companies by taxing those firms. Consequently it was not surprising that, in early October, shortly before the expiration of the trade treaty, Hull reemphasized the principle of the American position in a conversation with Ritter. He again explicitly rejected any acceptance of the German desiderata and stressed "that if we surrendered a portion of our trade agreements program it would severely discredit that program and render virtually impossible further progress with it." Consequently on 5 October 1935 Ritter telegraphed from Washington that, regarding German-American economic negotiations, in view of the strong opposition of the State Department and especially Hull, there was no agreement in sight.

Finally the negotiations concluded with extension of the German-American trade treaty without its centerpiece, the most-favored-nation clause. Thus it was hardly worth the paper on which it was written. When Berlin denied the US as of 12 October most-favored-nation status, this was understood in America as basically a hostile action. Although this step implied increasingly turning away from the US in favor of other countries and offended Washington, Berlin was not prepared to give in to American pressure, because if Germany gave in to Washington, that would be interpreted as "a sign of weakness." In this, the two different systems of trade policy had clashed violently and neither side seemed willing to yield to the other.

Competition for Third Markets

When Reich Minister of Economics Schacht inaugurated the "New Plan" in August, 1934, this brought Germany onto a collision course with the United States, as he changed German trade to bilateral settlement, abandoned the principle of treating trade partners equally and turned to currency control. These essential elements of the new German trade policy contradicted the principles of the RTAA agreed upon in June 1934 which called for an open world market, trade as free as possible, and most-favored-nation handling. They

> not only closed the door for the US in Germany, but took away from the United States the "equal chance" particularly in those places where National Socialist trade policy was able to achieve considerable success: in southeast Europe and Latin America.

In this, German-American antagonism in foreign trade policy manifested itself in the third markets.

1. The German "Monroe Doctrine" in Southeast Europe

Before the first World War, Germany was quite important in trade with southeast European countries and Weimar Republic was a major trade partner for the entire region which had acquired new territorial form after the Paris treaties. The countries in that area—with the exception of Czechoslovakia—remained peripheral or developing countries during the entire interwar period. The worldwide economic crisis at the end of the 1920s and the beginning of the 1930s had catastrophic results in that region because it came at a time of a farm crisis caused by structural problems. However, their value in Germany's foreign trade policy rose because at that time when order was collapsing in world and trade currency, protectionist practices and trends towards autarky were spreading and contending trade blocs were emerging, sufficiently secure export and import areas were of enormous significance. Whereas France led the countries of the gold standard bloc and London intensified its trade with the Empire in the sterling bloc and the US set its sights on a dollar-based trade zone, the Weimar cabinets moved towards currency control and laid the foundation orienting German trade policy towards bilateralism.

The southeast European countries, which had also adopted currency control during the world economic crisis, were seen by German politicians both as a natural sphere of influence and as a backyard. Although there had been no place for active German policy in southeastern Europe in Stresemann's view, that changed with the presidential regimes. They clearly followed the efforts of Wilhelmine Germany and tried to tie that area closer to Germany both economically and politically. The first step towards German preponderance in central and southeast Europe was the project for a customs union with Austria which began in 1930 and failed in 1931 because of inadequate preparation, reacting against the Briand plan which had a vision for all Europe and called for "independent national great power development."

In addition, the presidential cabinets turned to agrarian protectionism as a way to move the countries of that area to good conduct and lured them with preferential contracts. Offers made to Hungary and France's treaty partner Romania to sign preferential treaties in 1931 "were the actual start of a trade offensive by the German Reich in the southeast." Political calculations played a prominent role in this, as this step aimed at undermining the French security system in that region. "The transformation of growing economic power into political capital became the central theme of southeast European policy in the Foreign Office." This German initiative grew weaker through international protests, a constantly growing orientation towards interdependence and a lack of interest by von Papen. Among the governments which raised objections was first of all that of the United States. It clung to the most-favored-nation principle and did not agree to preferential customs duties. In this a future line of conflict was already apparent.

German industry also recognized the possibilities for economic development in that region. However, industrial branches oriented towards export did not view southeast Europe in any way as an alternative or substitute for the world market, but rather as a supplement thereto. The offer of preferential contracts to southeast Europe was critically evaluated, but nevertheless the RDI (*Reichsverband der Deutschen Industrie*—German Industry Association) and the *Deutsche Industrie- und Handelstag* (DIHT) adopted a "double strategy," which lined its sights along both worldwide export markets as well as a safe regional European market. They did not even consider withdrawing from the world market. They rejected exclusive orientation towards southeast Europe, because

> …such preferential systems lead to the inevitable result that they cause conflicts with the countries which did not join the system. It would not be wise, from an economic point of view if we risk 96.6% of our exports in order to secure 3.4% of our exports.

The further development of world trade, the emergence of economic blocs and the failure of the world economic conference in London in the summer of 1933 caused German industry to turn around, without, however, abandoning entirely its orientation towards the world market. Decline in world trade and the change in "Terms of Trade" which benefited the industrialized countries, and thus also Germany, because prices for primary products fell more than prices for partially -finished or finished goods, led to stronger concentration on the southeast European countries. However, in contrast to France, Berlin did not possess considerable financial power to make its influence felt and trusted the "consumer strength of a population of 60 million," i.e., the absorptive power of the German market. When the National Socialists came to power, there was a complete shift towards bilateralism. Two-sided agreements were generally preferred to multilateral ones. Indeed, Schacht's "New Plan" somewhat resembled Brüning's preferential policy which often lacked concept and was at least improvisational.

> …but the quality of goals and means had fundamentally changed in the meantime. The "New Plan" represented a revolutionary change in German foreign trade policy in that it dealt with the abandonment of the principle of the most-favored-nation clause and the increasing bilateralization of trade in the framework of a long range strategy.

Its aims were motivated by an economy based on rearmament and served "the National Socialist plans based on racial ideology, territorial expansion and world power." Southeast Europe was not to become entirely Germany's "informal empire."

In March 1933 when the German-Yugoslav commercial treaty expired, both sides agreed during the negotiations, which were held without delay, to an extension. Belgrade scarcely had any alternatives to association with Berlin. As counterpoint to the world economic conference held at the same time, and where there was at least a possibility for a multilateral strategy for coming to terms with the crisis, Berlin and Belgrade signed a provisional agreement on 29 July 1933 which became a genuine commercial treaty by May 1934. This agreement provided German preferences for Yugoslav agricultural exports and was accompanied by 20 secret additional agreements which confirmed the "central importance of Yugoslavia for Germany politically and for trade" at that time. This treaty also exemplified the fate in store for the southeast European countries according to the will of Berlin, for in the treaty Belgrade undertook an almost complete adaptation of its agricultural production to German import requirements. This was compensated for by the fact that Germany paid for about 60% of Yugoslav grain exports at a price which was 30% above the world market price. The German-Hungarian trade treaty of 21 February 1934 and the treaty with Romania in March 1935 were similar. The purpose of the latter was to undermine the Little Entente.

Parallel with this, Hitler entered new fields in foreign policy by seeking a rapprochement with Poland. At a ministerial conference on 7 April 1933 it was agreed that an understanding with Poland was neither "possible nor desirable," but Hitler disregarded the anti-Polish feeling in the Foreign Office. In so doing he emphasized his claim to leadership in the shaping of German foreign policy. The non-aggression pact with Poland of 26 January 1934 was important to Hitler for two reasons. He torpedoes the plan of French Foreign Minister Paul Boncour to create an East European pact system by feeding Poland's ambitions to become a great power. Poland itself, after French participation in the four-power pact with Great Britain, Italy and Germany (15 July 1933), which meant turning aside from Poland and the countries of the Little Entente, was thrown on its own resources. Thus, with this pact, Warsaw felt it had won security with respect to Germany and the USSR. Almost at the same time as the signing of the non-aggression pact, Hitler ended the trade war with Poland in the spring of 1934. In March 1934, in October 1934, and in November 1935 commercial and compensatory agreements were initialed. As with other countries in that area, Germany was trying to use the clearing system to bring Poland into the German sphere of influence. However, the Polish government avoided that by seeing that Germany did not accumulate clearing debts towards Poland which could be used by Berlin for political pressure, rather, that German exports to Poland and imports from Poland remained in balance.

After the Hitler government came to power, and especially from 1934 on, Germany pressed its southeast European policy and severely contained domestic political resistance to agricultural imports from that region. Conspicuous in this was the "striking coincidence" of the economic and security policies of bilateralism, documented by German withdrawal from the Geneva Disarmament Conference and the League of Nations in October 1933 and the commercial treaties and the German-Polish non-aggression pact. In order to achieve its political aims in southeast Europe, i.e., create an informal empire in that area, Berlin used instruments of foreign trade. Among these was the accumulation of clearing debts vis-à-vis its trading partners already mentioned.

In the second half of August 1934, the Foreign Office complained of the high levels of clearing which had gradually become "an intolerable burden" and were leading to a "new foreign indebtedness." Still, a fine means for political pressure could be made of it: the unspoken, but ubiquitous, threat of not paying these debts hung like a sword of Damocles over the governments of the southeast European countries. The German indebtedness in clearing with foreign countries thus became an intentionally created weapon in foreign economic policy, a "clever imperialism without money." Through this instrument, Germany exerted considerable influence over the economic development of those countries. Only Poland and Czechoslovakia, whose trade with Germany was not active, were able to escape this trap. Meanwhile people continued to look upon the importance of Germany as trade partner for the Danube countries as the main pillar for the German position in southeastern Europe. The Reich practically guaranteed them export for their products. With this—as Schacht put it during his trip to the Balkans in 1936—Germany became "His Majesty the Client." In this context, it was urged to the change the contractual system over to bilateralism. Thus, it was thought that it would be considerably more effective than the multilateral system because it broadened the domestic field of action.

Under the Four Year Plan Berlin increased its efforts in southeast Europe. In December 1936 the German economy was explicitly encouraged to expand its capital investments in southeast Europe. The results of these endeavors were satisfactory. At the end of April 1937 Ritter concluded a general directive from the Foreign Office with satisfaction that the realization had been implanted in the entire southeast European region that its economic prosperity depended on Berlin. He said that the use of bilateral agreements had succeeded and that from now on it would become increasingly difficult in that area to create economic groupings without or even against Germany. This was likewise true for the political sphere, which could scarcely be separated from it.

German military exports from 1935 to the southeast European countries (and Latin America) illustrate this nexus between politics and economy. They are to be looked upon "in the framework of political and economic development," according to an evaluation by *Reichsgruppe Industrie* (RGI), and served to soften southeast European complaints over German clearing debts and cemented the asymmetry in bilateral relations in favor of Germany. On 12 March 1938, Germany and Bulgaria signed a secret treaty concerning the supply of German military equipment to Bulgaria amounting to 30 million Reichsmarks. The two countries traditionally maintained friendly relations with each other and their economic interaction had increased significantly since the world economic crisis. In November of the same year, Wiehl, the head of the section on economic policy in the Foreign Office, approved an additional arms credit for Bulgaria of over 45 million Reichsmarks. In May 1938, the Reich Economic Ministry (RwiM) urged concluding an arms agreement with Romania, which was rich in petroleum, in order to guarantee delivery of aircraft fuel to Germany. In October 1938, Berlin and Bucharest agreed that Germany would import wheat and petroleum from Romania and in return would share in Romanian rearmament. In February 1939 the

Foreign Office supported Krupp's request for a comprehensive guarantee by the Reich to send arms to the Yugoslav government valued at 100 million Reichsmarks. Finally, after the Minister to Belgrade, Heeren, reported a Yugoslav feeler directed towards the Western powers, Belgrade was assured in May of a German arms credit of 200 million Reichsmarks. At the same time, Greece received a German arms credit of over 50 million marks and in economic negotiations with Turkey an armament deal was also signed. In June, Budapest made a similar overture to the Reich.

Also, in February 1939, Berlin was negotiating with Bucharest concerning a trade agreement. Romania agreed to guide its agricultural and lumber production towards German requirements and to exploit its minerals, as Germany promised support in building up its industry and in supplying military equipment for over 10 million Lei. The Foreign Office reasoned that this type of accord served as guide, as similar arrangements with Yugoslavia, Hungary, Bulgaria and Turkey were probable. In this way, Germany was making certain of being the "first power in southeast Europe." The governments of both countries initialed a development contract on 23 March 1939 which represented a "break in National Socialist foreign trade policy." In fact, the agreement bound Bucharest in a forced marriage with the economy of the Third Reich. Finally, on 8 July there was a secret protocol as a supplement concerning the delivery of aircraft and weapons, and on 10 December 1939 Romania and Germany signed an economic treaty whereby Germany agreed to receive 400,000 tons of wheat. With this German-Romanian economic treaty, relations with the countries in that region had reached a new level. The annexation of Austria in March 1938 had been an especially important step towards a German economic empire, an informal empire in Central and Southeast Europe, since Vienna was the key to the southeast European region. The occupation of the Sudeten territory followed in October 1938 and in March 1939, the occupation of Czechoslovakia. With the treaty between Berlin and Bucharest, which gave Germany broad influence over the production of goods in Romania, steered Romania's industrialization and directed it towards the German politico-strategic supply requirements, the structure and character of large-scale economy consequently assumed definite shape.

It was true in the period between the wars that trade with southeast European countries was "never attractive on purely economic grounds." For Germany, intensification of economic relations with those countries during the world economic crisis was at first economically motivated, as losses were suffered in traditional segments of the world market. But questions of trade policy and economics were quickly mixed up with political ambitions. The strategy of the German Reich aimed at a "colonial status" for the southeast European countries, that is, the establishment of a German sphere of influence, an expansionist economy whose intended functions, blockade-free and dealing with military economic matters, would act as a supplier of raw materials and foodstuffs. This was reflected in the words of Carl Krauch, General Commissioner for special questions of chemical manufacture and *spiritus rector* of the "New Military Economic Production Plan," who demanded at the end of April 1939 that

> Germany must so strengthen its war-making potential and that of its allies that the coalition is equal to the efforts of almost all of the rest of the world. That can only occur through new, large and joint efforts by all allies and an improved, at first peaceful, expansion of the large economic region in the Balkans and Spain according to the raw materials base of the coalition.

The German policy of setting up a commercial instrumentality for achieving its interests made the Reich actually the preponderant power in southeast Europe by the late 1930s. With its aim of creating an "informal empire" in southeast Europe, Berlin's policy after 1933 followed the tradition of Weimar foreign policy entirely, going back to Brüning's preferential policy in its concepts. However, National Socialist policy in southeast Europe went beyond that continuity, showing "a specifically National Socialist component." There were qualitative differences: on the one hand, the domestic opposition of agrarian interest groups was eliminated, having been quite visible in the later phase of the Weimar Republic; on the other hand, the rigidity with which that policy was converted, and finally the alignment of the bilateral relationships with the requirements of the German economy.

London and Paris were able to do little in opposition to this, like other European countries. Their economic and strategic priorities lay elsewhere. In the first half of the 1930s, France did nothing to defend the *status quo* in that area. Economic aid from Paris was bitterly missed in the southeast European countries and particularly in the Little Entente. Great Britain, overextended by its global imperial interests, looked upon this region not as an economically important area, but rather as a large bargaining chip, that is, a field where considerable concessions could be made in order to attain parity with Germany.

This situation in the international political economy led to the result that east and southeast Europe—including the Baltic states—had at this time no alternative to a "close economic dependency on the German economy." The advantages did not lie on the side of National Socialist Germany exclusively. In Reich trade with the countries of this region, there were favorable opportunities for complementary trade. For the agrarian countries of the region, the bilateral accounting system was of great economic importance, in some cases "the best means available for financing economic recovery." The marketing of agricultural products and raw materials from those countries was guaranteed in Germany with a view to the future. Besides, the Reich paid prices above the world market, which was favorable for the Terms of Trade in southeast Europe, and the German exports corresponded to the import requirements of those countries. For these reasons a certain complementarity could not be disputed. It affected primarily the economic sector, where both sides profited from the trade relationships, although not to the same degree. From a political point of view, the advantages lay clearly in Berlin. The economic favors given the southeast European countries were relatively easy to accept under the conditions of the rapid economic recovery in Germany and this assured their political application. Political opposition to the Reich incurred enormous economic penalties, whereas political good behavior was rewarded from an economic standpoint. The cost to be paid the Reich was political respect and willingness to adapt one's own production and in so doing the orientation of industrialization increasingly to German needs. This shifted the economic advantages as time went on successively to the German side, which assigned this area a clearly dependent status within the expansionist economy dominated by Berlin which at a higher level was to be autarkic (continental autarky). The presumably leading role of the Germans in the family of nations was cited to legitimize this situation.

From time to time children must be forced towards their happiness. Besides, in individual life as well as that of nations everyone must make sacrifices when the future and destiny of society are at stake. When one does not willingly demonstrate the necessary community feeling, he ought and must be forced to do so.

This German policy towards southeast Europe met with heavy criticism in the US, because the building and establishment of a one-sided economy under German leadership implied the exclusion of outside (*raumfremd*) powers like the United States from that region. Through this German trade system there would result enormous success whose effects would be felt beyond that area. It would mean a significant setback for Washington's attempt to create a more open, free and multilateral system of world trade and possibly seriously limit its chances of success. Thus, southeast Europe was an important ingredient in the German-American antagonism over foreign trade policy.

2. American Foreign Trade Policy in Latin America Challenged by the Reich

The first German-American rivalries in Latin America occurred in the second half of the 1920s, for example, in air travel, when Pan American Airlines competed against Scadta. Nevertheless they did not become acute until the National Socialists came to power when German trade ambitions in Central and South America were directed towards securing German import needs for raw materials, raw products and foodstuffs. The methods which Berlin used for this were based on Schacht's "New Plan" which converted German foreign trade policy to bilateral settlement of accounts and was diametrically opposed to the RTAA. They assigned different status to German trading partners, so that many countries came to enjoy preferential treatment which was not given to others. Now the Reich tried to convince the Latin American countries of the advantages of this trading system. This was interpreted by the US as a threat to vital American interests which included, besides economic, obvious political factors. Herein the western hemisphere became a "chief battlefield" for the two systems of foreign trade policy.

From July 1934 until January 1935, a German trade delegation headed by Otto Kiep traveled through nearly all South American countries. Their mission—the creation and expansion of trade relations—was crowned with success. There were trade and currency agreements with several of these countries, which placed the Reich on a collision course with the US. As early as the middle of 1935, Legation Counselor Hans Kroll, in charge of South American economic affairs in the Foreign Office, noted "that for several months a systematic and energetic campaign against the new German Latin American policy is being waged by the United States and England." However, Kroll was optimistic and gave the American measures only slim chances for success and spoke of

> Germany's new trade relations on a new basis full of hope and capable of expansion with the struggling South American continent which, with Germany, is advantageous economically.

In fact, Germany made considerable efforts to guarantee exports from those countries to Germany, which relied on importing their raw materials and products. For this purpose, Berlin paid prices which were in general 10 to 15% higher than world market prices. In addition, Germany granted extremely favorable credit conditions such as generous terms for repayment which further encouraged those countries to sign trade agreements with Germany. This development was carefully noted in Washington. The Latin American section in the State Department registered in 1935 successes of the German export offensive in 14 Latin American countries, excepting Cuba, Mexico and Panama, while there had been distinct German progress in trade with Central American countries. One year later Germany had even risen to become the most important trade partner for the ABC countries (Argentina, Brazil, and Chile). The widening of German commercial activity in Latin America at the expense of the US strengthened American criticism of the German trading system. According to Hull, the system for settling accounts drastically limited the amount of foreign exchange of the Latin American countries available for trade with other countries, so that bilateral trade undermined three-way commerce and thus was extremely detrimental to the US.

Consequently the Latin American trip by Max Ilgner of the IG was watched by Washington with distrust. Ilgner was in Latin America from August till December 1936. The purpose of his trip was to make contact with all agencies in Latin America involved with export, to discuss concrete projects and to collect information concerning the political and economic situation in the countries visited, the situation of IG representatives there and the activities of national and international competitors. In general, Ilgner evaluated the German position in Ibero-America as growing. He thought that this was due to German immigration and the success of National Socialist foreign policy. He also credited the activity of German air transport to and within South America through the Zeppelins and the Condor syndicate as increasing German prestige. This growth in prestige precipitated the drastic increase in imports from Germany. In any case, the South American market was at the moment the fastest growing and consequently offered the greatest possibilities for development, provided that a proper strategy could be found to get around the movements towards nationalization in that area. Competition in the region from the US, which continued to bear "colonial-imperialistic traits," was of particular interest. In this, the Pan American idea would fall positively on fertile soil. Ilgner's Latin American trip was automatically interpreted in Washington in the context of ambitions of the German government in that area, so that Dodd saw in Ilgner's mission an attempt to discredit American trade policy. When, in the middle of 1937, a German consortium led by Siemens received the bonus of the Rio Negro hydroelectric project, the Gabriel Tarra dam, it was viewed as a confirmation of that opinion. If this project was considered together with Ilgner's Latin American trip—it amounted altogethfer to about 50 million pesos (over 200 million Reichsmarks)—it gave the picture of "centralized direction of German commercial activities abroad."

German-American antagonism was not limited to the economic zone alone, but also extended to the political arena. Thus, both sides sought to bind the Latin American countries closer to themselves in a political way. In Berlin, American efforts to implement the RTAA in Latin America were followed with great care and maximum attention was paid to Washington's promotion of Pan-Americanism. The Reich steered against this politically by raising German legations in the ABC countries to the rank of embassies, thereby giving them greater diplomatic prestige. The governments of the three countries responded to this move towards closer relations at the political level by raising their missions in Berlin likewise to embassies. Thereupon Hull again took up the idea of continental solidarity and in 1936, at the Pan American Conference in Buenos Aires, urged banning war from the western hemisphere. Without its being mentioned, this also meant closer political cooperation. German diplomats perceived the Good Neighbor Policy as an "updated variation of the old Monroe Doctrine" and played upon similar fears of Latin American diplomats of a US-American imperialism.

Cooperation within the hemisphere continually acquired greater importance in Washington, since, in the eyes of American diplomats, the consequences of a successful Latin American strategy by the Third Reich would be enormous for the US. Under Secretary of State Sumner Welles, speaking of Brazil in July 1937, claimed for the United States the right for "equality of opportunity for its trade in other countries." But Germany, he said, was using unfair methods for promoting its trade with Brazil. Sumner Welles now called for steps to be taken against these methods, for

> ...their continued effect would be to weaken any commercial treaty arrangements based on other principles unless safeguards were taken against them; and with the weakening of these commercial treaty arrangements the underlying principles themselves will become inoperative.

The German foreign trade offensive in Latin America had to be countered if the US wanted to secure a breakthrough for its own philosophy of trade. Even Mexico, where until 1938 there had been no sign of Fascist ideology and where the Mexican government had sometimes refused barter deals with Germany in favor of exports from the US, frequently accepted barter trading with Germany at the end of 1938 and in early 1939. The Mexican firms delivered mostly petroleum to Germany. In addition, German deliveries of military goods in the second half of the 1930s to balance imports and exports to Argentina, which at that time was seeking a role of independent leadership in South America and came to be the most important opponent of

Washington at the Pan American conferences in Buenos Aires (1936) and Lima (1938), caused much irritation in the US.

In Berlin, on the other hand, the American attempts to sign most-favored-nation treaties with Latin American countries were perceived as a direct and coordinated maneuver against German policy. This was focused on the "test case" of Brazil and had to be opposed "with all appropriate means"—and here the German government was thinking of involving the NSDAP-AO. So Berlin went about strengthening the ideological part of its foreign policy, which was then looked upon with distrust in the US. German establishments in the western hemisphere were considered *per se* as potential "Fifth Columns," whether they were diplomatic delegations or branches of German companies.

Events in Europe, particularly the Munich Agreement and the German action against Czechoslovakia, encouraged this view and the Roosevelt administration adopted extensive countermeasures. Secretary of the Treasury Morgenthau proposed in October 1938 credits, debt relief and economic aid for Latin American countries. However, these were not seen at the German Embassy in Washington in the context of the political development, but were seen as resulting from the presumably successful economic policy of the German Reich in Latin America. Hull's address before the National Foreign Trade Council, mentioned previously, in which he unrelentingly insisted on recognition of the American trading system, was explained by Dieckhoff as due to the successes of German trade policy in Latin America (and in central and southeast Europe). He said that Hull was echoing the lament of American banking and industrial circles who, as though suffering from psychosis, were painting the threatening conquest of the South American market by authoritarian nations on the wall.

However, experience did not entirely confirm this view. Although the economic successes of the German Reich in Latin America were indisputable, it must be added that Great Britain suffered more from them than the United States. The Latin American section of the State Department was aware of this situation. Still, the impression persisted in the subjective feeling of many diplomats that Berlin's roll-back strategy to drive back US influence in the Latin American countries was succeeding. Among Cordell Hull's paper there is a untitled manuscript which he drew up after the outbreak of the World War. In it he described German policy in the western hemisphere as a large-scale attempt at penetration. Latin America was to be drawn into the German orbit by influence on the local press, the delivery of military goods, the activities of the Lufthansa daughter company Condor and Scadta, espionage, and especially through economic channels and a trade war. Consequently, this was pictured by him as an almost mortal threat to the US.

Washington's increasing calls for continental solidarity together with the economic incentives offered by the US brought their first successes towards the end of the decade. Thus, from 1938 on, more or less strongly, bad news came to the Foreign Office from German missions in Latin America. The US exerted massive political and economic pressure on Brazil, which showed some success in October 1938, at least from a political standpoint. Washington worked in Mexico and Uruguay through economic and trade measures against Germany; in Central America the US was probably behind anti-German campaigns in the press. Reports finally culminated in the opinion that American diplomacy was seeking

> ...by all means next to economic war to eliminate German political and cultural influence in South America in order to establish a Pan American bloc also in case of war.

These fears were confirmed in December 1938 after the Pan American Conference in Lima. Noebel, the German minister in Lima, drew the following conclusions from the talks. Although Washington had suffered a shipwreck with its plan for a military alliance under its leadership and the establishment of economic hegemony in South America, American diplomacy had achieved ideological success in strengthening Pan American solidarity and democracy. Distrust in Latin American countries of the "Big Neighbor to the North" had lessened significantly, so that the Reich did not have a single friend on the whole American continent. Thereupon Berlin tried to secure its influence in South America through military shipments. Further ideas on how to deal with the "cloudiness in relations" with the Latin American countries were discussed in June 1938 at a conference of German Latin American missions at the Wilhelm Straße. The ambassadors to the ABC countries and the minister to Uruguay met afterwards on 28/29 July in Montevideo for another discussion where a catalogue of measures was worked out which included, among other things, the signing of trade agreements over a period of several years with the Latin American countries, a reduction of AO activity as well as greater influence over the local press, and called for the assignment of military attachés. The plan for reining in the activities of the NSDAP-AO naturally met with immediate opposition. Hitler finally entered the conflict between the Foreign Office and the Nazi Party's overseas organization and decided in favor of the Wilhelm Straße position. On 3 September he confirmed the subordination of Party agencies to the diplomatic missions which had already been arranged in practice.

However, Berlin overlooked the fact that the alleged and actual successes of Washington's diplomacy were brought about less by efforts of the Roosevelt administration than by growing criticism of National Socialist policy and ideology in the Latin American countries themselves. Thus, the Argentine government decisively opposed the activity of the NSDAP-AO in Argentina from April 1938 on. After the outbreak of war, the countries of Latin American finally adopted a neutral stance, which proved the division among those nations during the German-American struggle. It was a gesture towards the United States, which was also remaining neutral, and at the same time, it was an attempt to continue economic relations with the Reich. But finally the American Good Neighbor Policy won out in Latin America. It was possible to block the German influence, especially after war began. At the end of July 1940, the participants in the Pan American Conference in Havana finally signed an agreement on the "Reciprocal Assistance and Cooperation for the Defense of the Nations of the Americas," which was, in fact, a defense treaty, brining continental solidarity a little nearer to reality.

A. *The example of Brazil*

Brazil, under President Vargas, showed in negotiations with the German trade delegations that it was receptive to the ideas of compensation arrangements and barter trade, since the central European markets were more advantageous for Brazilian export interests than the American market, which mainly received Brazilian coffee. Thus, in November 1934 a trade agreement with Berlin was signed. The State Department had also considered trade preferences for Brazil in order to counter the German export offensive. However, when it was seen that this meant stepping into bilateralism, those ideas were put aside. Brazil, which was striving towards leadership in its area, decided to exploit the strong interest of Washington and Berlin in Brazil opportunistically and pragmatically for its own purposes. In the end, the German offer to pay for Brazilian exports to Germany with military goods was decisive. In following years German military shipments became visibly larger, so that the areas of military-security policy and trade policy overlapped.

And yet, closer ties were made with the US also. Thus, after making the agreement with the German Reich, Washington was sounded out and in November 1935 a trade treaty was signed with the US. However, the United States took offense when, in December 1935, Brazil cancelled all treaties of most-favored-nation type dating from 1931 to 1934 and also delayed ratification of the treaty for several months. Additionally, in the same period Brazil's trade with the arch-rival in trade policy increased significantly and Brazil converted its representation in Berlin to the status of an embassy, emphasizing its willingness to further strengthen its relations with the Third Reich. Furthermore, an evaluation of the economic relations with Germany had a positive outcome, when, in June 1936, a secret "Gentlemen's Agreement" with Berlin was distributed, setting Brazilian trade relations with Germany until the war and even influencing Brazilian foreign policy. Following this agreement, German-Brazilian trade experienced renewed impetus. Thus, the treaty must be seen as a triumph for Berlin and a renunciation of the Good Neighbor Policy of the United States.

In Washington's view, the German challenge in Latin America obviously gave reason for concern. The State Department received correspondence from corporations that were alarmed by German trade practices, asking for help from the government. For example, Westinghouse complained in 1937 that it had lost a half-million dollar deal because of German actions to increase its exports in Brazil. American efforts were finally crowned with success when, in mid-July 1937, a treaty was signed with Brazil, spurring Berlin to intensify its endeavors in Brazil. When an extension of the German-Brazilian trade treaty came up in 1937, Berlin protested against US intervention in the economic and trade sovereignty of the Latin American countries which the Germans found inadmissible. Dodd replied that the United States wanted to be dealt with by Brazil exactly like Germany.

When a domestic political shift took place in Brazil towards the right with the "*Estado Novo*," Germany expected greater political advantages to follow, but it was quickly seen that only the economic relations were intensified, whereas the political relationship was clouded by Brazil's fear of German political expansion. For this reason, Brazil even forced the withdrawal of the German ambassador. Economically, the "*Estado Novo*" increased instability in Brazil and this encouraged arms purchases from Germany. Thus, in March 1938 an order was placed with Krupp for artillery shipments to Brazil in the amount of approximately 8.3 million pounds. As a counterpoint to this, the American Export and Import Bank issued a credit to Brazil in April of 20 million dollars. After a diplomatic rapprochement had been arranged in 1938, a consortium brought together by Krupp obtained the addition of an arms order amounting to 1.7 million pounds in July 1939.

Both agreements contributed to engaging Brazil more firmly to bilateral trade policy. Here, the connection between arms and trade policy was obvious. Neither the United States nor Great Britain was prepared for arms deals with Brazil and Germany stepped into this breach,, combining its arms sales with trade concessions. Brazil continued to withdraw from American efforts to close ranks in its own hemisphere and this made Brazil in the eyes of the US a fulfillment aide to National Socialist Germany. Not until the war, which closed European markets to Brazilian exports, was Brazil compelled to concentrate again more strongly on the western hemisphere.

It is exceedingly difficult to make a definitive judgement of German intentions in Latin America. There are justifiable doubts whether

> Berlin by the end of the 1930s had a clearly defined policy towards the Latin American countries at all if one puts aside the trade policy of involving those countries in supplying Germany with raw materials and foodstuffs without using foreign exchange.

There is no doubt that South and Central America had great importance for German trade policy, which brought that country into conflict with the US. The development of the German position in foreign trade with the Latin American countries aggravated the tensions in trade policy between Washington and Berlin because it was interpreted in the context of the antagonism between the systems. It was perceived not only as competition between trade systems, but also as part of the contest between sociological ideologies opposed to one another (democracy versus dictatorship). Although Latin America was only a "sideline" in German foreign policy and stood only on the margin of Hitler's "program," the German successes in foreign trade policy in that area in the later 1930s had for Washington also a political and even military nuance. For, in the American view, they threatened not only the economic security of the United States, but could also provide a base of military operations or various "Fifth Columns." Consequently, the intensive struggle for foreign trade in Latin America held a significance that went well beyond a purely economic one.

3. The Increasing Gravity of the Conflict Over Foreign Trade Policy From the Middle of the 1930s

The German successes in foreign trade policy in Latin American and southeast Europe led to a sharpened consciousness of the problem of the elementary antagonism in foreign trade policy in the American government. They demonstrated the significance for trade policy and the dissemination of the American foreign trade system that came not only from an economic, but also from a political point of view. There grew in the State Department, as in the Roosevelt administration overall, a willingness to be more strongly active in international politics. For example, Sayre composed a small memorandum with the title "America Must Act." In it he first stressed the involvement of the US in relations of interdependency. He said America was not a "hermit nation," but was dependent on its integration in world trade. To support this, the policy of bilateralism in trade, the antipode of an open system of world trade, must be opposed with determination, he continued. This question has an fundamental significance, for "war or peace in our time may hang upon the choice which nations are now making of the economic policy which is to rule the world." In this, American policy may be the determining factor. "The responsibility for leadership lies in Washington."

The debate over the collection of compensatory customs duties in 1936 may be interpreted as a first, small step in that direction. In view of the German measures to advance their exports, the Treasury Department aired a plan to collect these duties on German exports to the United States. This proposal was warmly greeted by many firms which complained of German trade methods like the subvention of exports and demanded government support measures. However, the Trade Agreements Division thought this was a wrong step, as likewise did cotton and tobacco producers and importers of certain German products, such as, for example, cameras and wine. Even the State Department was not entirely happy with this decision, as it was feared that there would be negative effects on trade with Europe and South America. Therefore, Sayre, at the beginning of February, made a new attempt to bring Germany around in a conversation with the director of the Reichsbank Puhl and Hartenstein of the Reich Economic Ministry. He said that it was desired to increase trade with Germany, but only if it was compatible with the principles of the RTAA. In order to strengthen this requirement, Washington refused the sale of 800,000 bales of cotton to Germany, because that was not in accord with the spirit of the RTAA.

From March/April 1936 there seemed to be hope for a meeting halfway on the part of the German government on the question of trade principles, for Berlin announced its interest in the reintroduction of most-favored-nations policy. Henry Grady, head of the Division of Trade Agreements, objected, however, that this did not mean abandoning the clearing system, but must be seen in the light of the debate over compensatory customs duties for German goods, for the collection of such duties was to be prevented by this. However, on 11 June 1936 the Treasury Department announced this step with Roosevelt's backing, as it saw in the Askimark system an unacceptable form of promoting exports. The compensatory duties, which were to be collected on the thirtieth day after announcement of the directive, were to amount to 22.5% up to 56% of the value of the goods, according to the product. Berlin protested officially against this decision within only a few days and Luther complained to Hull that this measure would hinder planning for talks on trade policy. Hull parried this by saying that the measures in question were the responsibility of the Treasury Department and he hoped that Germany could get the reason for these additional duties out of the way. The German government immediately promised to cancel its export promotion projects, since it was to be feared that countries with a customs system similar to that of the United States like Canada, Australia and South Africa might adopt similar measures. Consequently, the Treasury Department withdrew its directive on 4 August and shortly thereafter Berlin cancelled the export promotion measures. As a result, German-American trade came to a halt. This left a bitter taste behind in Germany, where the American action was looked upon as coercion. Because of this, German-American relations deteriorated further and "ties that in the past had helped draw the two nations together" were severed.

Consequently, Luther was greatly afraid of future developments, if Germany did not formally recognize the most-favored-nation principle. "It is possible that in some years there will only remain ruins of a once blossoming German-American trade." This skepticism was confirmed at the end of November when he had a talk with Sayre. Sayre told him that no German-American economic treaty was to be expected in the near future, as the German proposals for it had too little substance. Prior to this there had been Germany's refusal to sign the Three-Power Agreement of 25 September between the US, France and Great Britain on currency policy, and the recognition of the Spanish national government on 18 November. "Because of this, deep bitterness has grown against us in the past few weeks."

Afterwards, there was no change in position. Washington tried to bring Germany to support a free trade policy, while Germany clung to its clearing system. Berlin made its preference clear with the inauguration of the Four Year Plan (VJP). On 20 October 1936, in a cable to Hull, Dodd evaluated this as a clear limitation of Schacht's authority and at the same time an increase in Göring's power. In addition, he saw in this a great step towards autarky and emphasized the military aspects of industrial mobilization.

According to an opinion in the US government, trade policy could now be used as a means to deter Germany from that course. On 24 November 1936 Sayre stressed to Luther and Meyer of the German Embassy that the US did not want in any way to force its trade principles on the nations of the world. He suggested that the US would look benevolently on an offer from Germany which respected most-favored-nations and the basic principles of the RTAA. Negotiations on trade policy were explicitly understood as an instrument of peace strategy. Therefore, a memorandum drawn up by the Trade Agreements Division in December 1936 concluded

> that a refusal to negotiate a trade agreement with Germany... would not achieve its peaceful purpose, will further damage American export trade versus German competition abroad and will help to convince moderate German opinion, still influential in high circles, that, possibly, belief of the Party radicals in the sword as a solution for the Reich's difficulties may not be incorrect.... The extension of an economic hand of friendship may help to stem the direction in which the Reich is moving. Likewise, if an accord with Germany can be reached, the fulcrum of the bilateralistic front will have been removed and the major opponent of the trade agreements program scotched.

If the United States held to its position without change, Germany could not be restrained from waging war. But Hull did not want to hear of this and at the end of January took a position vis-à-vis Luther which did not vary an iota from his previous conviction and expressed his hope that his ideas on trade policy would spread throughout the world. If Germany did not recognize the principle of most-favored-nation status, as Sayre said in support, there could not be much progress.

Nevertheless, in the spring of 1937 a Trade Agreements Committee on Germany was formed, which was mandated to seek ways to harmonize the two conflicting systems of trade policy, but without damaging the essential points of the RTAA. What seemed to many as a squaring of the circle was seen by Sumner Welles only as a difficult problem of "adjustment for America commercial policy." German policy blew into the same horn when it referred constantly to the pressures which had driven Germany to this trade policy and let it be known that there was no basic opposition between the bilateral system allegedly followed by Germany and the most-favored-nation system." By the end of 1937 the opinion prevailed in the Trade Agreements Division that Washington's inflexible attitude was producing negative results not only for Germany, but also for the US, as the position of "all or nothing" meant "in fact to get nothing." Greater willingness to negotiate on the part of the US was needed, since an agreement with Germany could advance the cause of peace. Therefore, in the future, "any formal restatement of our commercial principles and policies, which the German Government has already been instructed in *ad nauseam* should be avoided." However, this was contradicted by Moffat in the European Section, who believed that if the US gave in now in trade policy and made an agreement with Germany, it would only be water over the dam of the German rearmament machinery, since, after Schacht's departure in November 1937, the Reich Economic Ministry had become an appendage of the Reich Air Ministry. Instead, he recommended adhering to the previous course, for

> ...the development of our trade agreements program will auto-matically put economic pressure on Germany and in this way we have a ready-forged weapon in hand to induce Germany to meet general world trade and political sentiments.

Special hopes were raised by the signing of contractual trade negotiations with the United Kingdom. This proposal to bring the Reich to make economic as well as political concessions by hemming it in by trade policy became more or less the official line of the American government. Washington's attitude in the question of trade policy remained inflexible, since "the economic value to the United States of a trade agreement with the Reich was limited." Although hope for an understanding with the US had not been entirely given up in the Foreign Office, still, disillusionment, even almost resignation began to spread. "Our present trade situation vis-à-vis America can be seen most clearly by the reflection that, by Hull's trade policy we are almost completely encircled." Hull's handling of negotiations was seen as dilatory, as he was about to "crown his work with the British treaty." Besides, Dieckhoff complained, "anti-German circles are in the majority in the State Department."

Meanwhile, on the German side, the government did not want to risk a complete break in relations with the US for political and economic reasons. Politically, it was feared that added respect for the US, especially in Latin America, would have a negative effect on German-American trade relations; economically, it was expected that there would be complications for German direct investments abroad, and with patents and industrial technology for German firms in the US. In addition, Berlin had to take into account that the countries which were subjected to the German Monroe Doctrine did not at all want to be members of the German informal empire. Thus, during the 1930s several east European countries expressed interest in concluding trade agreements with the US based on the principles of the RTAA. This was the case in Yugoslavia and Hungary in early 1935, Poland in 1937, and in Romania in 1937 and 1938. Even the annexation of Vienna by the Reich caused trade friction, for Hull complained at Berlin's assumption of the Austrian debts to the United States. But the German government rejected this firmly. Thereupon Washington removed Austria from the list of most-favored-nations, to which Germany objected.

Thus, the fronts on trade policy continued rigid. Although a few supporters for resuming negotiations on trade policy spoke out, such as the American ambassador in London, Joseph Kennedy, who was oriented towards isolationism, this was strictly rejected by the US. Messersmith justified this attitude in October 1938, saying that "we must stick to our principles. We must be prepared to do something actively in the defense and maintenance of these principles." Hull's position also remained unchanged. Reporting on a speech by Hull before the National Foreign Trade Council, Dieckhoff, the German ambassador in Washington, noted in particular "the great severity with which he called for the uncompromising recognition of his trade system at the end of his remarks." Dieckhoff saw in Hull's address

> ...the voice of an unbending doctrinaire who felt his system was being threatened and believed he had to defend it not only against the totalitarian powers, but above all against the considerable criticism in his own country.

Roosevelt also refused to start negotiations and Dieckhoff felt that a general "feeling of hate" was growing in the American public. In such a climate, where this kind of proposal was seen *per se* as a tactical maneuver, there was hardly a chance for serious moves to stimulate trade relations. As an example of this were the efforts of State Secretary Rudolf Brinkmann of the RwiM. At the end of October 1938, he suggested the adoption of an American Mark, in order by this technical means to revive German-American trade. The Board of

Trade for German-American Commerce (BTGAC) took up this idea and approached Hull, whom they tried to convince of the compatibility of the two trade systems. The American ambassador in Berlin, Hugh Wilson, recommended Brinkmann to the State Department as a liberal politician particularly friendly to the US and encouraged serious study of his suggestions, but Sayre saw scarcely any chance for its success.

4. In Practice: Barter Exchange

Below the official level of trade policy, barter exchange between German and American companies was supported by Berlin and was quietly tolerated and usually not hindered by the American government. This was an illogical and contradictory position for the US because in practice something was allowed which was vehemently opposed in theory. Large American companies with important business connections in Germany played a prominent role in this exchange of goods without money. In early 1935, Franz Klasen, the general representative of Standard Oil of New Jersey (SONJ) for Germany ordered two tankers from German shipyards which were to be "paid for" by the delivery of American kerosene and other petroleum products. Only a short time later, the American consul general in Hamburg, John J. Erhard, informed the State Department that the German-American Petroleum Company (DAPG), a daughter of SONJ, had placed orders with German shipyards for four tankers of 15,000 tons and two tankers of 6,000 tons. In order to compensate for the higher German prices with respect to prices on the world market in shipbuilding, German authorities allowed the DAPG a 35% discount as an export subsidy. The overall total thus came to 11.7 million Reichsmarks which was paid by the shipment of petroleum to Germany. Additionally, in April 1935 SONJ exchanged through DAPG several German finished products against petroleum valued at three million Reichsmarks. The DuPont company also developed barter deals with Germany. In the first quarter of 1935 they purchased chemicals from several German firms, including IG, valued at 10 million Reichsmarks for which DuPont supplied American cotton.

By the end of 1937, DAPG, German Vakuum Öl AG and the Atlantic Refining Company of Germany (GMBH)—daughter companies of SONJ, Socony Oil Company and Atlantic Refining

Company—were dealing with the German authorities using a modified exchange procedure. According to this, the American petroleum producers also sold their oil to American firms who wanted to import good from Germany. Those who delivered these goods then sold the petroleum to German oil companies. These companies justified the system saying that there was no alternative other than giving up the German trade, which would be of advantage to British and Dutch competitors on the world market. Barter exchange with cotton and also copper likewise continued almost unhindered. This barter exchange was practiced until March 1939 and gave many American companies the opportunity to do business with Germany. Usually these were firms which believed that they depended on the quality of certain German products, such as cameras for photography. They purchased set quantities of petroleum, cotton or copper, and exchanged them for German products. However, the American government definitely refused involving official agencies in this continuing exchange of goods. This attitude was reflected in the instructions which Sayre sent Wilson in Berlin on Hull's behalf. In them he said to Wilson,

> ...the Embassy should not become involved in the German system of barter. However, so long as Germany has its present system of control, trade must run along strictly business channels and such business as can be consummated must rest on the business arrangements which American exporting interests can make with the appropriate German authorities and buying agencies.

This communication took place after the annexation of Austria by Germany in March 1938 and shows that it was possible to separate the macropolitical level from the microeconomic one. In mid-November 1938 a memorandum on trade with the US was prepared by Legation Counselor Becker in the Foreign Office section for economic policy. According to this, Germany was receiving primarily cotton, petroleum and petroleum products, and cooper from the US; on the other hand, German exports to the US included all types of German industrial finished goods. The major portion of the trade was due to barter deals. Despite the cul-de-sac in which German-American foreign trade policy found itself, economic relations between the German Reich and the US were maintained. However, the conditions under which this exchange took place became successively more restrictive and complicated, so that the volume of German-American trade was reduced.

5. American Strategy of Containment as Foreign Trade Policy

A. *The Anglo-American Commercial Treaty*

The English factor played a prominent role in American government thinking, since the British preferential system for the Empire which dated from the Ottawa Agreement of 1932, was taken to be an antonym in foreign trade to the RTAA program. In order to break up the British trade bloc, the US and especially Hull had enormous interest in drawing Great Britain, a significant commercial power, into the American system. Hull hoped that this would be a complete breakthrough for the RTAA. With this, it might also be possible to increase cooperation between Washington and London in important questions of international policy which had only been developed in a rudimentary way up to now. Thus, in early 1936, Hull tried to convince the British ambassador in Washington, Sir Ronald Lindsay, of the advantages of multilateral world trade, vehemently criticizing British bilateral trade and Empire policy. Meanwhile, London saw no reason to accede to the American wishes for the time being.

Finally, the American government found the key to open the English economic bloc in Canada which, as a member of the Commonwealth, entertained close relations with Great Britain. In November 1935, Canada and the United States concluded a trade agreement which ended the unofficial trade war between the two countries and at the same time inaugurated closer cooperation in security policy. With this diplomatic coup Washington improved the conditions for an understanding with London. In later negotiations the British expressed their desire to enlist Washington in a more active role for world order. A commercial treaty would contribute significantly to that end. By 1937-1938 essential differences had been resolved and the agreement was signed on 17 November 1938. This resulted in an American-Canadian-British system of trade agreements which represented a clear center of gravity in world trade and at the same time at first "the democracies' answer to the Axis threat to western Europe." In Hull's view, the Anglo-American treaty was perhaps the most important building stone, because, with a network of trade treaties based on the principles of the RTAA, he felt that he could isolate Germany on the world market and thereby move her to make political concessions. Schröder shared this view when he referred to the treaty as a "pillar of American containment strategy using economic means" and as the "highest point of Washington's foreign and particularly German policy."

On the other hand, Roosevelt did not share this opinion. He turned out to be right, for the effect of the treaty did not meet expectations. For one thing, the British preferential system remained closed to the American economy and, furthermore, its influence on the political development in Europe was marginal. British industry even adopted a strategy of appeasement in mid-March towards Germany, as shown by the Düsseldorf agreement. In addition, the Anglo-American trade treaty did not in any way affect the divergence of British and American interests, for the Chamberlain government did not want to be taken in tow by the United States. The idea of a "joint policy of containment" would not take hold until 1939.

B. Trade Policy Measures Against Germany

The incompatibility of the foreign trade policies and the growing realization of the imminence of the National Socialist threat, particularly from German rearmament, led to the fact that Washington finally paid more attention to the goods which were actually exchanged and the conditions under which that took place. After the annexation of Austria, when the export of a considerable amount of helium to Germany came to debate, voices were heard approving the deal. Wilson approved of the export, in order to guarantee a fair treatment of American citizens and interests in Germany, and in so doing he echoed Göring's line of argument. On the other hand, others pointed to the possible military significance of helium and opposed the deal. In May, the American government finally refused to allow the helium export. Harold L. Ickes, Secretary of the Interior, who did not consider helium a product of military importance, felt that the determining factor was that this refusal represented a moral penalty for Germany's immoral conduct.

A few months later, the Treasury Department was intensely occupied with the barter system as it was being practiced between German and American firms. It was suspected that on the German side there was a hidden subsidizing of exports. In October 1938

Secretary of the Treasury Morgenthau described this as follows: An American interested in German goods buys mostly copper or cotton for dollars at world market prices and ships them to Germany after having found a buyer there. However, the latter pays in Reichsmarks a price far above the level of the world market into a settlement account, where the amount is immediately blocked. Then the American importer can "purchase" goods in Germany up to the amount his German client had deposited. Morgenthau saw this as an unacceptable promotion of exports. For this reason there was again discussion of charging compensatory customs duties on German goods. But this decision was not fully acceptable to the State Department. Hull opposed it, because he feared, among other things, a negative reaction to American efforts to facilitate departure from Germany. So he proposed to inform Berlin ahead of time of the intended measures. The Trade Agreements Division also voted against the charging of compensatory customs duties, as this would affect American foreign trade negatively and would deprive the moderate elements in the German government of their commercial base.

The domestic political trend in Germany strengthened those circles in the government which opposed resumption of trade negotiations. In this context the pogrom against the Jewish population on the "*Kristallnacht*" of 9 and 10 November 1938 and a series of anti-Jewish decrees issued by the government thereafter should be mentioned. On 14 December 1938 the American government formally protested against the decree eliminating Jews from trade, which also included discrimination against American citizens in Germany on the basis of their race or religion. At the same time Germany was also informed that this would bring German-American trade negotiations into a more desolate situation and that there was even danger of a complete break in relations. For this reason, Dieckhoff emphatically urged a more moderate German policy, but a study made by the Foreign Office at the end of November 1938 judged that the effects of a break in relations, despite great disadvantages, were entirely tolerable. Thus, the cost of dissolving interdependencies was viewed as acceptable.

After the National Socialist government had occupied Czechoslovakia in March 1939 and proclaimed the Reich Protectorate of Bohemia and Moravia, the Treasury Department finally decided on 18

March to renew the 25% compensatory duties on German deliveries in the US and justified this by the unacceptable German subsidies on exports. The American press went further. In its comments, they were clearly convinced that no end to German expansion was to be expected and the US must work harder than before for the cause of democracy, especially in the western hemisphere. Thomsen, the chargé d'affaires in the German Embassy in Washington, protested against this politically motivated measure and considered harsh countermeasures. He thought, on the German side, of a drastic reduction in cotton imports from the US. But this suggestion remained only an episode.

In view of the fact that the bilateral trade relations had almost dried up (see Chapter II) and only a little trade still existed, that kind of threat was almost laughable, although it had great symbolic importance. Only three days later Thomsen reported that one could scarcely anticipate support for withdrawal of the compensatory duties from business circles in the US interested in trade with Germany because they also looked upon this measure as a political action and felt that they were exposed to an anti-German climate in public opinion. People seemed resigned to the fact that business with Germany was now definitely finished. They wanted to import increasingly from Germany until the duties took effect and then turned to other sources of supply. On 30 March, it was finally decided at the Foreign Office to abandon the plan of German countermeasures and to make concessions to the Americans. Through a stoppage in export subsidies, Washington was to be encouraged to put an end to the compensatory duties. Despite Thomsen's prediction of reluctance by the transnational economic organizations and associations, the BTGAC came out in favor of the German position. Its members were interested in continuing importation of German goods and protested to Hull against the new duties. Representatives of large companies also approved of bilateralism in trade relations with Germany, urged an increase in imports from Germany, condemned the boycott of German wares and called for cancellation of the compensatory duties. Graeme Howard, Mooney's successor in GM's overseas division, criticized Hull's trade policy with great vehemence and deeply regretted that he had not signed an agreement with totalitarian states.

However, suspension of the compensatory duties would only be considered by Washington if Germany withdrew its measures promoting exports. Hull made it unmistakably clear in April 1939 that "any obstacles which German trade faces in the United States as compared with any and every other country are entirely the result of German policy and practices." Finally, on 1 August 1939 Washington was informed that Germany was prepared to abandon the settlement system by which American goods were sold in Germany at an extremely high price, which had the effect of subsidizing German exports. Besides the question of customs duties, other complications arose from the territorial expansion of the German Empire. As in the case of Austria previously, there was the question of the trade status of the former Czechoslovak areas. For Washington, the situation was clear: the US handled Bohemia and Moravia as German territory and refused them most-favored-nation status. Although the German government protested against this, it was only pretense, as those regions officially belonged to the German customs area from April 1st on.

The uncompromising attitude of the US grew out of the development of American foreign trade. This was the way Hull commented on American trade statistics with visible satisfaction on April 18. They showed that the US, with it RTAA program had been considerably more successful in expanding trade relations than the Germans with their compensatory system and barter. He interpreted this situation optimistically. "Every advance made by the trade agreements program is an advance for the cause of economic sanity and peace." Reich Minister of Economics Funk accused the American government of stubbornness in foreign trade policy. "In Germany we are practicing an economic policy based on common sense; dogma is the foe of business." And the Steuben Society seconded this, criticizing Hull's "hostile position towards Germany." In the American business world the assessment was that the world was divided into two groups—here, the democracies; there, the authoritarian states—gained more and more adherents. Winthrop W. Aldrich, Chairman of the Board of the Chase National Bank in New York, was alarmed by the growing governmental control of the economy in the authoritarian systems. This led him to conclude that "there is no possible compromise ultimately between the conceptions underlying the democratic and authoritarian systems."

In this atmosphere, German-American trade fell by 1939-1940 to ephemeral levels, as we showed in Chapter II. This was only small trade, of only marginal importance for the two national economies. After the outbreak of war, particularly in 1940, the Roosevelt administration urged American companies still remaining in Germany to sell their investments in Germany. Many US firms did so, and the overall American investments in Germany fell from nearly 720 million dollars (1938) to 393 million by the end of 1940.

Analysis of the Antagonism in Trade Policy

Foreign economic policy was looked upon differently within the American administration. Secretary of State Cordell Hull saw in free world trade a means for overcoming the world economic crisis and also an instrument of great value in peace strategy to guarantee peace and a liberal world order. For President Roosevelt, on the other hand, trade policy was only a political instrument to be used as opportunity arose; for him, as opposed to Hull, free trade was "a step on the way to a comprehensive peace order, but not the order as such." In his view, the RTAA was not a "cure-all to establish world peace." As an internationalist, he became more and more convinced during the 1930s that peace could only be maintained by agreements on security.

However, the domestic political climate for a long time prevented taking that road, as, through the neutrality laws, it was isolationist in nature and Roosevelt had to take that into account. Roosevelt could only combat isolationism by partisan strategy (G. Weinberg). In this situation, foreign economic policy was the most important instrument of American foreign policy until 1939. This substitution of trade policy for foreign policy also occurred in policy towards the German Reich. Here, Roosevelt used the "weapon of trade policy" to "emphasize to the Hitler regime his dissatisfaction with its policy of expansion." In this connection the refusal to deliver helium, as described above, in the context of the annexation of Austria, and the leveling of compensatory duties after the occupation of Prague should be mentioned.

The employment of foreign economic policy as containment strategy against Germany was evident in the conclusion of the British-American trade agreement. In this Washington was in no way following a strategy of appeasement. In contrast to British policy which aimed at peaceful coexistence with the German trade system, the Roosevelt administration believed that Germany should be brought by economic pressure, trade encirclement and economic containment to return to a multilateral and liberal system of world trade. In this way, Germany would fall first under massive economic pressure and then automatically under political pressure. This should cause Berlin to recognize international interdependencies and to abandon the course of foreign political aggression. Thus the RTAA program was not only an essential part of the Roosevelt crisis therapy but at the same time an important instrument in Washington's foreign policy before the outbreak of war. This calculation often paralleled views concerning America's "mission." The world economic crisis, economic nationalism, and the disintegration of the world economy into separate regional economic blocs became, as it were, a new "frontier," a testing ground for America where the RTAA program had to prove itself. The Secretary of Commerce, Daniel C. Roper, wrote in 1936:

> Our responsibility not only to ourselves but to the world is to prove that democracy, or the ability of the people to rule themselves, is successful and will be strengthened in the crucible of time.

Hull's view of foreign trade, which was practically a substitute for foreign policy and which was fully supported by diplomats like Moffat and Messersmith, overlooked the possibility—for Roosevelt, even *probability*—that Hull's "economic liberalism and moral persuasion were insufficient to combat Germany's new order." In the end, Roosevelt was right, "for the policy of economic containment could not compensate for political abstinence in the European power game" and military participation in the struggle against Hitler was necessary.

German economic foreign policy with autarky on a large geographic basis may be interpreted as a "conscious antithesis to a universal world market" and resulted, together with Japan's challenge to the United States, in a worldwide threat to the "Open Door" policy. National Socialist Germany and Japan meant the danger of dividing up the indivisible world market and thus threatened at the same time the American economic system. However, this alone did not cause Washington to take up arms. In the case of Japan the economic rivalry had turned into a *casus belli* a few years earlier than in Europe, because it had been connected to Japanese military expansion since 1931. Thus an economic factor was joined to the politico-military element. But this connection did not take place in Europe until 1938. The clearly recognizable scenario of a relatively autarkistic world falling into separate trade blocs represented one viewpoint among the internationalists around Roosevelt on the question of America's entrance into the war. In this regard, German foreign trade policy and its objectives were felt to be especially threatening. However, this economic challenge alone was still not a *casus belli*. The United States considered the challenge by the Third Reich to mean that the "Fascist Internationale" would also reach out to America during the war. The interpretation of German policy as a ubiquitous threat to the security of the United States was decisive for Roosevelt. It was a syndrome of political, ideological and economic motives which formed the "critical mass" that led to entry into the war. Here, the foreign economic threat had to be "enriched" by the military security threat which stemmed from the opposition of ideologies.

This chapter on differences in foreign trade policy between the US and the Third Reich showed how separate economic points of conflict, part of which dated from the era of presidential cabinets, became explosive in foreign trade policy after Hitler came to power and in third markets like Latin America nearly reached the stage of genuine trade wars. The contrasting principles of the "New Plan" and the RTAA (bilateralism versus multilateralism, preferential treatment versus unconditional most-favored-nation status) were interpreted by the American government (with some opposing voices) as irreconcilable. On the other hand, the German side looked at the matter rather pragmatically. This uncompromising attitude by America and its rigidity was due to the struggle for parts of the world market in the "shapeless world economy" of the 1930s (Kindleberger). With this there also gradually came the politico-ideological antagonism. With the limitations placed on foreign policy by isolationism, it was possible to clearly disapprove of the activities of the Reich in foreign policy, which were seen as a visible threat to the society of nations and world peace. Thus foreign trade policy became an instrument of foreign policy. It should be added as a restriction, that it lost its effect, because economic exchange relations in practice did not follow official announcements, but were carried out within the limits set by the German economic system and mostly with methods which were officially prohibited. However, the dualism of the foreign economic systems continued to be a visible sign of tension in German-American relations and their growing tendency towards conflict. This antagonism in ideology, politics and foreign trade policy contrasted with the intensive economic cooperation of transnational concerns, as will be seen in the following chapters. Against the background of increasing political conflicts, and the continuing regression in the close interdependency relations of the 1920s which were discussed in this chapter, transnational cooperation presents an interesting phenomenon, apparently going in the opposite direction.

IV
GERMAN-AMERICAN BUSINESS RELATIONS BETWEEN THE WARS*

The Automobile Industry

At the beginning of the 20th century American industry had catapulted to first place in the world. Alert contemporaries interpreted this development as the start of the "Americanization of the world." The First World War consolidated this position, because at this time European competition largely disappeared from world markets. This was also true for the automobile industry, the most important branch of American industry. In this, the industrial superiority of the US stood out most clearly. Progressive production methods with mass production and Taylorization and the gigantic domestic market assured considerable profits and gave this sector immense advantages not only in production but also in the area of management.

Since the end of the 19th century dozens of independent manufacturers had fallen victim to a process of concentration within this branch of industry. For example, the General Motors Corporation (GM) in Detroit, Michigan, had by 1909 incorporated nine formerly independent firms, including Buick, Cadillac, Oldsmobile and Pontiac and even tried, unsuccessfully, to take over the Ford Motor Company in Dearborn, near Detroit. By 1920 GM had purchased 12 additional firms, including Chevrolet; in 1925 it sought, again unsuccessfully, to purchase Dodge. In 1922 the Ford Motor Company annexed Lincoln Motors, Chrysler in 1923, Chalmers and Dodge in 1928. Between 1923 and 1926, 43 companies in this field closed down; by 1935 only ten firms remained. But even this number is deceptive regarding the actual situation, for, in the 1920s the American market was controlled by the "Great Two"—Ford and GM—with Ford dominating in the first half of the decade and GM in the second. Mistakes in Ford's

---

* The reader is referred to the original German text for detailed footnotes.

commercial policy on the one hand, and GM's good business policy on the other led to the situation that, in the late 1920s, GM visibly came to symbolize the "automobile and automotive age itself." Or, in Schuler's words, "Sloanism" triumphed at the end of the Roaring Twenties over "Fordism"—marketing over pure production. This described a process within the automobile sector which was referred to as a "transition from an early entrepreneurial stage dominated by the Henry Fords to a corporate phase dominated by the Alfred Sloans." From 1928 the Chrysler Motor Corporation from Detroit closed ranks with both and from then on it was a triumvirate—the "Big Three"—that dominated the market, in which GM was *primus inter pares*.

However, the triumphal march of American automobile manufactures in the 1920s was not limited to the American market, but was worldwide and seemed to be irresistible. Almost from the start, the Detroit automobile companies were hardly inferior to New York's Wall Street banks in international direction and interest in opening up to foreign markets.

AMERICAN AUTOMOBILE VENTURES IN GERMANY

Besides the various activities spread out over the entire world, the engagement of the American automobile industry in Germany seemed at first like a small tile in a mosaic, because in 1924 the German automobile manufacturers, with an annual production of approximately 18,000 vehicles, only came fourth on the list of European factories after France, Great Britain, and Italy. But four years later Italy had been surpassed and in another seven years Germany had become the largest European producer after Great Britain. The following table illustrates this development.

These figures confirm the estimate of the American firms. The industrially progressive German Reich, with its broad market seemed to offer extraordinary possibilities over the short and long term. The starting point for the engagement of American automobile companies in the Weimar Republic was the fragmentation and technological backwardness of the German automobile industry.

TABLE 8*
THE ANNUAL AUTOMOBILE PRODUCTION OF THE
MOST IMPORTANT EUROPEAN COUNTRIES
(in thousands)

Country	1913	1924	1928	1935
Great Britain	34	133	212	404
Germany	14	18	90	240
France	45	145	210	165
Italy		35	55	44

Source: Foreman-Peck, 1982:871.

Besides competition from France, the German contingency system hindered business until 1925. Through the intervention of the Deputy American Commercial Attaché Herring in Berlin and the head of the Tariff Commission in the Bureau of Foreign and Domestic Commerce Henry Chalmer—which occurred with the support of President Calvin Coolidge—as well as the bribing of responsible officials in the German office for approval of imports and exports (who were employed after 1925 by Ford), the US automobile industry succeed from 1924 to 1925 in increasing its quotas step by step. Likewise, the umbrella organization of the automobile industry, the National Automobile Chamber of Commerce, obtained a reduction in the customs duties for the imported automobiles. In 1930, German efforts to again adopt a contingency system and higher customs duties for imported automobiles were blocked by the American commercial attaché in Berlin and the American producers.

In the 1920s the American firms initially only exported separate parts of their vehicles to Europe where the parts were then assembled. Thus it was automobiles of American design that reached Europe in this manner. European requirements (economical fuel consumption, smaller vehicles, lower, less taxable engine power, etc.) were largely ignored. When this was brought up by clear-sighted employees like the head of the GM Foreign Section, James D. Mooney, they were

---

* Table 9 in the original German text.

opposed by management. It was gradually realized that it would be advantageous to take the wishes of the European customers into account. Ford did so from about 1930 and GM from 1932.

This process was also a result of changes in the manner of engagement. In the beginning, when the automotive manufacturers contented themselves with creating distribution organizations, assembly plants were immediately established. The creation of complete production installations, which were understood to be an adequate way to control the market, was the final phase in development. While the Department of Commerce clearly voted for the establishment of sales organizations and against the creation of production plants, enthusiasm for building such production facilities gained momentum by the fact that in 1927/28 the German automobile industry expressed higher interest levels for imported automobile parts and equipment. The desire to offset American competition had the opposite effect, as the network of branches of American companies in the German Reich increased. The overall investments of the nine largest American firms (GM, Ford, Ambi-Budd, Chrysler, Hudson-Essex Motors, Willy-Overland, Graham Paige, Durant Motors and Studebaker) reached 211.5 million reichsmarks (*RM*) by 1931, according to data from the US Commercial Attaché H. Lawrence Groves.

GENERAL MOTORS AND OPEL

1. Purchase of Opel by GM

Contrary to Ford, GM found itself prior to 1920 in a deep crisis. Quarrels over management and trade policy between the founders of the company, the Durant brothers, on the one hand, and Pierre S. Du Pont and John Raskob from the headquarters of the Du Pont in Wilmington, Delaware, on the other, led favorably towards the latter. As a result, by 1921 Du Pont held over 36% of all GM shares and thus, in fact, controlled the firm. Besides, the crisis was intensified by the American depression after war's end in the early 1920s. When control of the company was taken over by the Du Pont family business, there followed a reorganization of the company structure in the first half of the 1920s, essentially an adoption of the Du Pont management structure. Alfred P. Sloan, a member of the board of directors along with Haskell, Raskob and Du Pont, and an outstanding genius in organization, was primarily responsible for these changes. Under him, GM evolved into a company with a decentralized structure. "Decentralized word under coordinated control" was his maxim. Although the idea of decentralization based on Sloan's self-assessment is a myth, the fact remains that this was vastly more efficient company structure.

Parallel to the change in organization, a clear concept was worked out concerning the vehicle program, which—differing from Ford—took account of the customers' wishes and from 1923 on anticipated the introduction of new models and types of automobiles. It was based on a "policy of a car for every purse and purpose" and a philosophy of "producing more for less." These two developments laid the groundwork for the commercial success of the coming years. GM attacked the position of Ford as a leader of the market. In the first half of the 1920s GM's share in the American market climbed of about 45% and thus became the largest American producer. In the four-year period between 1926 and 1929, GM earned a profit of nearly one million dollars, of which 63% was extracted for dividends while the remained was assigned to self-financing.

GM's involvement overseas, influenced by Ford building a factory in Great Britain, dated from 1919 when a 50% share in the French manufacturer Citroën was being considered. This plan did not succeed because of opposition by the French. Basically, GM was facing these alternatives: to be exporter or overseas manufacturer. It chose the latter because of European attempts to oppose the overpowering American competition in automobiles through trade barriers. When the projected acquisition of British Austin failed in 1924/25, GM took over the relatively small Vauxhall Motors Ltd. in Great Britain in 1925. In terms of company policy, this was considered a trial balloon, an experiment in overseas production.

In the same year, GM opened an assembly plant in the free port of Hamburg and a sales office in Berlin. At about the same time, the Opel family offered GM the purchase of Adam Opel AG in Rüsselsheim. However, this proposal was not accepted at first. In the spring of 1927 GM moved the assembly plant from Hamburg to Berlin-Wittau and purchased buildings in Berlin-Borsigwalde. A year later, GM's overseas program had taken on more definite dimensions. In 1928, James D. Mooney, the head of the overseas division of GM, stated that the Americans had set about building a great American economic empire based on business alliances and personal contacts, on capital and individuals.

> Instead of appropriation of territory there is a penetration of ideas, an infiltration of practices, the building of an industrial and commercial empire. The world has seen nothing of its like before. American business to-day knows no boundaries. The markets of the world are the markets of American business. And we must be prepared to defend this great industrial empire...in this new era that is upon us—an era in international trade of a scope and potentiality such as the world has never known before.

Against such a background, the directors of GM returned that same year to Opel's offer and acquired the right to priority for purchase. The American Commercial Attaché in Berlin, F.W. Allport, considered a merger of Opel and GM to be only a rumor, for he did not believe that "General Motors would want to get into such a mess." However, GM's decision had been well thought out. A delegation from the Dodge company which had visited the Opel works in 1927 found almost American production methods. In 1928 Opel held a 44% market share and thus was the largest German manufacturer with a distribution organization which covered the territory; finally, it was well established in the lower price area—which was favorable for GM's production policy. That segment of the market was also becoming more important in the US, so that it was expected that this would be aided by the Germans. Besides, Germany was considered a good export market with much promise for the future. This was the feeling of the GM leadership, whose policy in the second half of the 1920s was a "broadening of the source of supply of cars and trucks by engaging in manufacturing operation in countries strategically located." So, in 1929 GM finally acquired an 80% majority in Opel.

In Germany the takeover of Opel was seen as a turning-point. The *Frankfurter Zeitung* even wrote: "Not often does one experience in industry historical moments." Some feared that the acquisition of Opel would lead to penetration of the German economy by the Americans. Thus, for many, Opel was "from an economic standpoint an American automobile factory in Germany." Fear of a successive extinction of German producers was shared also by American living in Germany. Allport described the situation as follows: "It is as if the rest of the German automobile manufacturers have little between time and extinction." In the *Opel Plant History* by Hauser, on the other hand, we read:

> Recognizing the limits of their strength, brothers Wilhelm and Fritz are taking each other's hand across the ocean which lies between them. Most of the Opel family shares are going over to General Motors with this bold and difficult decision.

Afterwards Opel experienced a transfer of American personnel, know-how, equipment and finance to Rüsselsheim. GM invested two million dollars alone for the installation of new machinery at the Rüsselsheim plant. Two years later, in October 1931, in the midst of the spreading recession, the transaction was concluded with the acquisition of the remaining 20% of Opel, according to the agreement. With this, GM had taken over the entire Adam Opel AG for $33,362,000 or 155 million *RM*. At the same time, GM gave itself a national color, i.e., although the firm was in American hands, it presented itself under a well-known, renowned German name, which could only have a positive effect on business. In Rüsselsheim, it was hoped that Opel was now armed as well as possible for the future through this sale.

> The Opel Works can now live through the next difficult years unshaken by bank crises, low exchange rates, black Fridays on the stock exchange, supported by the strongest world power that exists in automobile manufacture.

2. Opel and GM in the Depression

The purchase of Opel and Vauxhall and the general diffusion of GM on the world markets changed the character of the Detroit company. GM changed "from a national to an international manufacturer" prepared to seek market opportunities "wherever they existed, and to support these markets by factories, assembly plants and organizations, if the circumstances justified it." The annexation of Opel and Vauxhall, like the opening of agencies abroad, meant a noticeable and lasting change in foreign trade, as, for example, the 1933 sales of Vauxhall and Opel were larger than the exports of vehicles made in

America. The share of automobiles produced in the US in foreign markets sank from 52.1% in 1929 to 26.8% in 1938. However, neither Opel nor Vauxhall nor any other overseas branch of GM attained greater importance for the overall business in this period. In design policy the overseas branches were neglected; vehicles were being built for American tastes and European preferences were not taken into account.

In contrast to Ford, in early October 1929 at GM headquarters it was feared that economic expansion was at an end and that a recession was beginning. An effort was made to increase profits through greater efficiency and lowering of prices, but the world economic crisis meant gigantic losses for GM; the market value sank by one-third in the first year of the crisis, from 1.5 billion dollars in 1929 to 983 million in 1930. Even though the American and Canadian GM manufacturing plants were still able to sell 1.9 million units in 1929, profits declined at the same time from $248 million to $165,000. By 1932 GM was producing at less than 30% of its capacity. In order to face the Depression, wages and salaries were cut, production and distribution were restructured partially by combining and closing plants, and changes in the desires of clients were followed. In 1933 the lowest price group of the automobile market comprised 73% of the overall market, as opposed to 52% in 1926. In addition, investments were drastically reduced during the five years from 1930 to 1934 when only the modest sum of $81 million was invested altogether, with the bottom in 1932 of only $5 million. The number of employees at GM was reduced in three years by about 50%, from 233,000 in 1929 to somewhat over 116,000 in 1932. Opel's business trend also was not rosy. For example, in 1930/32 Opel suffered a loss of 16.4 million *RM* and the staff was reduced from 12,000 to 6,650 at the beginning of 1933.

3. Opel and GM in the 1930s: Transnational Cooperation in
   a Difficult Political Atmosphere

Moments of political crisis were added to the economic ones. In the first months of the National Socialist domination people in Detroit were quite uneasy because, through growing nationalism and popular demand for autarky, the possibility of being forced out of the German market, perhaps even expropriated, hung over GM like the sword of

Damocles. These fears had a substantial basis. On the one hand, voices were raised within the NSDAP from an anti-capitalist, anti-big industry camp—mostly from the SA—demanding the breakup of big industry and the halting of subsidies to large companies. These circles had already announced in 1932 that they would not approve of foreign control of Opel. On the other hand, with the growth of nationalistic trends, demands were heard for the re-Germanizing Opel. In March 1933, the Opel family seriously considered buying back their former property.

For these reasons, GM made an effort to obtain from German officials a guarantee that American capital was safe in Germany. In this connection GM President William S. Knudsen traveled to Germany in October 1933, where he was received by Göring. This high-ranking visit clearly showed how concerned the managers were in Detroit, for such top-level visits were rare. In 1933/34, GM was immediately ready to take the Opel family into the Opel Company or even to negotiate selling Opel to the family. However, complications arose in the talks over the value of the shares. Moreover, GM held the trump card that up 'til then, Opel was selling its products abroad through GM's international distribution network. However in early 1934 after Hitler had forcefully guaranteed "that he would not allow any discrimination against foreign capital invested in Germany for legitimate purposes," these negotiations dried up. When Mooney, who had been in Germany to have this matter clarified, left the country in May 1934, Hitler expressed his admiration for his efforts and his "firm confidence in Germany's stability and lasting prosperity."

Apparently the Detroit company had made an arrangement with the new regime. Besides the valid reasons for GM's presence in Germany, during the world economic crisis trade barriers had accumulated that made it difficult to place American automobiles in Europe. In addition, competitive pressure on American firms increased, as European manufacturers adopted American technologies and used them to produce automobiles geared to European tastes. It was therefore economically sensible in the framework of world market strategy for GM to remain in the German market.

This inertia was not immediately profitable because it was not possible to transfer profits, but Opel's economic success promised favorable luck in the market over the long term in continental European countries. After the relatively satisfactory change in the political parameters, the economic situation of the company appeared advantageous. Table 9* on the following page gives an impression of the business development of Opel and its position in the German automobile industry.

In 1933 Opel realized a profit of something over 5 million *RM*. In the same year, Opel manufactured 33.5% of all German passenger cars and trucks. In 1935, Opel's production represented 42.2% of German automobile production; in 1937, Opel's share was 37%, and in 37.1% in 1938. The company profited from the National Socialist transportation policy and the rearmament program. On 11 February 1933, at the opening of the International Automobile Exposition in Berlin, Hitler announced a transportation program which provided for the motorization of the German nation and thereby an increase in automobile production, as well as tax reduction for car owners, promotion of automotive sports and an immense expansion of the highway network. As part of the rearmament, from 1935 on Opel received defense contracts which at that time dealt mostly with the delivery of heavy trucks of the "Blitz" model, an adaptation of an American one. This business proved to be so lucrative and extensive that in April 1935 Opel planned on building a truck factory. Thus, after contact with German government agencies, the largest truck factory in Europe was built at Brandenburg an der Havel, considerably farther to the east and thereby far safer from air attacks, which was of great importance to the government. It cost 14 million *RM* and began production in mid-November 1935. It was officially opened on 7 January 1936 and was devoted almost exclusively to fulfilling government contracts.

Opel also found itself in an enviable position of liquidity because the German government had prohibited the transfer of profits overseas after the National Socialists assumed power. Thus, the profits, which in reality ought to have been transferred to Detroit, remained in the country. The management in Rüsselsheim seized this opportunity and in following years reinvested the money in modernizing and enlarging its factories and carried out a program of massive expansion. The company set about increasing the number of its models, so that by 1934 Opel was able to offer a comprehensive palette of products. The

---

* Table 10 in the original German text.

TABLE 9
SUMMARY OF THE BUSINESS DEVELOPMENT OF ADAM OPEL AG

Year	I	II	III	IV	V	VI	VII	VIII	IX
1929	6002.9	4611.8	138.3	146066	5.3				-2.3
1930	4181.5	3167.5	96.1	101755	5.6	26312	25.9	5.1	-12.2
1931	3086.1	2305.3	68.3	79563	14.1	26355	33.1	26.9	-3.4
1932	1973.0	1327.0	48.3	58280	17.2	20914	35.9	32.5	-0.8
1933	2549.7	1786.3	92.3	104449	11.7	39295	37.6	19.5	5.0
1934	3402.9	2364.8	150.3	163366	8.0	71665	43.9	11.8	2.0
1935	4563.4	3352.8	201.2	224568	10.4	102765	45.8	11.0	19.8
1936	5515.0	4130.7	245.1	281174	12.8	120397	42.8	13.0	19.9
1937	5774.5	4250.5	244.5	312892	21.9	128370	41.0	25.4	9.6
1938	3873.3	2384.4	248.8	326919	23.9	139631	42.7	26.1	13.8
1939									15.6
1940									5.2

I	— world auto production (in 1000s)		VI	— bought from Opel
II	— production in USA and Canada (in 1000s)		VII	— portion sold in Germany (in %)
III	— production in Germany (in 1000s)		VIII	— portion of exports (in %)
IV	— sold in Germany		IX	— profits and losses (in Mio. RM)
V	— export quota of German auto industry (in %)			

Sources: Columns I-VI, VIII: Thirtieth Annual Report of General Motors Corporation. Year Ended December 21, 1938. BAP, 80, Ba 1. Mr/ 7958, Bl. 140: 14, 22. Column VII: Eigene Berechnungen anhand der Spalten IV und VI. Column IX: Jahre 1930-1934: Berechnet nach den Angaben des Ford-Managers Heine in Manager's Report to Directors, 11.1.1933. Jahre 135-1940: Berliner Börsenzeitung, Nr. 157 vom 3.4.1938; Nr. 134 vom 20.3. 1939; Nr. 261 vom 5.6.1940; und Nr. 309 vom 5.7.1941.

Rüsselsheim works were enlarged and new facilities were installed. In August 1937 Opel's plans for expanding the Rüsselsheim and Brandenburg works were discussed in GM's Administrative Committee. As these investments could be made entirely from Opel's portfolio, no objections were raised in Detroit against these plans. A glance at the balance sheet confirmed Opel's rosy commercial situation. From 1931 to 1936 Opel invested 60 million *RM*, that is, an amount equal to its entire stock, in new factories and new machinery. In 1936 alone Opel reported a profit of 19.9 million *RM* and made new investments of 33 million *RM*. In 1937 Opel was the largest European manufacturer and employed more than 20,000 workers. Although Opel had to pay nearly 33 million *RM* in taxes in 1938, the firm remained extraordinarily liquid, primarily because of the German prohibition on the transfer of profits. They rose from under 9.6 million *RM* in 1937 to nearly 13.8 million in 1938. In that year Opel made investments of 7.4 million *RM*.

The parent company in Michigan was also helpful in other ways. Mooney always emphasized his opinion from 1932: "Our interests as an industry lie always in trade expansion, never in trade restriction." For this reason he said vehemently on several occasions, as in September 1935, that American imports from Germany should be increased. With this he hoped to accomplish, as he explained his abstruse ideas in January 1937, to calm "Germany's hungry belly, the cause of the ugly face with which Germany confronts her European neighbors." Although Mooney only intended to express his basic conviction of the advantages of trade as free as possible and at the same time gain a few plus points for GM's German interests, one could also interpret these words as supporting Germany's National Socialist interests. Berlin was constantly promoting such an increase. This ambivalence was further shown when Mooney also opposed customs penalties and the American boycott movement, always stressing the "inherent friendliness" between the American and German people and rejecting a larger economic conflict between the US and Germany. On the contrary, he was of the opinion that "the economic background of Germany and the United States supplement each other in a rather ideal way."

In any case, his statements were welcomed in Berlin, as Mooney's 1938 award of the Cross of Merit in the Order of the

German Eagle, 1st Class, must be interpreted. But in the US his statements caused irritation. The following statement was sent to the State Department by the widespread movement to boycott German goods in the US as a reaction to the German domestic and foreign policy:

> There seems to be a direct conflict of interest between the General Motors Company in Germany and General Motors here. When General Motors officially attack the boycott, or the countervailing tax, they seem to speak for General Motors foreign subsidiaries and against the interest of the parent company. It seems to be the case of the tail wagging the dog.

When German production threatened to stop in 1936 because of a shortage of rubber, R.A. Fleischer, Opel's treasurer, and Karl Luer of the Dresden Bank and also a member of Opel's board of directors, flew to talks in New York in the autumn of 1936. They asked Mooney for $1,000,000 to finance Opel's rubber requirements. Detroit accepted this request under the condition that the money would be repaid through barter trade and Opel exports which were to be handled through the GM international distribution network. This was carried on at least until April 1939.

During those years the transnational GM, through Opel, enjoyed high esteem in German government agencies. They orchestrated transnational contacts largely for their own purposes. They divided the rubber supplies in such a way that GM felt that it had to help. In this way the German government relieved the German shortages in raw materials. In the same way it increased the export of German goods, particularly by Opel, and by this means took pressure off the tight foreign exchange situation. GM led the transnational cooperation from which Berlin, but also Opel, at first profited more than GM, because, "if foreign investment is to continue, it must recognize the responsibilities it has to the country of domicile and to the people of that country."

But GM, through its weight, was able to force the government to make concessions. Shortly before his visit to Berlin, Mooney had learned on 27 March 1939 in London that Karl Stiefs, Opel's chief engineer, Prigges, head of the Rüsselsheim patent division, and Heinke, another Opel employee, had been arrested by the Gestapo.

They were accused of industrial espionage. It was alleged that they had betrayed plans for the Volkswagen project to the US. Mooney took the matter up and on 1 April spoke with Meissner of the German Chancery. He made it clear that "there was the very important consideration of how this present situation would affect relations between the German government and General Motors." He expressly mentioned the great dissatisfaction of the GM stockholders and said the he "had been criticized for so strongly upholding operations in Germany, having confidence and faith in that policy and in the cooperation of the German government." Meissner finally had to realize that the whole affair would have a "seriously deterrent effect" on relations between GM and the German government. After Dieckhoff, the German ambassador in Washington, had also entered the scene, the Opel employees were freed on 6 April 1939. Although this incident illustrates the power of a transnational entity vis-à-vis a government, it should not be overlooked that there was far greater advantage in the transnational relations between GM and Opel for the German state than for the two companies.

Towards the end of the 1930s, following increasing gravity in the worldwide political situation, there was more uneasiness in Detroit concerning the situation in Germany and its assets frozen there amounting to $33.4 million. Indeed, in early 1939 there were thoughts among the managers of investing in the growth and expansion of the Opel works, increasing in this way their commitment to the German Reich. However, the Policy Committee of GM—against the background of the invasion of Czechoslovakia by the Wehrmacht— logically abandoned this suggestion. That panel also tried to set clear limits on Opel's activities. GM made it clear to Rüsselsheim that military production was strictly forbidden. This position was not entirely convincing because the delivery of trucks to the German military was taking place with the knowledge and approval of Detroit. However, the manufacture of explicitly military products, like the entry of Opel into the production of airplane motors which was considered by the management at Rüsselsheim in early 1939, was rigorously forbidden. Also, after the outbreak of the World War, when the German government approached the Opel management and, like an ultimatum, demanded the production of ammunition, Detroit rejected such plans.

4. Opel in the World War: The End of Transnational Cooperation

However, the German government had a longer breath. The parent company in Michigan was becoming less and less the manager of the Opel works. For Opel produced during the Second World War annually about 300,000 3-ton "Blitz" model trucks for the army and in 1942 designed the half-track "Maultier" together with Ford. In 1943 Opel produced about 27% of these vehicles. Furthermore, GM manufactured power systems for bombers and fighter planes of the Messerschmitt 262 type and also tanks, according to FBI data from 1941. Opel delivered about 50% of the motors for the Junkers JU-88 middle-range bomber. In 1943 Opel manufactured over 9,000 power trains and towards the end of the war, from October 1944 on, Opel produced 954 ME-262s completely.

This loss in control and the growing distance between parent and daughter company was accompanied by a withdrawal of GM employees in Opel's production and company management. After 1 September 1939, GM began the transfer of American personnel in Opel management from Germany. Early in March 1941, the last American GM employee left Germany. Although at first there was a nominal representation of GM officials on Opel's board of directors (GM President Sloan, GM Vice Presidents Mooney, Graeme K. Howard and John T. Smith), this was significantly accompanied by relinquishment of control over Opel's course. In addition, by 3 September 1939, the German government assigned a purely German management for "daily operations." So logically it is a mistake when Snell wrote that GM was in "complete management control" until the appointment of Karl Luer as administrator of the Rüsselsheim works on 25 November 1942. In June 1940 Opel was officially nationalized and at the latest, at the time of Pearl Harbor, GM withdrew entirely from Opel. This formal, but in no way actual, representation of GM in the leadership of Opel continued throughout the entire period of military conflict. Opel remained, according to the letter, a GM possession, but the actual control lay outside the legal property relations. The situation cannot be precisely reconstructed for the period from September 1939 until at the latest December 1941. It can no longer be determined to what extent GM employees took part in Opel's military production and how far they were aware of these activities. However, one can assume that Detroit was well informed of the situation in the Opel works, because internal company communications across the Atlantic were not cut off until 2 September 1941. But one could only watch helplessly: there was no longer any possibility for action.

5. Transnational Relations as an Instrument of Politics and Diplomacy: Roosevelt and Mooney's Trip to Germany in 1940

When war broke out, the commercial contacts between GM and Opel were used by the Roosevelt administration for diplomatic purposes. During the 1930s James D. Mooney, with whom Roosevelt made contact, had supported German trade policy wishes, called for an increase in American imports from Germany, approved barter exchange and attacked the boycott movement. He was convinced of the "inherent friendliness between our two peoples," as he had said before the BTGAC when greeting the new German ambassador to the US, Hans Dieckhoff, on 27 May 1937. In order to avoid war in Europe, Mooney had said in January 1937, Germany had to be turned away from its "warpath." One could take part in this, if one realized that "Germany's belligerency is only a symptom: it is the result of hunger." If Germany could be supplied with food and raw materials, perhaps through a Bread Fund, Berlin could be brought back to the road of peace. His activity for the improvement of bilateral relations between the German Reich and the US had been rewarded by the German government with the Order of the German Eagle, 1st Class, in 1938. Mooney was thinking in 1939/40 of ways to avoid a war, and when it broke out, of how to end it as quickly as possible. These activities were based naturally on concern for GM investments not only in Germany, but in all Europe.

In October and November 1939 Mooney explored, chiefly at Germany's suggestion, but with silent support of the State Department, in Germany and Great Britain chances for ending the war. Washington gave Mooney free reign because it was hoped that he could shed some light on German, as well as British, intentions. This first mission of Mooney's led to no tangible result. Soon afterwards, in early 1940, Roosevelt approached Mooney directly, asking him to sound out the situation in Germany and offer American mediation. At the same time he was to stress that the US was not aiming at world domination. In February 1940 Mooney went to Europe and conferred with Hitler and Göring in Germany. He was impressed by the explanations of his German interlocutors. They expressed great interest in strengthening German political and economic relations with the US. Mooney reported to Roosevelt on 19 March 1940 regarding his conversation with Göring, during which he expressed "a strong desire for improved economic and commercial relations between Germany and the United States" and had urged the US to increase its imports from Germany. Mooney, who was convinced of the strategic effectiveness of economic relations in seeking peace, was impressed by German diplomacy. He left Germany under the impression that that country wanted to reestablish peace and misunderstood that Hitler and Göring were only intent on claming the US and making sure of American neutrality.

In February 1941 Mooney wrote a letter to Roosevelt, asking him to clearly state American aims in the European conflict. Mooney himself suggested avoiding American intervention and recognizing the new German power in Central and East Europe as a buffer against the Soviet Union and cooperating with Germany and Great Britain to build a new world order. As Mooney saw it, these suggestions were in accord with American national interests, but presupposed that Germany would end hostilities and withdraw its troops from the occupied areas. The US "will never lend its cooperation to Germany in a program for the restoration of political and economic order without German assurance of political autonomy for the small democracies of Western Europe." These actions, with Roosevelt's partial agreement, irritated the American public. Vagueness, assumptions and rumors about the involvement of Mooney and GM in German arms production were reflected in surveillance of the officials in the overseas division by the secret service. Mooney in particular was the subject of investigations and the scrutiny of the press. In mid—1940, he worked out a plan to use the political, economic and even military resources of America, "the greatest power in the world," to press for the beginning of peace negotiations. Washington was in a strategically and tactically favorable position because "Germany's greatest anxiety is the possibility that America may enter the struggle. On the other hand, the greatest anxiety of England is that we may not." This position could be used to bring about a quick end of the war. But Mooney's activities met with opposition. GM's leaders disapproved of Mooney's methods, which unavoidably brought the name of General Motors into the headlines. If Mooney were to be suspected of being too pro-German, or even of sympathizing with the National Socialists, that would automatically affect the whole corporation. That could raise doubt about GM's national loyalty, which would have a negative effect on business. In particular, Alfred P. Sloan was afraid of trouble if GM ventured so far into politics. On 27 August 1940, he wrote Mooney the following message which was equivalent to a reprimand:

> I think it is very dangerous for anybody in your position, or in my position, or for any of the rest of us in General Motors, to deal, in view of the atmosphere that prevails to-day, with questions involving politics, patriotism or religion.... What I would recommend is, that we confine ourselves to our industrial responsibility, feeling free to deal with the problems that affect us and that contribute to a better order of things, industrially.

In this message, he was referring to articles in the press linking Mooney with Hitler and National Socialism. Furthermore, in addition to the press, the State Department and also the secret service were becoming involved. The diplomat George Messersmith, who was assigned to duty in Cuba at that time, explained the Mooney "case" as follows:

> Mooney is fundamentally Fascist in his sympathies.... He is obsessed by this strange notion that a few business, including himself, could take care of the war and the peace. I am absolutely sure that Mooney is keeping up his contact with the Germans because he believes, or at least still hopes, that they will win the war, and he thinks if they do that he will be our Quisling.

On the other hand, R. Geist did not see Mooney as a Nazi sympathizer since, as is often overlooked, he was no longer the head of the Overseas Operations Department, but was coordinating GM military production. According to information from Special Agent L.I. Tyler of the FBI, that was not at all reassuring, because Graeme K. Howard, Mooney's successor in the Export Division, was more of a Germanophile than Mooney. According to another report from Special Agent L.A. Langville, Mooney's conduct was due to GM's immense investments in Europe. He estimated them at the outbreak of war at \$125 million in parts of Europe under German control.

> Mooney therefore realized that if General Motors was to recoup any of this investment, it must remain in a position where it will not give offense to the Nazi government and he, personally, is endeavoring to conduct himself in such a way that he would be in a position after the war to return to Germany and with his contacts salvage as much as possible of this investment.

Therefore, his conduct stems from economic considerations and there is no reason to doubt his patriotism and loyalty. Altogether, Mooney and GM were cleared of the accusation of supporting National Socialism.

Thus, when Snell claims that GM (and Ford) "retained the economic and political power to affect the shape of governmental relations both within and between these nations in a manner which maximized corporate global profits," he is not supported by the facts. He even added the theory of a conspiracy, saying that the two firms "were able to shape the conflict to their own private corporate advantage." The power of the companies was clearly overstated here for the purpose of creating the picture of an enemy. Besides, Snell sees the transnational structures as too monolithic; he ignored the tendencies towards dissociation within the worldwide GM network. The firms are often tempted to look upon themselves as being entirely independent of political restrictions or of standing above them. Thus the management of GM at first underestimated the power of the war to penetrate the company. On the eve of the German invasion of Poland, Sloan expressed the view to some stockholders that GM was "too big" to be affected by "petty international squabbles."

But he learned better, as the politico-military developments had, by the end of 1941, pulled the rug out from under the transnational intra-company relations between GM and Opel. Although they had been used by Roosevelt as a potential diplomatic instrument, that remained only an episode after Mooney's mission to Europe. In the political climate of that time the transnational transfers between Opel and GM involved security policy and thus were considered a possible source of danger because they might include the transfer of sensitive —that is, militarily useful—materials and production technology. Because of this, the contacts between GM and Opel became politically and economically inexpedient and consequently were broken off. Transnational cooperation had to give way to political developments after all.

FORD IN GERMANY

1. The 1920s: Ford's Start on the German Market

The rise of Henry Ford and his Ford Motor Company (FMC), established at Dearborn, Michigan, near Detroit, in 1903, is like a modern fairytale. The success of the "Tin Lizzie," which made Henry Ford a multimillionaire, was based on the work-sharing organization of the production process and economies of scale. They made FMC the largest, most successful and most renowned automobile company in the world and the man at its helm the herald and prophet of a new industrial age.

From the beginning, the firm followed a world market strategy aimed at omnipresence. For this purpose, branch factories were set up in various countries before and after the World War. FMC entered Germany through its Danish branch. On 1 December 1924 it leased a liaison office in Berlin on Unter den Linden. Business developed well, so that, together with Ford-Great Britain, headed by Sir Percival Perry, the Ford Motor Company was founded on 5 January 1925, located in Berlin. Perry was likewise its manager. In August of the same year, the firm became an Aktien Gesellschaft (AG). The new FMCAG was not only a distributing organization, but also a partly production company. One year later an assembly plant was established at Berlin-Westhafen.

In the second half of the 1920s, when it was realized in FMC that, for reasons mentioned in the preceding chapter, the company was visibly falling behind GM and losing competitiveness in the world markets, a reorganization of the worldwide structure of the Ford empire was begun. In Europe, this pretentious "1928 Plan" primarily involved the factory at Dagenham (UK) which, as Henry Ford intended, was to become Europe's Detroit. But important changes were also envisaged for the German offspring. The motto was business expansion and establishment of a full-producing independent plant, since the business report for the Berlin factory in 1929 showed a profit of more than 2.1 million *RM*. Search for a proper location extended to cities like Frankfurt, Regensburg, Essen, Neuss, Düsseldorf and Cologne. On 18 October 1929, the mayor of Cologne, Konrad Adenauer, offered Perry land for a Ford manufacturing plant near Cologne under extremely favorable conditions. Perry promptly accepted. However, Adenauer did not approve the deal until Ford had said he was willing not only to transfer the production plants, but also the administrative headquarters from Berlin to Cologne.

The financing caused small difficulties. As the banks were not prepared to admit the FMCAG to the stock exchange, contact was made with IG, which was known to be seeking capital in the US to establish a daughter company. It was possible that an arrangement could be agreed upon to benefit both sides. Finally, Dr. Carl Bosch, the IG manager, guaranteed FMCAG. The latter agreed with the condition that Edsel Ford, Henry's son, should join the board of directors of the American IG (AIG). The agreement also provided that FMC would become a shareholder of AIG and that IG would acquire 35% of the stock in FMCAG, which was running at 15 million *RM*. Sixty percent lay with Ford Great Britain and the remaining 5% with suppliers.

On 2 October 1930 the cornerstone was laid in Cologne in a buttress of the powerful retaining wall on which the words were engraved "*Und trotzdem vorwärts* — Henry Ford." This was meant as a program, for Henry Ford did not want to acknowledge the Depression. He still clung to one of his basic ideas, according to which one could make "prosperity continuous and universal." In more difficult times like these it is even more important than before for the businessmen to be leaders; in this way he strengthened his unlimited control over the Ford empire:

> The sea captain sails by his charts; he can do that because the sea route has been charted. But American business is now sailing over seas that have never passed before.... What American business is depending on is the man on the bridge—the living manager—whose only charts are his foresight and his insight and his sense of the new trade winds that are beginning to blow...business to-day is an explorer's ship.

In addition, financial control of the company remained with him alone. He could therefore avoid many suggestions for reform which were, among others, also brought to him by his son Edsel, the president of FMC. Henry shut himself off rigidly from his son's ideas and the latter soon resigned because of the uselessness of his work. Relations between father and son remained quite strained. Henry rejected, for example, the system of "performance control" used by GM and even eliminated his central office. If, from a superficial view, this gave the impression that Ford was serious about decentralization, the real effect of this measure was aimed at tightening his domination of the industry. It was clearly illustrated in a brochure for the 30th anniversary of Ford Motor Company how Henry Ford had drawn away from reality and changed conditions when he wrote: "All of the principles we laid down (in 1903) are still operating; we find that they have great survival value for the future."

2. FMCAG during the Depression

The assembly plant in Berlin which still registered profits over 3.2 million *RM* in 1930 continued operations until 15 April 1931. Afterwards, the equipment was brought to Cologne, where the first vehicle was produced on May 4th and by 12 June 1931 the factory had completely opened. Altogether, investment there amounted to 23.3 million *RM*, of which about $1.7 million went toward the expansion of FMCAG's own production of automotive parts in order to obtain the desirable label *"deutsches Produkt"* (made in Germany). All previous efforts in that direction had not yet succeeded. From 1930 FMCAG was even confronted for three years with supplementary taxes. Those pulling the strings behind these maneuvers were mostly the Reichsverband der Deutschen Automobilindustrie (RDA) whose aim, since the mid-1920s, had been to force American manufacturers out of the German market.

These annoyances added to the effects of the world economic and bank crisis. The Cologne plant was producing at a capacity of only 13% and one month after its opening it even had to temporarily close its doors. FMCAG's portion of the market fell from 9.9% (in 1930) to 2.2% (in 1932). If that shows "in what a catastrophic way Ford had declined vis-à-vis competing brands," it must also be taken into account that in the economic circumstances of that time new automobiles could hardly be sold. So it is not surprising that in 1931

FMCAG had to record a loss of 1.7 million *RM* which could be only be reduced to a short 1.2 million *RM* by carrying over the profit from 1930. In the next year the loss was about 6 million *RM* and a year later nearly 4 million *RM*.

Insecurity was so widespread that even the Dearborn staff who held stock in the Ford plant at Cologne tried to divest themselves of it. With this, the somber predictions of Heinrich Albert, attorney and deputy chairman of the board of directors of FMCAG, were confirmed. At the close of 1931, he had expressed highly pessimistic views concerning the company's future because of the drastic fall in the purchasing power of the population and the trend towards the lowest price level with a minimum taxation, both of which were negative developments for Ford. To improve the situation, he urged investment in the Borsig Works in Berlin, which had been unofficially offered in 1932 by government agencies and the Reichsbank. In so doing, Ford could become almost "German" and thus give itself a stronger national color.

Perry, chairman of the board, whose word was practically law for FMCAG, recognized the risks in that FMCAG was "still subject to almost malicious agitation as foreigners" and as "an American enterprise with whom true Germans ought not to do business." But he rejected participation in Borsig, which he justified by saying that he fully shared Ford's policy of "isolation of political motive from industrial enterprise." He believed, as Edsel Ford also did, that this transaction would not reconcile the Cologne plant with the government. Wilkins and Hill rightly draw a gloomy conclusion against this background: "Ford's German operation was a wasteland. It was an expensive manufacturing plant with no market for its products." But the promises of one of the most important and largest retail markets in Europe, combined with rivalry with GM/Opel (a result of the competitive motive) induced FMC to continue its presence in the German market.

When it was introduced to the market in 1928, the "Model A" had difficulty. Therefore, FMC at first saw the light at the end of the tunnel in the "Baby Ford," the "Model Y," which was sold in Germany under the name "Köln." With the "Köln," FMC intended to regain lost terrain. Production was to begin on 2 January 1933. Meanwhile, regulations concerning what were considered German products had changed so that Ford was compelled to manufacture the vehicle entirely at Cologne, otherwise, there would be considerable taxes to pay and commercial disadvantages to suffer. Whereas it was initially thought to assemble the car in Cologne with parts coming mostly from Great Britain and the US, now the company had to try to produce as many parts as possible in Germany itself. This implied market and production losses for Dagenham, which evoked Perry's displeasure and meant a significant shift in priorities within Ford's global organization.

Even with these changes, Ford's problems did not diminish. FMCAG continued to be faced with an anti-American mood which grew worse during 1933. Hitler's great admiration for Henry Ford's achievements could do nothing to change this. Relations between the firm in Cologne and the German authorities remained tense. As a result of the miserable economic situation and the difficulties with the German authorities. Ford's losses in mid-1933 fell just short of 7.6 million *RM*. This was a very serious sign, for that sum represented more than half of the total capital of 15 million *RM*. Perry, in a letter to Dearborn, could not avoid recommending refinancing of the Cologne factory as a step urgently required. At the same time in Cologne managers were racking their brains to find an appropriate business strategy. However one twisted and turned, one always came to the same conclusion, namely "the necessity of producing a 100% German car," as CEO Edmund Heine put it at a meeting of the board of directors on 7 June 1933. In October 1933, Heine was able to report some partial successes to Dearborn. Not only had production increased a little, but efforts to obtain recognition as a German firm had borne their first fruits. The four-cylinder and the truck from the Cologne plant were recognized as German products. Still, this was no reason for overflowing optimism, as the RDA was continuing its obstructionist campaign against FMCAG. And Heine anticipated further difficulties from that direction.

3. Intra-Company Relations Between FMC and FMCAG and National Socialist Germany

A. The precarious situation of FMCAG until the mid-1930s

In 1933/34 Detroit was in now way satisfied with events in Cologne, since Ford-USA, in view of the company's tense economic situation, had to take over the financing of Cologne and increase its share in the company to 34.2%. In later adjustments Detroit's share grew at the expense of Dagenham. The extent of the malaise became apparent when, in 1934, the Cologne plant could only function between 15 and 38% of its capacity. In addition, the dealers complained of the quality of the products which were often defective. However, there was no question of leaving Germany because, on the one hand, FMC did not want to lay themselves open to their arch-rival GM, and on the other, they calculated that there would be good opportunities before long in the German market. The comprehensive program of motorization which Hitler had announced in February 1933 offered unforeseen possibilities.

Although the situation remained uncertain through all of 1934, there was a weak upward trend later on. During that year, sales increased a little and for the first time a profit, albeit a small one of about 3,900 *RM*, was recorded. But within the management at Cologne internal quarrels arose because of what was considered an extremely unsatisfactory business situation. It became increasingly clear that Heine could not handle the situation. The flames were fanned further by the intrigues of Prince Louis Ferdinand, the FMCAG representative in Hamburg, who wanted to expand his position of power within the company. He recommended to the management in Cologne, of which he was not a member, that they accept the Volkswagen project of the National Socialist government and support Hitler's program of standardization aimed at the interchange of parts in the automobile industry. In this context Louis Ferdinand worked actively to have the Cologne plant transferred to Hamburg. This proposal was brought before the directors of the company by the German authorities who were interested in having FMCAG share in the Volkswagen project for reasons of military strategy. Keppler, responsible for economic questions in the Chancellor's office, had written to the prince on 9 August 1934, while he was in Dearborn, that he should Ford to take account of "reasons of country defense" when making new investments and selecting their location. By this Keppler was referring to the transfer of the Cologne factory to Hamburg on the Elbe or to central Germany.

This question was discussed in Detroit on 4 September 1934. Albert and Prince Louis Ferdinand spoke for FMCAG and Lange and

Wirtz for the Hamburg city government. During this discussion, Lange attempted to bring pressure on Ford by pointing out that Opel and GM had already agreed to participate in the Volkswagen project and have even agreed to build a new factory. But Albert "pointed out that Mr. [Henry] Ford is almost a fanatical supporter of the idea, that the Government should in no way interfere with business, which has to be left to private initiative." The Hamburg representatives were powerless against this joint opposition from Detroit and Cologne. FMCAG remained in Cologne. Although Keppler was a little disgruntled over this decision, it did not prevent him from holding onto his ties with FMCAG. His contact person was Albert who, although he had opposed moving to Hamburg as proposed by the government, still had great interest in maintaining relations with the German government and since mid-1934 saw a way to improve the delicate situation of the company. In December 1934 Albert and Keppler had their first dinner together, on which Albert reported to Dearborn. In his report, he said expressly that he wanted to preserve this contact and expected that it would be useful for the company. Above all, it became clear in Cologne that allying the company with the National Socialist government would be accompanied by commercial advantages. The people in Cologne who supported this idea met with bitter resistance from Perry who, despite the assumption of financial control of the Cologne plant by the parent firm in Dearborn, still had an important voice in operations there. For him, there was no question of a rapprochement with the German government. He feared too deep an involvement in the somber machinations of the German regime:

> I think we should avoid politics so far as possible, and particularly should not consider that any arrangements made to comply with the requirements of the existing dictatorship will be permanent or reliable.

These objections were shared in Dearborn; the trend towards rapprochement with the government was greeted with mixed feelings. Charles E. Sorensen, technical manager for FMC, felt that Albert was "too impressed with the necessity of cooperating with the Government Authorities." Discussion of business policy swayed between these two poles until 1935. The members of the board in Dearborn, like Perry, were mostly opposed or at best hesitant, whereas the managers in Cologne and especially Albert increasingly saw cooperation with the government as a cure-all for the company's difficulties. They also approved as far as possible adoption of German norms in the question of standards. In April 1935, Albert pointed out at conference that Opel had adopted the metric system as part of its standardization and he felt that this had led to its disproportionately more favorable commercial situation. This policy of Opel's had opened the door for German government contracts, particularly with the Defense Ministry.

Besides these basic differences over company policy there arose misunderstandings between Heine, whose lack of ability was becoming more apparent, and Albert, who was becoming more and more a decisive personality in Cologne. The disagreements came to a head in early 1935 and in the end could not be bridged. Albert turned to Dearborn. Besides Albert, the other members of the board—Bosch, Perry and Davies—also wrote to Edsel Ford on 22 January 1935. They said that they were in an "unworkable situation" in Cologne since Heine "has entirely run out of control of directors." The latter was ordered to Dearborn at the end of January 1935 and in March, Dearborn finally reached a decision. Heine was encouraged to retire and Erich Diestel, "a babe in the motor car woods," was appointed his successor. Meanwhile, the main responsibility for the plant at Cologne was transferred to Albert. It was hoped in Dearborn that this decision would clarify relations in the German daughter company. This was urgently needed: in his report, A.L. Burns, who had been sent from Dearborn to test the situation there, came to the crushing conclusion that "the whole situation here is anything but encouraging." That report called attention to various weaknesses, but especially criticized the coordination problems between the sales, purchasing and production departments. Under these obscure conditions production of the V-8 was begun in Cologne. For this, a capital of about 4.5 million *RM* was needed. FMC participated in the financing to a considerable degree. While Ford's European Finance Company in Luxemburg provided 2 million *RM*, Dearborn sent the remaining 2.5 million, not in cash, but in the form of machines and spare parts. This required authorization from the RwiM, which was requested in March 1935 and granted.

B. *The turn upwards after 1935*

The year 1935 was a turning-point for FMCAG. From then on business improved, which was also due to the fact that Hitler and Göring both had visited the display of FMCAG at the International Automobile Exposition (IAA) in Berlin in 1935. This was interpreted as a sign that the ice was beginning to thaw between FMCAG and the German authorities, an assumption which proved to be correct. This made the people visibly happy in Cologne. In September 1935 it was reported to R.I. Roberge, head of the International Division in Dearborn, that when Hitler was dealing with the Volkswagen project he no longer paid court to GM and Opel alone but was also more obliging towards FMCAG.

> Hitler has already told the German auto manufacturers that they are too weak and inexperienced to do the job that is needed [developing the Volkswagen] and that there is room for foreign capital and ability, particularly such companies as Ford and GM.

The budding relaxation in relations between the companies and the German government became apparent to the public, which was subsequently reflected in the number of sales. Sales were stabilized in the second and third quarter of 1935 and the manufacturing volume rose to about 40%. Contributing to this success was the fact that FMC and Dagenham were willing to include the German plant to a larger degree in export business than had been the case in the past, although this forced them to make a sacrifice, i.e., their business volume overseas. To effect this agreement the approval of the RwiM was again necessary and on 26 October 1935, FMCAG signed an export agreement with the RwiM. Accordingly FMC received an export bonus of 25% on the value of merchandise up to 600,000 *RM* for products sent through Cologne to Dearborn for use there or for further export. Thus, the Hitler government gave FMC preferences by subsidizing these German export products and thereby promoted German exports. Furthermore, Berlin's acceptance of this agreement implied withdrawal from the uncompromising position it had held on the question of standards because by transferring to the metric system, the FMCAG parts could not be used by FMC.

The management problems relative to coordinating the separate sections were also solved little by little. These organizational changes pleased Roberge, who visited Cologne in June 1936 and said optimistically that "the ground work has been laid for the future." In addition, FMCAG began to go its own way in model production and in production technology and even more in design to become separate from its American parent company. In both the "Eifel" and the "Taunus" models, Cologne turned out its own models which took greater account of the requirements of the European public. These efforts bore fruit, for the in the autumn of 1935 the Reich Transportation Ministry informed the FMCAG that as of 1 February 1936, the Ford automobile could bear the official phrase "*Deutsches Erzeugnis*" (made in Germany).

Although glad for that news, it was depressing for the managers in Cologne to make comparisons with their rival Opel, which was the market leader in Germany. Opel had gained an enviable 40% market share and in 1935 had built a new factory in Brandenburg. It was especially painful for the managers in Cologne that, in contrast to FMCAG, Opel was receiving large government contracts. Furthermore, FMCAG still had to struggle against its image as a foreigner and the accompanying prejudice. This had to be eradicated and it was Albert who thought of a clever strategy to do so. Writing to Edsel Ford, he complained at first against the decisions made to establish the firm at Cologne, which had later proven to have serious disadvantages. "We are suffering from the fact that we did not appear on the scene in the German cloak from the outset, as Generals Motors has done." He continued, painting a grim picture of the situation and proffered a prediction of disaster. "The time is no longer distance when the Opel Werke will prevail exclusively in the market." He considered the measures which had been taken up until then as insufficient. Finally he outlined his concept that, on the one hand, consisted in increasing production in order to lower costs and, on the other, a more comprehensive acceptance of the wishes of the German government. The first was set in motion half a year later with the expansion of the plant at Cologne. He made the latter more concrete later on by recommending participation in the Volkswagen project and again encouraged joining a German producer in order to give Ford a strong German anchor.

C. Adaptation to the German government: the Stoewer transaction

In this context Albert was thinking of the purchase of the Stoewer Works in Stettin. He and Carl Bosch of the board of directors had already made this proposal to Sorensen in December 1935. By doing so, Albert hoped to kill several birds with one stone. First, the Stoewer firm was reputed to be a well-managed, renowned, German company; second, it enjoyed government contracts, and third, it operated a carrosserie (body) factory, so that eventually its one-sided direction towards its previous supplier, Ambi-Budd, could be reduced. However, it came out little by little that Stoewer was more or less bankrupt. While the matter was over for Perry and the board in Dearborn when they learned this, the purchase was nevertheless approved in Cologne because in their view, the advantages mentioned above outweighed the pending insolvency.

In support of their argument, they also used their relation to the Opel Works. General Manager Diestel wrote in early March to Sorensen that there would be "dangers threatening in case Opel with their immense financial resources further reduce prices and make the situation generally difficult." In taking stock on 6 April 1936, the managers feared that soon the people in Rüsselsheim would hold 50% of the trade in automobiles and thus control the entire market. It was pointed out emphatically in this context that this was "also being influenced by their good contact with the government." At most FMCAG could reach 10% of German automobile production because its price level was too high, it had no contacts with the government, and an attitude of rejection was still apparent in the public. This could be countered by the merger with Stoewer it was argued. During 1936 Albert and Erhard Vitger received support in this matter from the board in Cologne. At a meeting on 13 May 1936 it was agreed that the "purpose of a merger with the Stoewer Works mainly is to profit from a possibility offered to remove the well-known discrimination of Ford Motor Company AG and their products" and approved the purchase. It was calculated that about 5 million *RM* would be needed for this transaction. A preliminary agreement was indeed reached on 15 May 1936 in the presence of Sorensen from Dearborn with Stoewer, but this did not remove FMC's scruples. Finally the whole project failed because of the stubborn opposition of Dearborn to the investment of so great a sum for a comparatively exhausted company like Stoewer.

here is reason to believe that these arguments were only adduced by
ie company management and that the actual motive for the rejection
as fear for the safety of the investments in Germany. Given the rela-
vely uncertain situation in Germany, one was not inclined to risk
ich a great amount of money at once.

During the discussions with the Stoewer company, the mere
ossibility of a merger had a positive effect on business, as German
overnment agencies were urging the takeover. In his speech at the
AA in February 1936 in Berlin, Hitler specifically expressed his
dmiration for FMCAG and Henry Ford's accomplishments. When he
ppeared on that occasion at the Cologne stand and a few days later
Jöring even personally ordered an Eifel Cabriolet—almost like the
rst government order—this was rightly viewed as a sensation and the
tart of future business with the German government. Hitler's and
Jöring's step was in no way just a pleasant gesture, but sprang from a
vell thought out calculation: because of the government program of
notorization, the FMCAG could not be neglected out of hand. Hence,
ie failure of the Stoewer merger would only mean a temporary set-
ack. In the midst of greater preparations for war following the
nnouncement of the Four-Year Plan, the German government would
ot bother with such trifles. There were more important things to do
nd all resources were to be used for the great purpose.

). *Aid from the parent company*

After German government agencies had severely limited rubber
istribution as a result of difficulties in obtaining raw materials, the
ack of rubber was deeply felt at FMCAG by August 1936. On 30
August this bad news from Cologne landed on Edsel Ford's desk:

> Tire Situation Catastrophic. The only chance left is to import raw
> materials ourselves and have this manufactured into tires. If no further
> compensation business can be soon arranged, plant must shut down
> October first. [...] We suggest that you arrange supply of raw material
> we pay through extended export to USA, Canada, Mexico, Japan,
> British India and Dutch East Indies.

In this connection Albert was thinking of paying for the shipment
of rubber from Dearborn with the export of wheels, chassis parts and
ball bearings. This was actually a return to barter exchange in modern

form. Albert had Dearborn check whether—as in the case of SONJ—it might be possible to ship products other than those of FMCAG "to USA on a large scale with the help of the Ford organization." This, however, did not happen. In September 1936 Diestel again described the dramatic situation to Sorensen and stressed that they were instructed to seek larger possibilities for export. For this Dearborn's support was needed. He went on: "If we are denied such cooperation, I fear we will be worn out between Opel on the one and the whole German automobile industry on the other side." After this reference to their GM competitor, Dearborn agreed to the proposal and reached an understanding with Cologne by which Cologne shipped V-8 motor parts and accessories to Michigan. From there some of them were exported further to other countries. In return, Cologne was supplied with caoutchouc which was processed by Continental in Hannover and sent on to Cologne. Sorensen especially supported this agreement in Dearborn; his intervention in favor of the requests from the Cologne factory made it possible first to export spare parts made in Germany to Dearborn and later also to northern Europe.

On 7 November 1936 Albert sent Dearborn more bad news. The German government required that from then on 30% of the rubber supplied by Dearborn should be sent not to FMCAG but to the German agencies. FMC was offered a higher price of from 25 to 30 percent. In his evaluation of the situation, Albert thought it would be a mistake "to hesitate in submitting to the conditions of the government, be it only for a moment." Such an agreement would ensure, when there was continued support from Detroit, an adequate basis for production in the coming years, since there was a distinct possibility that "the scarcity of rubber may so greatly increase that our company will be far ahead of all the other competitors." FMC was under pressure. It was learned that, under Göring's orders, FMCAG (and also Opel) would, from 15 December 1936, be entirely exempted from the rubber rationing of the control agencies. This order was justified by the fact that they were in a position to guarantee their requirements through foreign contacts and export activity. Cologne was not at all pleased by this and angrily wrote to Göring that other firms at lease received government contracts.

FMC Cologne, however, has never got government orders; it did not profit of the rearmament boom and still to-day is exclusively dependent on its own private production. Secondly, FMC Cologne, owing to its American character, has hitherto not enjoyed equal rights with the other German factories. It would, therefore, be unreasonable if now when once and quite exceptionally the fact of FMC Cologne's American affiliation happens to be advantageous to it the German authorities would demand equal rights in favor of the other factories.

But all of the protests came to nothing. The orders must be followed. Along with this, Albert continued his efforts to obtain government contracts, as "they would imply the official recognition of our works and lessen also the obstacles standing in the way of private sales." In order to facilitate such business, he suggested in forestalling servility, as it were, and in anticipation of possible difficulties, replacement of the Jewish manager Diestel. A German was needed. This brought criticism in Dearborn, where it was felt that Albert was going too far in his friendly efforts to get government contracts. But he did not let himself be turned away by this.

It was with satisfaction that the sales increase for 1936 was reported at close to 53% in comparison with the previous year and exports increased nearly three times as much. It was the best business outcome in years, with a profit of nearly 900,000 *RM*. There had also been progress in the question of recognition in Germany. There were orders from government agencies and requests from the army ordnance branch. However, one dared not be content with these successes. Hence, the annual report explicitly stressed readiness to collaborate fully with the Four-Year-Plan. Only that would guarantee further commercial success, for "according to present German ideas, an enterprise in Germany is only justified to exist insofar as it submits to the general political and economic requirements of the State." Albert was strengthened in his position by the fact that, due to blockages in the supply of raw materials in Germany, the factory had to be closed for ten days in February. Government rationing of raw materials was an efficient tool to force the companies to conduct themselves properly and consequently this episode seemed to drastically confirm the need for establishing a consensual relationship with the government. On the other hand, Diestel considered the breakthrough already complete. The government had to recognize that FMCAG, together with Opel, was leading in the field of two- and four-ton vehicles. Besides, their export activity was "of special importance within the German economic system."

Fortunately, recognition as a German firm made further progress. After the RwiM (January 1937), came the Wehrmacht (Department of Defense) on 18 June and on 1 September the Reichsverkehrsministerium (RVM – Reich Ministry of Transport). This recognition by German governmental agencies was of vital importance for FMCAG in view of the shortage of raw materials in Germany and the arbitrariness of the government rationing system and required good behavior on the part of FMCAG. Although this policy put the company on a slippery slope, there was no alternative and in fact, this business policy was accepted. After all, because of the hasty readiness to cooperate with the government, three agreements with German agencies were signed on 1 April 1937 which practically guaranteed the basic supply and thereby the existence of FMCAG to a degree. In the agreement on iron ore, Cologne was promised 32,000 units of ore, as long as 8,000 of them went to export; in the metal agreement, 75% of what Cologne had used the preceding year was guaranteed for non-iron metals; the rubber agreement supplied FMCAG with half of its requirements. The other half of the rubber as well as the other materials arrived through the international Ford network and particularly through Dearborn to Germany. On the other side, Cologne was exporting automotive parts.

At the end of May a report arrived in Dearborn from Cologne concerning its export activities. An annual production of 32,000 units had been approved by the German authorities, but under the condition that 25% of them, i.e., 8,000 units, be exported. Cologne—and in the end also Dearborn—could do nothing other than accept these conditions. Besides, Opel, whose export activity was likewise increasing, did not want to fall short. Thus Cologne products mostly found their way to European countries, but also to Egypt. This method was quite promising, so that FMCAG began to make further plans. It announced its interest in distributing automotive parts to additional European countries as well as overseas. Up until now this had been done with the US, Canada, and Great Britain. FMC agreed, in order to stabilize the business in Germany. After this, FMCAG distributed truck transmissions, tachometers, axles, mufflers, spring suspensions and other items abroad.

The assistance which the Dearborn headquarters provided the plant in Cologne was not limited to supplying rubber and increasing Cologne's share in export, but also included the supply of spare parts and materials such as raw iron and non-iron metals which, in the Germany of 1937, were difficult to obtain. In the days that followed this also presented a considerable problem. The company, which next to Daimler-Benz, was the only German manufacturer in 1937 which was able to increase its production in comparison with 1936, believed its production program was in serious danger. The firm received the announcement that the German agencies responsible for the distribution of raw materials had assigned a quota of 40,000 units to FMCAG for 1938, reducing its own planing by 8,000 units. Adding to the difficulties, the RwiM withdrew its dollar credit for the purchase of pig iron, while the exports from Cologne just covered the rubber imports. On 20 September 1937, Albert Sorensen described the need for raw materials urgently and asked Dearborn to help in the distribution of pig iron. These shipments were to be paid for by additional exports from Cologne. Should Dearborn refuse, the consequences were unpredictable, indeed catastrophic.

> If you now leave Cologne in the lurch, the effort of an increased program breaks down—not only for 1937, but also for 1938 as the negotiations with the authorities about the again increased program for 1938 are based on your readiness to provide us with pig iron.

Dearborn approved. But assistance from the parent company also had its limits. It was not prepared to invest more money in Germany. Solicitude did not extend that far, for there was a "serious question as to whether or not any additional investment should be made in the absence of definite possibilities of repayment."

E. Albert's strategic victory

Continuing efforts were made to establish a successful relationship with the German government. To this changes in the management of the Cologne enterprise made an important contribution. In June 1937 Perry, who had been chairman of the board of directors, resigned and Albert became his successor. In addition, the executive committee was increased by two members—Erhard C. Vitger and Robert H. Schmidt—so that the most important positions of the enterprise were filled with German nationals, reflecting greater independence in personnel. This greater distance between parent and daughter firms was also documented in a symbolic way by a directive sent by Dearborn to the daughter company in the autumn of 1937. According to this, the well-known Ford emblem would only be permitted on American products in the future, whereas Ford branches throughout the world would use their own emblem.

At the same time, further efforts were made to expand the enterprise, which were welcomed (and supported) by the government. With Edsel Ford's permission, construction of a foundry was planned, which was approved by the city fathers of Cologne. Adenauer arranged for FMCAG to have a one-year option to purchase land north of the factory for the price of 3.50 *RM* per square meter. Additionally, towards the end of the year the construction of a small factory was started next to the production area of Ambi-Budd in Berlin-Johannisthal which was first intended to produce an eight-cylinder limousine, but a year later trucks for the government.

The German authorities included the Cologne Ford factory more and more in their plans and at the close of 1937 the German government made a project proposal to the company management. Together with Ambi-Budd and an unnamed third firm, three-axle vehicles were to be produced from October 1938 for the German government. First, 250 trucks and then 50 per month were to be made. However, Wibel, the director of purchasing in Dearborn, saw in the three-axle a "product which clearly comes under the head of 'war munitions'" and asked Sorensen to "cable Dr. Albert to be careful as to what he promises the German government before he has the official consent of our people here as to the commodity to be manufactured." But Albert found this a unique opportunity to obtain government contracts in greater number and insisted on carrying out the three-axle project, as "cooperation with government on this subject was of vital importance for future business." After he had frequently intervened with the authorities in Dearborn on this subject, the plan was finally approved in mid-January although scruples in Dearborn had not been removed entirely. In particular, Henry Ford had often clearly stated that, although he did not reject government contracts in general, they were only acceptable as long as they did not include supplying explicitly military goods, such as, for example, tanks or half-track vehicles.

One thing must have been decisive for Michigan's approval: that Albert was able to win Sorensen in Dearborn over to his view during the discussion. "Sorensen had no qualms about working for the government. He scoffed at the danger of war, and felt that orders from the regime would simply help the company." Besides, one could take comfort in the fact that neither military goods nor weapons in the true sense, but only part of the traditional line of products were being given to government agencies. Finally, financing was largely guaranteed by a considerable profit in 1937 of over one million *RM* from business in Cologne.

The gradual increase in production can be seen in the rate of productivity in the installations. Although the capacity in 1936 varied from 46% to 63%, it increased in the following year to between 47% and 93%. In 1938, it swung between 78% and 100%. This development resulted in rising profits which were reinvested due to the prohibition of transfer of profits.

TABLE 10
THE BUSINESS DEVELOPMENT OF THE COLOGNE WORKS

Year	Profits	Turnover	Employees	Sales
1934	-3,900.00	30.0	1139	10018
1935	62,778.76	42.6	1707	12768
1936	368,900.49	65.0	2297	20843
1937	1,014,303.55	94.3	3383	31720
1938	1,213,358.56	120.9	4262	36582
1939	1,377,154.86		3847	35364
1940	-1,700,000.00		3871	17557

Source: "Ford Werke A.G. Cologne." HFM&GV, Acc. 713, Box 2, Folder 2-1. Die Zahl für 1934 stammt aus dem Geschäftsbericht für das Jahr 1934. Ebd., Acc. 38, Box 19, Folder Cologne. Die Zahl für 1940 ist aus Albert an E. Ford., 1.4.1941. Ebd., Acc. 6, Box 369, Folder Ford Motor Co, – Cologne.

The FMCAG policy grew into commercial success, while government contracts increased in volume. In mid-1938, FMCAG received the first large comprehensive government contract for production of 3,150 trucks of V-8 type. Albert felt that this large contract had justified his policy. In order to remove the last doubts in Dearborn, he telegraphed Sorensen that this development showed how foresighted and profitable for the future the decision to establish an assembly plant at Berlin-Johannisthal had been. The German government also sought to gain the good will of the company's eccentric owner. A month later, the Grand Cross of the German Eagle was bestowed on Henry Ford on his 75th birthday "in recognition of Ford's pioneering work in motorization and in making automobiles available to the masses."

Therefore the business report for the third quarter of 1938 praised the arrangement with the government: "Business with the authorities developed extraordinarily and the demand could only be satisfied by importing a considerable number of American trucks." After that, government business grew to such an extent that deliveries could no longer be completely filled and even American trucks had to be imported. Work on government contracts was given absolute priority, so that finally a separate section was set up for that.

The outlook for the future was more promising still. On 24 November FMCAG was called to a conference at the Reich Aviation Ministry at which the other German automobile manufacturers were also present. They were subjected to harsh criticism. Its subject was the unsatisfactory quality of the German cars since—as Göring and von Schell, in charge of automotive questions, explained—they did not satisfy German military requirements. The plan, as von Schell then sketched it, involved standardization and reduction in the multiplicity of types. But the specter of stronger government intervention in production lost its chill when he explained to the public that the army was planning mostly for acquisition of 100,000 three-ton trucks. A few days later, Diestel, who had attended the conference, learned in a conversation with Colonel Zuckertort and Major Schmiedel that the army was thinking primarily of deliveries by FMCAG and Opel.

The move to rapprochement, even familiarity, with the German government was continued and even intensified. In order to dispel any last doubts of the loyalty of the Cologne enterprise, Albert reiterated, during talks with Edsel Ford, Sorensen and Perry in Dearborn on 14/15 November 1938, his old idea of replacing the Jewish business manager Diestel and suggested as a successor the Oberbürgermeister of Cologne, Karl Georg Schmidt. Surprisingly, all of those present approved of that proposal. On 15 December 1938 Diestel was replaced. This episode can proved that in 1938 Cologne had "long been autonomous," for the fact that Albert could dare reprise a proposal that had already been rejected and that he was able to have it approved spoke volumes about the relationship between parent and daughter companies. In connection with the rapprochement with the German government, there occurred shifts in the firm's structure which afforded the German branch more flexibility. On the other hand, the importance of the truck deal for the German government can be gauged by the fact that FMCAG was completely exonerated from the requirement to adopt metric standards and the import of American trucks was permitted.

F. Continued assistance from Dearborn

When deliveries were made from Cologne to the United States, in view of the mood in the US which was increasingly critical and hostile towards Germany, the origin of these products was concealed. At the end of July 1938 the following request from Cologne was discussed:

> ...that we [in Detroit] investigate the possibilities of their shipping German merchandise to us in the States, we to find ways and means of denationalizing the German units by assembly other parts to them and then claiming duty refund and shipping to our various export markets.

It was quite clear that these were dangerous waters indeed, and an official request to the Treasury Department about the legality of this procedure was to be avoided at all costs. After Dearborn had accepted this transaction and the German deliveries were set, certain precautions were taken to avoid unnecessary attention. "To avoid any reaction from outside interests that might be anti-German, it is desirable that the material be split over weekly sailings during November and December." Thus Dearborn was well aware of the explosive nature of this undertaking. A letter from Dr. Robert Rosen, chairman of the Boycott Committee of Jewish War Veterans of the United States, to Edsel Ford on 9 July 1938, in which he requested information about Dearborn's imports from Germany and urged a rearrangement of purchases, indicates how justified it was in Dearborn's view to keep this shrewd system secret. Similar letters mentioned the continuing exchange relationships and accused Dearborn of supporting Germany "in its efforts to subjugate many small innocent neutral nations."

In early 1938 it became clear that the planned increase in production at Cologne from 32,000 units in 1938 to 46,000 units in 1939, based almost entirely on government raw contracts under the Schell Plan, could scarcely be realized. Only the supply of machinery from Dearborn for the manufacture of gear-boxes could remedy this, so that they were forced to help the Cologne factory out. The Cologne management sent Dearborn a similar request in April, 1939. This involved an additional order for 1,500 to 3,000 trucks intended for the Sudetenland. FMCAG would only receive the subsidy for this project, however, if the quantity of deliveries of materiel from Dearborn and the transfer of German goods, which would not be limited to products of the automotive industry, to the US could be increased. At the instigation of the German government, an attempt was obviously being made to bring other German products to American customers and thus advance German exports. It was felt that this could be not be avoided, for

> We are anxious to receive at least 1500 of this order because this means that we get cars into a district where there are so far practically no Ford cars running, in fact very few cars at all. We would then be able to secure a good market for the future.

For that reason Dearborn was asked to find people interested in German goods in the US. Here again they were meeting the wishes of Germany halfway.

> As regards the supply of foreign raw materials to enable the operations of our Cologne company to continue...it was necessary for this company to arrange for the sale of German manufactured products abroad...in order to create the foreign exchange necessary to purchase the raw materials. The entire arrangement was unsatisfactory...but the alternative was to close down our Cologne operations or to sell out the Ford interest to German capitalists, with little or no chance of being able to convert the proceeds of this sale into dollars.... It was a case of

having a substantial investment in a country and attempting to protect
it in the hope that eventually the situation would improve so that we
could continue our business in a more satisfactory manner.

4. The War and its Consequences for Intra-Company Relations

In cases like those just mentioned, the desires of the German
government for increased sales and profit were followed, thus killing
two birds with one stone. On the one hand, the program of rearmament proceeded and on the other, German resources were preserved
through the use of company deliveries from the US. When war began,
these were stopped at first by Dearborn. But in late September 1939,
Cologne announced its interest in retaining this system and continuing
it, describing the supply shortages in drastic terms. In October 1939
Cologne received an import authorization and wrote to Dearborn:
"We trust you will see your way to ship these [ball bearings] to us
without delay." Dearborn then delivered, until 1940/41, materials such
as milling machines and placed orders with American manufacturers
that were intended for Cologne.

These deliveries from the company headquarters took place
despite the tendencies towards separation of the parent from the
daughter firm. The gap in the production line increased with the
"Taunus," the successor to the "Eifel," from April, 1939, as it was
largely an independently German development. It was symbolic of the
greater independence that the name of the Cologne factory was
changed on 25 July 1939 from Ford Motor Company AG to Ford-
Werke AG. With the outbreak of war, the situation of the Cologne
factory changed. While deliveries from Dearborn were at first assured
after a short interruption, deep cuts had to be made in production. The
production of passenger cars ceased relatively soon; in essence, trucks
were being made. For the moment, there was no break in the favorable
business environment. The report for 1939 showed an increase in
sales of 17.5% and a rise in profits of 10% from the previous year. At
this time, the process by which Detroit was losing control of the
German Ford factories reached its zenith. The American V. Tallberg,
who was working as an engineer for Ford in Cologne and had not had
access in 1938/39 to the truck works in Berlin-Johannisthal, was at
Cologne from May to September 1940 and observed a large new
factory site next to the firm's property in Cologne. His research

revealed that this was a lot of the Arendt Company, registered under the name of the two heads of the Ford Works, Albert and Schmidt. At this factory, according to Wilkins and Hill, with machinery from the Ford stocks, parts for the V-2 turbines and Junkers were produced.

In the course of the German conquests in the first years of the war there arose the question of what should become of the Ford branches in those countries. The Cologne company made an effort to retain control of those branches. Thus in June 1940 Albert and Schmidt cabled Edsel Ford: "Trying with approval authorities to safeguard your interest for plants in occupied territory," for which Edsel Ford expressly thanked them later on. In fact, on 13 June 1940, the German authorities named R.H. Schmidt director of the Ford works in Holland and Belgium. In this capacity he showed "such loyalty to Ford interests as his official role permitted." Following the example of other German firms and adopting the official argument of the government, Albert strove for closer cooperation between the factories in Cologne, Antwerp, Amsterdam and Paris. In September, 1940, he explained this as follows:

> ...that the greater part, if not the whole, of Europe will economically form one unit and that import and export will be possible only according to a uniform plan and that also in the motor car business a united program as mentioned before may have to be set up for the whole of Europe, Germany taking the lead.

As a result, this meant that "Ford, Cologne, became the administrative center for almost the entire Ford organization in Europe and adopted a very authoritarian attitude towards the other Ford works." This and the restructuring of production required a financial shot in the arm. This increase in capital of altogether 12 million *RM* was to be realized by the issue of new shares, as approved by Edsel Ford in December 1940. Thus an extraordinary general assembly at Cologne approved on 24 March 1941 an increase in the basic capital of 32 million *RM*. On 1 April 1941 Albert informed Edsel Ford of this increase in capital and again assured him that the share of 52% held by the parent firm remained entirely untouched. This news report to the Dearborn headquarters had only a symbolic character at the time; the views, suggestions and directives from distant American had no real significance for Cologne any more. the separation of parent and daughter had taken place *de facto*, but not *de jure*.

> Until 1939, although the management of the firm was in German hands, all important maters of policy were settled from America, but after the outbreak of war American influence decreased and ceased altogether in 1941.

Besides, as communication with Dearborn was becoming noticeably more difficult, Albert did not see any other solution but "to carry on using our own judgement at the best of our knowledge in Germany as well as in the occupied territories." With this statement, Albert pointed out politely, but clearly, that the German daughter company was in fact unconditionally independent and he again stressed its claim for leadership at least with regard to the Ford works in continental Europe. At the same time he succeeded in showing his service to the overall concern, although he was to be arrested later because of his involvement in the attempt on Hitler's life on 20 July 1944. Albert's conduct may be partially, if not entirely, explained as a tactical measure, as shown in an statement from company headquarters:

> Our recollection is that Dr. Albert was constantly pressed by the German government authorities to eliminate or minimize the American interest in the Cologne company.... This company, of course, did not wish to lose control of the German Ford company and consequently requested Albert to resist the efforts of the German authorities. To do so he had to use logical reasoning which would appear advantageous to the German government.

After the German declaration of war and the American entry into it in December, 1941, Schmidt was appointed trustee of the Cologne works. This prevented the takeover of company management by the military.

Data concerning the activity of the Ford works during the war are contradictory. Whereas Rosellen wrote that, in the view of the authorities, Cologne was to produce tanks and armored reconnaissance cars in 1942, which Schmidt refused to do, Wilkins and Hill and Seherr-Thoss give other information. According to these authors, from 1940 in Berlin Ford produced the open country vehicle SPKW and later on (from 1942) the half-track "Maultier," delivered at the end of 1942. The government requests, in their view, could hardly be refused, unless one wanted to run the risk of losing control of the firm perhaps to the military. Although there is no indication of the exact time when vehicles were produced which were not part of the traditional production plan, it is obvious that they were part of arms production and it is nevertheless clear that the Ford works were involved in the manufacture of military goods. Thus, the company produced in 1943 60% of the three-ton half-track vehicles intended for the German army. By doing so, Ford-Germany became a willing instrument in Hitler's hands and he acted cleverly in the matter. Hitler

> did not expel the alien company which his German automotive firms would have liked him to banish. Rather he permitted it to grow and thrive but in the process tamed it thoroughly. In the end it became a favored unit and when the tocsin of war sounded, was a convenient instrument in his hands for the prosecution of his ruthless policies.

The German government obtained considerable capital from the intra-concern relations because, through the transnational relations, the raw material situation could be relieved and export increased at the same time. The separation process between parent and daughter company which was forced after the second half of the 1930s occurred as with Opel in only short and more rare visits by delegations from the parent company, a company-wide phenomenon which facilitated this at the same time. It reduced the possibilities for Dearborn to intervene to a minimum. FMC could not hinder the "*liaison dangereuse*" between the Hitler government and FMCAG. The transnational relations could be used by a national entity, namely Germany, for its politico-military purposes. The world market strategy of the parent company, which was primarily motivated by economics, and the constraints of global competition played a part in this development. They brought it about that the German base was not given up in spite of the political situation there and in spite of the obvious deterioration for Detroit in company relations due to politics. Remaining in Germany was legitimized afterwards by "corporate identity" as a global, internationally oriented enterprise, possessing a characteristic strategy aimed at peace. "Ford's operations during the 1930s represented a gallant effort in internationalism in an era of fervent nationalism."

For that reason FMC still delivered to FMCAG merchandise which indirectly aided German arms production, but the deliveries were stopped by 1941 at the latest. At that time the relations between FMC and the Ford works acquired in the United States an enormous political importance, particularly regarding security policy, which was interpreted negatively. FMC reacted to these political interferences by breaking off business relations. Political momentum was now winning out also in the US over transnational policy. The examples of Ford and Opel consequently both show a similar pattern. In both cases, transnational relations took on a configuration through political decisions by public persons and a politicized public. Governments channeled and manipulated private business contacts according to their own political ends. The Hitler government exploited them for military purposes; the Roosevelt Administration tried to use them for diplomatic ends leading to peace. Thus politics set the parameters within which the transnational relations could develop and determined the point at which they could no longer be accepted and so had to be broken off.

SELECTED BIBLIOGRAPHY

1. UNPUBLISHED SOURCES

Bundesarchiv Koblenz (BAK)
> Bestand R 2 (Reichsfinanzministerium)
> Bestand R 7 (Reichswirtschaftsministerium)
> Bestand R 13 (Wirtschaftsgruppen)
> Bestand R 25 (Reichsamt für Wirtschaftsausbau)
> Bestand R 43 (Reichskanzlei)
> Bestand NL (Nachlässe)
> Bestand ZSg 126 (Wirtschaftsarchiv des Instituts für Weltwirtschaft und Seever-
> kehr, Univ. Kiel)

Bundesarchiv Potsdam (BAP)
> Bestand 09.01 (Auswärtiges Amt, Akten der Abteilung III)
> Bestand 25.01 (Deutsche Reichsbank)
> Bestand 31.01 (Reichswirtschaftsministerium)
> Bestand 31.02 (Statistisches Reichsamt)
> Bestand 80 Ba 1 (Dresdner Bank)
> Bestand 80 IG 1 (Bestand IG Farben)

Detroit Public Library – Automotive History Collection (DPL-AHC)

Ford Motor Company Archives, Dearborn (FMCA)
> Accession 6: Office of the President – Edsel B. Ford Papers
> Accession 38: Production Records
> Accession 46: Executive Correspondence – Branch Correspondence 1938
> Accession 285: Henry Ford Office
> Accession 390: Purchasing – A.M. Wibel
> Accession 507: International Division – General
> Accession 572: Selected Research Papers
> Accession 708: International Division – Finance
> Accession 712: International Division – Correspondence
> Accession 713: Records/International Division – Russell I. Roberge, 1936-1950
> Accession 940: Frank Hill Research Papers
> Accession 951: Ford Non-Serial Imprints
> Oral History Section, July 1956. The Reminiscences of Mr. V.Y. Tallberg
> (Appointed Chief Engineer and Chief Inspector at Cologne)

Franklin D. Roosevelt Library, Hyde Park, NY (FDRL)
> Official Files (OF)
> President's Personal Files (PPF)
> President's Secretary's Files (PSF)
> Adolf A. Berle Papers
> Harry Hopkins Papers

Georgetown University – Special Collections (GU-SC)
The Papers of James D. Mooney

Hagley Museum – Du Pont Archives, Wilmington, DE (HM-DPA)
Accession 228: Irénée du Pont
Accession 473: Papers of John J. Raskob
Accession 500: Records of E.I. du Pont de Nemours & Co., Series II, Part 1
Accession 500: Records of E.I. du Pont de Nemours & Co., Series II, Part 2
Accession 1334: F. Donaldson Brown Collection
Accession 1489 ADD: Philip J. Kimball Collection

Harvard Business School, Baker Library – Special Collections, Boston, MA (HBS-SC)
Accession Copies of Documents of Oil Companies
Accession General Motors Collection. Papers Relating to General Motors, received from Alfred D. Chandler, Jr., September 1971
Accession Standard Oil Co. (New Jersey). Interviews 1944-45

Harvard University, Cambridge, MA – Houghton Library (HU-HL)
The Papers of William Philipps: The Diary of William Philipps

Library of Congress – Manuscript Division, Washington, D.C. (LOC-MD)
Collection: The Papers of Josephus Daniels
Collection: The Papers of William E. Dodd
Collection: The Papers of Felix Frankfurter
Collection: The Papers of Cordell Hull
Collection: The Harold L. Ickes Papers: The Harold Ickes Diaries
Collection: The Papers of Francis B. Sayre

National Archives, Washington, D.C. – Record Groups (NARG)
Record Group 20: Records of the Special Advisor to the President on Foreign Trade. Files of the Secretary of Records
Record Group 59: Records of the Department of State. Decimal File [DF] 1930-39. Decimal File 1940-4
Record Group 59: Records of the Department of State Relating to Internal Affairs of Austria, 1930-1944. Decimal File 863
Record Group 122: Records of the Federal Trade Commission. Bureau of Economics. Records of Roy A. Prewitt, 1939-1950
Record Group 151: Records of the Bureau of Foreign and Domestic Commerce. Records Relating to Commercial Attaches' Reports [CAR]. General Records [GR], 1914-1958
Record Group 165: Records of the George M. Shuster Commission
Record Group 226: Records of the Office of Strategic Services
Record Group 238: Records of the United States. Nuernberg War Crimes Trials. United States of America v. Carl Krauch et al. (Case VI), August 14, 1947–July 30, 1948
Record Group 242: Collection of Seized Enemy Property
Record Group 243: Records of the U.S. Strategic Bombing Survey

Record Group 259: Records of the Interdepartmental Advisory Committee on
    Hemisphere Communications. Files on the IT&T Corp., 1930-1945
Record Group 287: Publications of the Federal Government. Congress.
    Committees of Congress, Senate

Politisches Archiv des Auswärtigen Amtes, Bonn (PA-AA)
Bestände R
    Handakten Kroll
    Handakten Clodius
    Handakten Wiehl
    Abteilung III
    Abteilung W

Werksarchiv der BASF AG, Ludwigshafen (WA-BASF)
    Dokumentengruppe A 261 (Beteiligungen)
    Dokumentengruppe B 4
    Dokumentengruppe B 5
    Dokumentengruppe M 1104 (Aktenbestand Dr. Pier)
    Dokumentengruppe T 72
    Dokumentengruppe Z 0/4

Werksarchiv der Bayer AG, Leverkusen (WA-BL)
    Dokumentengruppe Bayer 1/6.6. (Verkauf)
    Dokumentengruppe Bayer 6/14 (IG-Firmenbeteiligungen)
    Dokumentengruppe Bayer 9/A (Farbenfabriken Bayer)
    Dokumentengruppe Bayer 19/A (Verträge)
    Dokumentengruppe Bayer 62 (Wirtschaft)
    Dokumentengruppe Bayer 67/3 (Vowi-Berlin. Ausarbeitungen)
    Dokumentengruppe Bayer 81/2 (Amerika)
    Dokumentengruppe Bayer 600/1 (Fremdfirmen A-Z)

Werksarchiv der Hoechst AG, Frankfurt/M. (WA-Hoe)
    Unterlagen des Technischen Ausschusses (TEA-Büro)

2. PUBLISHED SOURCES AND CONTEMPORARY LITERATURE TO 1945

AEG AG (Hg.) (1983). Einhundert Jahre: 1883-1983. Informationen zum
    100jährigen Jubiläum der AEG-Telefunken AG im Jahre 1983. Frankfurt-am-
    Main.

Akten zur Deutschen Auswärtigen Politik 1918-1945 (ADAP)
    Serie C: 1933-1937. Das Dritte Reich: Die ersten Jahre. Göttingen, 1971-1981.
    Serie D: 1937-1945. Baden-Baden, 1950-1970.

Albrecht Kraus Verlag (1981). Hitlers Politisches Testament. Die Bormann-Diktate
    vom Februar und April 1945. Hamburg.

Armstrong, Hamilton Fish (1937). 'We or They'. Two Worlds in Conflict. New
    York.

Ausschuß zur Untersuchung der Erzeugungs- und Absatzbedingungen der deutschen Wirtschaft (1932). Der deutsche Außenhandel unter der Einwirkung weltwirtschaftlicher Strukturwandlungen. 2 Bde. Berlin.

BASF AG (Hg.) (1990a). BASF – Stationen ihrer Geschichte. Ludwigshafen.

BASF AG (Hg.) (1990b). 125 Jahre BASF. Stationen ihrer Geschichte. Ludwigshafen.

Buell, Raymond L. (1937). Chaos or Reconstruction? Foreign Policy Pamphlets No. 3. January 1937. New York.

Commager, Henry Steele (Hg.). (1968). Documents of American History. 2 Bde. Bd. 2. 8. Aufl. New York.

Daitz, Werner (1943). Lebensraum und gerechte Weltordnung. Grundlagen einer Anti-Atlantikcharta. Ausgewählte Aufsätze. Amsterdam.

Deutsches Institut für Bankwissenschaft und Bankwesen (Hg.) (1937). Probleme des deutschen Wirtschaftslebens. Erstrebtes und Erreichtes. Eine Sammlung von Abhandlungen. Berlin/Leipzig.

Domarus, Max (1963). Hitler. Reden und Proklamationen 1932-1945. Kommentiert von einem deutschen Zeitgenossen. Neustadt a.d. Aisch.

Duisberg, Carl (1930). Die Zukunft der deutschen Handelspolitik. Leverkusen.

Duisberg, Carl (1933). Abhandlungen, Vorträge und Reden aus den Jahren 1922-1933. Berlin.

Dutton, William S. (1942). Du Pont. One Hundred and Forty Years. New York.

Eichholtz, Dietrich/**Schumann**, Wolfgang (Hg.) (1969). Anatomie des Krieges. Neue Dokumente über die Rolle des deutschen Monopolkapitals bei der Vorbereitung und Durchführung des Zweiten Weltkrieges. Berlin (Ost).

Ford Motor Company (1933). Thirty Years of Progress 1903-1933. Dearborn, Michigan.

Ford, Henry (1926). Today and Tomorrow. Garden City, New York.

Ford, Henry (1931). Moving Forward. London.

Ford, Henry (o.J.). Mein Leben und Werk. Einzig autorisierte deutsche Ausgabe von Curt und Marguerite Thesing. 16. Auflage. Leipzig.

Foreign Relations of the United States. Diplomatic Papers. 1933-1941. Washington, D.C. 1949-1959.

Fried, Ferdinand (1931). Das Ende des Kapitalismus. 5. Aufl. Jena.

Gapinski, Felix (1931). Die Stellung der deutschen Elektroindustrie innerhalb der internationalen Elektro-Wirtschaft in der Gegenwart. Diss. Köln.

Gay, Edwin F. (1932). The Great Depression. In: *FA*, 10, 4, 529-540.

Gebhardt, August (1932): Die Expansion der amerikanischen Elektro-Konzerne in Europa. Diss. Heidelberg.

Greiling, Walter (1941). Chemie erobert die Welt. Berlin.

Hauser, Heinrich (1937). Opel – Ein deutsches Tor zur Welt. Frankfurt-am-Main.

Hess, Eugen (1931). Elektropolitik und Weltvertrustung. Amsterdam.

Hexner, Ervin (1945). International Cartels. Chapel Hill, N.C.

Hill, Leonidas E. (Hg.) (1974). Die Weizsäcker-Papiere 1933-1950. Bd. 2. Frankfurt-am-Main/Berlin/Wien.

Hillgruber, Andreas (Hg.) (1967). Staatsmänner und Diplomaten bei Hitler. Vertrauliche Aufzeichnungen über Unterredungen mit Vertretern des Auslandes 1939-1941. Frankfurt-am-Main.

Hillgruber, Andreas (Hg.) (1970). Staatsmänner und Diplomaten bei Hitler. Vertrauliche Aufzeichnungen über Unterredungen mit Vertretern des Auslandes 1942-1944. Frankfurt-am-Main.

Hilzinger, Paul (1935). Die Entwicklung der Außenhandelsverflechtung Deutschlands während der Weltwirtschaftskrise. Diss. Heidelberg.

Hitler, Adolf (1933). Mein Kampf. 44. Aufl. München.

Hoenicke, Rudolf (1933). Die amerikanische Automobilindustrie in Europa. Diss. Berlin.

Hooker, Nancy H. (Hg.) (1956). The Moffat Papers. Selections from the Diplomatic Journals of Jay Pierrepont Moffat 1919-1943. Cambridge, Mass.

Howard, Graeme K. (1940). America and a New World Order. New York.

Hull, Cordell (1948). The Memoirs of Cordell Hull. 2 Bde. New York.

Hupka, Benno (1932). Der mittelbare Protektionismus in der Handelspolitik der Nachkriegszeit. Diss. Göttingen.

Jentsch, Gerhart (1942). Triebkräfte und Grundlagen der Roosevelt'schen Außenpolitik 1941. In: *JAP*, 8, 47-74.

Jochmann, Werner (1960). Im Kampf um die Macht. Hitlers Rede vor dem Hamburger Nationalklub 1919. Frankfurt-am-Main.

Jochmann, Werner (Hg.) (1980). Hitler, Monologe im Führerhauptquartier 1941-44. Die Aufzeichnungen Heinrich Heims. Hamburg.

Kiesewetter, Georg (1929). Der Welthandel III: Elektrotechnische Erzeugnisse. In: *Wirtschaftsdienst*, 14, Nr. 50 vom 13.12.1929, 2164-2170.

Klemm, Friedrich (1929). Die Hauptprobleme der Entwicklung der deutschen Automobilindustrie in der Nachkriegszeit und der Wettbewerb dieser Industrie mit dem Ausland, insbesondere mit den Vereinigten Staaten von Nordamerika, Diss. Marburg.

Kocka, Jürgen (Hg.) (1979). Emil Lederer. Kapitalismus, Klassenstruktur und Probleme der Demokratie in Deutschland 1910-1940. Ausgewählte Aufsätze. Göttingen.

Koops, Tilmann (Hg.) (1982). Akten der Reichskanzlei. Weimarer Republik. Das Kabinett Brüning I. Boppard am Rhein Jahr 1982.

Laum, Bernhard (1933). Die geschlossene Wirtschaft. Soziologische Grundlegung des Autarkieproblems. Tübingen.

Lederer, Emil (1932). Gegen Autarkie und Nationalismus. Rede im 'Verein für Sozialpolitik' am 29. Sept. 1932. In: **Kocka** (Hg.) 1979: 199-209.

Levy, Hermann (1933). Die europäische Verflechtung des amerikanischen Außenhandels. In: *WWA*, 37, 1, 164-192.

Lochner, Louis P. (Hg.) (1948). Goebbels Tagebücher aus den Jahren 1942-43. Zürich.

Loose, Paul A.F. (1939). Deutschlands Handelsvertragspolitik der Nachkriegszeit. Diss. Marburg.

Lütke, Heinz (1941). Zusammenbruch und Neuaufbau der Weltwirtschaft. Berlin.

Mahlin, Sybille (1937). Die Außenhandelspolitik der Vereinigten Staaten von Amerika von 1929 bis 1936. Diss. Berlin.

Michalka, Wolfgang (Hg.) (1985a). Das Dritte Reich. Dokumente zur Innen- und Außenpolitik. Bd. 1: 'Volksgemeinschaft' und Großmachtpolitik 1933-1939. München.

Michalka, Wolfgang (Hg.) (1985b). Das Dritte Reich. Dokumente zur Innen- und Außenpolitik. Bd. 2: Weltmachtanspruch und nationaler Zusammenbruch 1939-1945. München.

Minuth, Karl-Heinz (Hg.) (1983). Akten der Reichskanzlei. Die Regierung Hitler I: 1933/34. Boppard am Rhein.

Muir, Ramsay (1932). The Interdependent World and Its Problems. London.

Musil, Robert (1922). Das hilflose Europa oder Reise vom Hundertsten ins Tausendste. In: **Musil** 1978: 1075-1094.

Musil, Robert (1978). Gesammelte Werke, Bd. 2. Hrsg. von Adolf Frisé. Reinbek bei Hamburg.

Nixon, Edgar B. (Hg.) (1969). Franklin D. Roosevelt and Foreign Affairs. First Series: Vol. I-III. Cambridge, Mass.

Obst, Erich (1942). Die Großraumidee in der Vergangenheit und als tragender politischer Gedanke unserer Zeit. In: **Schaeder et.al.** (Hg.) 1942: 178-200.

Opitz, Reinhard (Hg.) (1977). Europastrategien des deutschen Kapitals 1900-1945. Köln.

Picker, Henry (1963). Hitlers Tischgespräche im Führerhauptquartier 1941-1942. Stuttgart.

Posse, Hans E. (1937). Die Hauptlinien der Deutschen Handelspolitik. In: **Deutsches Institut für Bankwissenschaft und Bankwesen** (Hg.) 1937: 481-513.

Pound, Arthur (1934). The Turning Wheel. The Story of General Motors Through Twenty-Five Years 1908-1933. Garden City, NY.

Predöhl, Andreas (1937). Die Beziehungen zwischen Währung und Handelspolitik. In: *ZfS*, 97, 71-84.

Radiis, Guido Radio von (1938). Die deutsche Außenhandelspolitik unter dem Einfluß der Devisenbewirtschaftung von 1931 bis 1938. Diss. Zürich.

Rasmussen, Ove (1934). Die Konkurrenzfähigkeit der deutschen Automobil-Industrie unter besonderer Berücksichtigung der letzten Erfahrungen. Diss. München.

Rauschning, Hermann (1940). Gespräche mit Hitler. 2. Aufl. New York.

Regierung der Vereinigten Staaten (Hg.) (o.J.). Präsident Roosevelt. Amerika und Deutschland 1936-1945. Auszüge aus Reden und Dokumenten. o.O.

Ribbentrop, Joachim von (1937). Vierjahresplan und Welthandel. Berlin.

Roorbach, G.B. (1932). Foreign Trade or Isolation? In: *FA*, 11, 1, 37-50.

Roosevelt, Elliott (Hg.) (1950). F.D.R. His Personal Letters. 2 Bde. New York.

Ross, Colin (1936). Unser Amerika. Der deutsche Anteil an den Vereinigten Staaten. Leipzig.

Salter, Sir Arthur (1932). The Future of Economic Nationalism. In: *FA*, 11, 1, 8-20.

Schacht, Hjalmar (1932). Grundsätze deutscher Wirtschaftspolitik. Oldenburg.

Schaeder, Hans Heinrich et al. (1942). Die Großraumidee in der Vergangenheit und als tragender politischer Gedanke unserer Zeit. Breslau.

Schewe, Donald B. (Hg.) (1979). Franklin D. Roosevelt and Foreign Affairs. Second Series: Vol. IV-XVI. New York/Toronto.

Schmitt, Carl (1939). Völkerrechtliche Großraumordnung mit Interventionsverbot für raumfremde Mächte. Ein Beitrag zum Reichsbegriff im Völkerrecht. Berlin/Wien.

Schönemann, Friedrich (1934). Amerika und der Nationalsozialismus. Berlin.

Siemens & Halske AG (1935). Werner Siemens und sein Werk. Berlin.

Sorensen, Charles (1956). My Forty Years with Ford. New York.

Southard, Frank A. (1931). American Industry in Europe. Boston/New York.

Standard Oil Company (New Jersey) (1957). The Lamp. 75th Anniversary of Jersey Standard. New York.

Statistische Jahrbücher für das Deutsche Reich, 42. Jg., 1921/22 - 59. Jg., 1941/42.

Statistisches Reichsamt (1936). Statistisches Handbuch der Weltwirtschaft. Berlin.

Taussig, F.W. (1933). Necessary Changes in Our Commercial Policy. In: *FA*, 11, 4, 397-405.

Taylor, Paul B. (1938). Problems of German-American Relations. In: *FPR*, XIV, 9, July 15: 98-108.

United States. Bureau of the Census (1949). Historical Statistics of the United States 1789-1945. A Supplement to the Statistical Abstract of the United States. Washington D.C.

United States. Bureau of the Census (1961). Historical Statistics of the United States. Colonial Times to 1957. A Statistical Abstract Supplement. 2. Aufl. Washington D.C.

United States Senate (1970). Development of United States Foreign Policy. Addresses and Messages of Franklin D. Roosevelt. Reprint. New York.

Ursachen und Folgen. Vom deutschen Zusammenbruch 1918 und 1945 bis zur staatlichen Neuordnung in der Gegenwart. Eine Urkunden und Dokumentensammlung zur Zeitgeschichte.

> Bd. 9: Das Dritte Reich. Die Zertrümmerung des Parteienstaates und die Grundlegung der Diktatur. Berlin 1963.

> Bd. 10: Das Dritte Reich. Die Errichtung des Führerstaates. Die Abwendung von dem System der kollektiven Sicherheit. Berlin 1965.

Wagenführ, Rolf (1936). Die Bedeutung des Außenmarktes für die deutsche Industrie-wirtschaft. Hamburg.

Weinberg, Albert K. (1940). The Historical Meaning of the American Doctrine of Isolation. In: *APSR*, 34, 539-547.

Weinberg, Gerhard L. (Hg.) (1961). Hitlers Zweites Buch. Ein Dokument aus dem Jahr 1928. Stuttgart.

Weizsäcker, Ernst von (1950). Erinnerungen. München/Leipzig/Freiburg i. Br.

Wergo, Herbert (1928). Freihandel und Schutzzoll als Mittel staatlicher Machtentfaltung. Untersuchungen zur Problematik der Handelspolitik. Jena.

Wickel, Helmut (1932). I.-G. Deutschland. Ein Staat im Staate. Berlin.

Wilhelm, Karl (1931). Die AEG. Berlin.

Winkler, John K. (1936). The Du Pont Dynasty. 3. Aufl. New York.

3. SECONDARY SOURCES

Adams, Willi Paul (Hg.) (1987). Die Vereinigten Staaten von Amerika. Frankfurt/M.

Adams, Willi Paul/**Krakau**, Knud (Hg.) (1985). Deutschland und Amerika. Perzeption und Realität. Berlin.

Adler, Selig (1969). The Uncertain Giant, 1921-1941. American Foreign Policy Between the Wars. London.

Aldcroft, Derek H. (1978). Die Zwanziger Jahre. Von Versailles zur Wall Street 1919-1929. München.

Ambrosius, Lloyd E. (1976). The United States and the Weimar Republic: America's Response to the German Problem. In: **Davids** (Hg.) 1976: 78-104.

Angermann, Erich (1973). Die weltpolitische Lage 1933-1935: Die Vereinigten Staaten von Amerika. In: **Hauser** (Hg.) 1973: 110-145.

Angermann, Erich (1987). Die Vereinigten Staaten von Amerika seit 1917. 8. Aufl. München.

Arends, Folko/**Kümmel**, Gerhard (i.E.). From Double Crisis to National Socialism: Germany. In: **Berg-Schlosser/Mitchell** (Hg.) (i.E.a).

Aron, Raymond (1963). Frieden und Krieg. Eine Theorie der Staatenwelt. Frankfurt/M.

Aron, Raymond (1966). The Anarchical Order of Power. In: *Daedalus*, 95, 2, 479-502.

Ashley, Richard K. (1986). The Poverty of Neorealism. In: **Keohane** (Hg.) 1986: 255-300.

Axelrod, Robert (1981). The Emergence of Cooperation among Egoists. In: *APSR*, 75, 2, 306-318.

Axelrod, Robert (1984). The Evolution of Cooperation. New York.

Backes, Uwe/**Jesse**, Eckhard/**Zitelmann**, Rainer (Hg.) (1990). Die Schatten der Vergangenheit. Impulse zur Historisierung des Nationalsozialismus. Frankfurt/M. – Berlin.

Bäumler, Ernst (1963). Ein Jahrhundert Chemie. Hrsg. zum Hundertjährigen Jubiläum der Farbwerke Hoechst AG. Düsseldorf.

Bäumler, Ernst (1989). Farben, Formeln, Forscher. Hoechst und die Geschichte der industriellen Chemie in Deutschland. München.

Ball, George W. (1970). Cosmocorp: The Importance of Being Stateless. In: **Brown** (Hg.) 1970: 330-338.

Barkai, Avraham (1988). Das Wirtschaftssystem des Nationalsozialismus. Ideologie, Theorie, Politik 1933-1945. Erweiterte Neuausgabe. Frankfurt/M.

Bay, Achim (1962). Der nationalsozialistische Gedanke der Großraumwirtschaft und seine ideologischen Grundlagen. Darstellung und Kritik. Diss. Erlangen – Nürnberg.

Beck, Earl R. (1968). Germany Rediscovers America. Tallahassee, Florida.

Becker, Josef/**Hildebrand**, Klaus (Hg.) (1980). Internationale Beziehungen in der Weltwirtschaftskrise 1929-1933. München.

Becker, William H./**Wells**, Samuel F. (Hg.) (1984). Economics and World Power. An Assessment of American Diplomacy Since 1789. New Haven.

Behrens, Henning/**Noack**, Paul (1984). Theorien der Internationalen Politik. München.

Behrman, Jack N. (1970). Multinational Corporations and National Sovereignty. In: **Brown** (Hg.) 1970: 114-125.

Behrman, Jack N. (1973). The Multinational Enterprise and Nation States: The Shifting Balance of Power. In: **Kapoor/Grub** (Hg.) 1973: 411-425.

Bellers, Jürgen (1988). Außenwirtschaftspolitik und politisches System der Weimarer Republik und der Bundesrepublik. Münster.

Bellers, Jürgen (1991). Nationale und internationale Steuerungsfähigkeiten in und von Nationalstaaten. In: *PVS*, 32, 4, 685-694.

Bennett, Edward W. (1979). German Rearmament and the West, 1932-1933. Princeton, N.J.

Benz, Wolfgang/**Graml**, Hermann (Hg.) (1976). Aspekte deutscher Außenpolitik im 20. Jahrhundert. Aufsätze Hans Rothfels zum Gedächtnis. Stuttgart.

Berg, Hartmut (1976). Internationale Wirtschaftspolitik. Göttingen.

Berg, Manfred (1990). Gustav Stresemann und die Vereinigten Staaten von Amerika. Weltwirtschaftliche Verflechtung und Revisionspolitik 1907-1929. Baden-Baden.

Berg, Peter (1963). Deutschland und Amerika 1918-1929. Über das deutsche Amerikabild der zwanziger Jahre. Lübeck – Hamburg.

Berg-Schlosser, Dirk/**Mitchell**, Jeremy (Hg.) (i.E.a). Crisis, Compromise, Collapse. Bd. 1: Conditions of Authoritarianism, Fascism and Democracy in Inter-War Europe. Basingstoke – London.

Berg-Schlosser, Dirk/**Mitchell**, Jeremy (Hg.) (i.E.b). Crisis, Compromise, Collapse. Bd. 2. Basingstoke – London.

Berge, Wendell (1946). Cartels. Challenge to a Free World. Washington, D.C.

Bergmann, Jürgen et.al. (Hg.) (1979). Geschichte als politische Wissenschaft. Sozialökonomische Ansätze, Analyse politikhistorischer Phänomene, politologische Fragestellungen in der Geschichte. Stuttgart.

Bergsten, C. Fred/**Keohane**, Robert O./**Nye**, Joseph S, Jr. (1975): International Economics and International Politics: A Framework for Analysis. In: **Bergsten/Krause** (Hg.) 1975: 3-36.

Bergsten, C. Fred/**Krause**, Lawrence B. (Hg.) (1975). World Politics and International Economics. Washington, D.C.

Berle, Adolf A. (1973). Macht. Die treibende Kraft der Geschichte. Hamburg.

Bernholz, Peter (1966). Außenpolitik und internationale Wirtschaftsbeziehungen. Frankfurt/M.

Bessel, Richard (1992). The International Economic Order between the Wars. In: **McGrew et.al.** 1992: 157-173.

Beyme, Klaus von et.al. (Hg.) (1987). Politikwissenschaft. Eine Grundlegung. Bd. 3: Außenpolitik und Internationale Politik. Stuttgart – Berlin – Köln – Mainz 1987.

Biersteker, Thomas J. (1993). Evolving Perspectives on International Political Economy: Twentieth-Century Contexts and Discontinuities. In: *IPSR*, 14, 1, 7-33.

Birken, Andreas (1979). Das Verhältnis von Außenhandel und Außenpolitik und die Quantifizierung von Außenbeziehungen. Beobachtungen zum 'Zeitalter des Imperialismus' 1880-1913. In: *VSWG*, 66, 3, 317-361.

Birkenfeld, Wolfgang (1964). Der synthetische Treibstoff 1933-1945. Ein Beitrag zu nationalsozialistischen Wirtschafts- und Rüstungspolitik. Göttingen – Berlin – Frankfurt/M.

Blaich, Fritz (1983). Wirtschaft und Rüstung in Deutschland. In: **Bracher/Funke/ Jacobsen** (Hg.) 1983: 285-316.

Boeckh, Andreas (Hg.) (1984). Internationale Beziehungen. Theorien – Organisationen – Konflikte. Pipers Wörterbuch zur Politik 5. München – Zürich.

Böhnke, Rolf (1977). Nationale Sicherheit und multinationale Unternehmen. In: *PVS*, 18, 1, 3-24.

Boelcke, Willi A. (1971). Die Waffengeschäfte des Dritten Reiches mit Brasilien. In: *Tradition*, 16, 177-200 und 280-287.

Böttcher, Bodo (1968). Internationale Zusammenhänge. In: **Zentralverband** (Hg.) 1968: 89-104.

Bollmus, Reinhard (1970). Das Amt Rosenberg und seine Gegner. Studien zum Machtkampf im nationalsozialistischen Herrschaftssystem. Stuttgart.

Booth, Ken (1991). Security in Anarchy: Utopian Realism in Theory and Practice. In: *IA*, 67, 3, 527-545.

Borchardt, Knut (1977). Wirtschaftliche Krisen als Gegenstand der Unternehmensgeschichte. In: *ZfU*, 22, 1, 81-90.

Borchardt, Knut (1979). Zwangslagen und Handlungsspielräume in der großen Wirtschaftskrise der frühen dreißiger Jahre: Zur Revision des überlieferten Geschichtsbildes. In: *JBAW* 1979: 85-132.

Borkin, Joseph (1979). Die unheilige Allianz der I.G. Farben. Eine Interessengemeinschaft im Dritten Reich. Frankfurt/M. – New York.

Bracher, Karl Dietrich (1955). Der 'Frontier-Gedanke': Motiv des amerikanischen Fortschrittsbewußtseins. Ein ideologienkritischer Versuch. In: *ZfP*, 2, 3, 228-236.

Bracher, Karl Dietrich (1964a). Demokratie als Sendung: das amerikanische Beispiel. In: **Bracher** 1964: 313-336.

Bracher, Karl Dietrich (1964b). Über das Verhältnis von Innen- und Außenpolitik. In: **Bracher** 1964: 337-372.

Bracher, Karl Dietrich (1964). Deutschland zwischen Demokratie und Diktatur. Beiträge zur neueren Politik und Geschichte. Bern – München – Wien.

Bracher, Karl Dietrich (1976). Zeitgeschichtliche Kontroversen. Um Faschismus, Totalitarismus, Demokratie. München.

Bracher, Karl Dietrich (1982). Zeit der Ideologien. Eine Geschichte politischen Denkens im 20. Jahrhundert. Stuttgart.

Bracher, Karl Dietrich (1984). Die Auflösung der Weimarer Republik. Eine Studie zum Problem des Machtverfalls in der Demokratie. Düsseldorf.

Bracher, Karl Dietrich (1990). Der historische Ort des Zweiten Weltkrieges. In: **Hildebrand/Schmädeke/Zernack** (Hg.) 1990: 347-374.

Bracher, Karl-Dietrich/**Funke**, Manfred/**Jacobsen**, Hans-Adolf (Hg.) (1983). Nationalsozialistische Diktatur 1933-1945. Eine Bilanz. Bonn.

Bracher, Karl-Dietrich/**Funke**, Manfred/**Jacobsen**, Hans-Adolf (Hg.) (1992). Deutschland 1933-1945. Neue Studien zur nationalsozialistischen Herrschaft. Bonn.

Braeman, John (1981). American Foreign Policy in the Age of Normalcy: Three Historiographical Traditions. In: *AmSt*, 26, 1, 125-158.

Brandes, Detlef (1976). Die Politik des Reiches gegenüber der Tschechoslowakei. In: **Funke** (Hg.) 1976: 508-523.

Bredow, Wilfried von (1972). Vom Antagonismus zur Konvergenz? Studien zum Ost-West-Problem. Frankfurt/M.

Bredow, Wilfried von (1978). Carl Schmitt lesen. In: *liberal*, 20, 6, 432-444.

Bredow, Wilfried von (1983). Europa? Zwischen Ost und West?. In: *liberal*, 25, 4, 285-299.

Bredow, Wilfried von (1991). Nation-State and International Relations in the 1990's. In: **Pal/Schultze** (Hg.) 1991: 351-360.

Bredow, Wilfried von/**Brocke**, Rudolf H. (1981). Einführung in die internationalen Wirtschaftsbeziehungen. Stuttgart – Berlin – Köln – Mainz.

Bredow, Wilfried von/**Jäger**, Thomas (Hg.) (1994). Regionale Großmächte. Internationale Beziehungen zwischen Globalisierung und Zersplitterung. Opladen .

Bredow, Wilfried von/**Noetzel**, Thomas (1991). Die Wiederkehr der Politik. Unveröff. Manuskript. Marburg.

Broszat, Martin (1970). Soziale Motivation und Führerbindung des Nationalsozialismus. In: *VfZ*, 18, 4, 329-409.

Broszat, Martin (1976). Deutschland – Ungarn – Rumänien. Entwicklung und Grundfaktoren nationalsozialistischer Hegemonial- und Bündnispolitik 1938-1941. In: **Funke** (Hg.) 1976: 524-564.

Broszat, Martin (1983). Zur Struktur der NS-Massenbewegung. In: *VfZ*, 31, 1, 52-76.

Broszat, Martin/**Schwabe**, Klaus (Hg.) (1989). Die deutschen Eliten und der Weg in den Zweiten Weltkrieg. München.

Brough, James (1987). Die Ford Dynastie. Ein Industrie-Imperium. Drei Generationen. München.

Brown, Courtney C. (1970a). Prologue to a New World Symphony? In: **Brown** (Hg.) 1970: 3-12.

Brown, Courtney C. (Hg.) (1970). World Business. Promise and Problems. New York – London.

Brown, Seyom (1991). Explaining the Transformation of World Politics. In: *IJ*, XLVI, 2, 207-219.

Brunner, Otto/**Gerhard**, Dietrich (Hg.) (1961). Europa und Übersee. Festschrift für Egmont Zechlin. Hamburg.

Bühl, Walter L. (1978). Transnationale Politik. Internationale Beziehungen zwischen Hegemonie und Interdependenz. Stuttgart.

Bühl, Walter L. (Hg.) (1975). Funktion und Struktur. Soziologie vor der Geschichte. 11 Aufsätze. München.

Büttner, Ursula (1989). Politische Alternativen zum Brüningschen Deflationskurs. Ein Beitrag zur Diskussion über 'ökonomische Zwangslagen' in der Endphase von Weimar. In: *VfZ*, 37, 2, 209-251.

Bull, Hedley (1980). The Anarchical Society. A Study of Order in World Politics. Reprint. London – Basingstoke.

Bull, Hedley (1990). The Importance of Grotius in the Study of International Relations. In: **Bull/Kingsbury/Robert** (Hg.) 1990: 65-93.

Bull, Hedley/**Kingsbury**, Benedict/**Robert**, Adam (Hg.) (1990). Hugo Grotius and International Relations. Oxford – New York.

Bullock, Alan (1972). Hitler. Eine Studie über Tyrannei. Vollst. überarb. Aufl. Düsseldorf.

Burke, Bernard V. (1966). American Diplomats and Hitler's Rise to Power, 1930-1933. The Mission of Ambassador Sackett. Diss. University of Washington.

Burke, Bernard V. (1972). American Economic Diplomacy and the Weimar Republic. In: *MA*, 54, 4, 211-233.

Burns, James M. (1970). Roosevelt: The Soldier of Freedom. New York.

Camilleri, Joseph A./**Falk**, Jim (1992). The End of Sovereignty? The Politics of a Shrinking and Fragmenting World. Aldershot – Brookfield, Vermont.

Carr, Edward H. (1961). International Relations Between the Two World Wars (1919-1939). London.

Carr, Edward H. (1966). The Twenty Years' Crisis 1919-1939. An Introduction to the Study of International Relations. Reprint. New York.

Carr, William (1972). Arms, Autarky and Aggression. A Study in German Foreign Policy, 1933-1939. London.

Carroll, John M. (1988). American Diplomacy in the 1920s. In: **Carroll/Herring** (Hg.) 1988: 53-70.

Carroll, John M./**Herring**, George C. (Hg.) (1988). Modern American Diplomacy. 2. Aufl. Wilmington, Delaware.

Caves, Richard E. (1991). The Multinational Enterprise as an Economic Organization. In: **Frieden/Lake** (Hg.) 1991: 146-160.

Chamberlain, John (1963). The Enterprising Americans. A Business History of the United States. New York – Evanston.

Chandler, Alfred D. (1964). Giant Enterprise. Ford, General Motors, and the Automobile Industry. Sources and Readings. New York.

Chandler, Alfred D. (1976). Strategy and Structure. Chapters in the History of the Industrial Enterprise. 9. Aufl. Cambridge, Mass. – London.

Chandler, Alfred D. (Hg.) (1979). Managerial Innovation at General Motors. New York.

Chandler, Alfred D./**Salsbury**, Stephen (1971). Pierre S. Du Pont and the Making of the Modern Corporation. New York – Evanston – San Francisco – London.

Cole, Wayne S. (1983). Roosevelt and the Isolationists, 1932-45. Lincoln – New York

Compton, James V. (1968). The Swastika and the Eagle. Hitler, the United States, and the Origins of the Second World War. London – Sydney – Toronto.

Conybeare, John (1985). Trade Wars: A Comparative Study of Anglo-Hanse, Franco-Italian, and Hawley-Smoot Conflicts. In: *WP*, 38, 1, 146-172.

Conybeare, John A.C. (1987). Trade Wars. The Theory and Practice of International Commercial Rivalry. New York.

Conze, Werner/**Raupach**, Hans (Hg.) (1967). Die Staats- und Wirtschaftskrise des Deutschen Reiches 1929-1933. Stuttgart.

Cooper, Richard N./**Nye**, Joseph S., Jr. (1985). Ethics and Foreign Policy. In: **Huntington/Nye** (Hg.) 1985: 23-41.

Costigliola, Frank (1976). The United States and the Reconstruction of Germany in the 1920s. In: *BHR*, 50, 4, 477-502.

Costigliola, Frank (1984). Awkward Dominion. American Political, Economic, and Cultural Relations with Europe, 1919-1933. Ithaca – London.

Cox, Robert W. (1986). Social Forces, States and World Orders: Beyond International Relations Theory. In: **Keohane** (Hg.) 1986: 204-254.

Cox, Robert W. (1987). Production, Power, and World Order. Social Forces in the Making of History. New York.

Craig, Gordon A. (1953). The German Foreign Office from Neurath to Ribbentrop. In: **Craig/Gilbert** (Hg.) 1953: 406-436.

Craig, Gordon A. (1984). Amerikanische Außenpolitik und Deutschland, 1919-1983. Einige Überlegungen. In: **Köhler** (Hg.) 1984: 200-213.

Craig, Gordon A. (1985). Roosevelt and Hitler: The Problem of Perception. In: **Hildebrand/Pommerin** (Hg.) 1985: 169-194.

Craig, Gordon A./**Gilbert**, Felix (Hg.) (1953). The Diplomats 1919-1939. Princeton, N.J.

Czada, Peter (1969): Die Berliner Elektroindustrie in der Weimarer Zeit. Eine regionalstatistisch-wirtschaftshistorische Untersuchung. Berlin.

Czempiel, Ernst-Otto (1963). Der Primat der Außenpolitik. Kritische Würdigung einer Staatsmaxime. In: *PVS*, 4, 3, 266-287.

Czempiel, Ernst-Otto (1981). Internationale Politik. Ein Konfliktmodell. Paderborn – München – Wien – Zürich.

Czempiel, Ernst-Otto (1986). Friedensstrategien. Systemwandel durch Internationale Organisationen, Demokratisierung und Wirtschaft. Paderborn – München – Wien – Zürich.

Czempiel, Ernst-Otto (1991). Weltpolitik im Umbruch. Das internationale System nach dem Ende des Ost-West-Konflikts. München.

Czempiel, Ernst-Otto (Hg.) (1969). Die anachronistische Souveränität. Zum Verhältnis von Innen- und Außenpolitik. Köln – Opladen.

Czempiel, Ernst-Otto/**Rosenau**, James N. (Hg.) (1989). Global Changes and Theoretical Challenges. Approaches to World Politics for the 1990s. Lexington, Mass. – Toronto.

Czempiel, Ernst-Otto/**Rosenau**, James N. (Hg.) (1992). Governance Without Government: Order and Change in World Politics. Cambridge, Mass.

Dallek, Robert (1968). Democrat and Diplomat. The Life of William E. Dodd. New York.

Dallek, Robert (1981). Franklin D. Roosevelt and American Foreign Policy, 1932-1945. Oxford – New York – Toronto – Melbourne.

Dassbach, Carl H. A. (1989). Global Enterprises and the World Economy. Ford, General Motors, and IBM. The Emergence of the Transnational Enterprise. New York – London.

Davids, Jules (Hg.) (1976). Perspectives in American Diplomacy. Essays on Europe, Latin America, China, and the Cold War. New York.

Deist, Wilhelm (1978). Die deutsche Aufrüstung in amerikanischer Sicht: Berichte des US-Militär-attachés in Berlin aus den Jahren 1933-1939. In: **Fischer/Moltmann/Schwabe** (Hg.) 1978: 279-295.

Deist, Wilhelm et.al. (1989). Ursachen und Voraussetzungen des Zweiten Weltkrieges. Aktual. Ausgabe. Frankfurt/M.

Delius, Friedrich Christian (1976). Unsere Siemens-Welt. Eine Festschrift zum 125-jährigen Bestehen des Hauses S. Erweiterte Neuausgabe. Berlin, 1976.

Dengg, Sören (1986). Deutschlands Austritt aus dem Völkerbund und Schachts 'Neuer Plan'. Zum Verhältnis von Außen- und Außenwirtschaftspolitik in der Übergangsphase von der Weimarer Republik zum Dritten Reich (1929-1934). Frankfurt/M. – Bern – New York.

Deutsche Bundesbank (Hg.) (1976). Währung und Wirtschaft in Deutschland 1876-1975. Frankfurt/M.

Diepes, Volker (1969). Die führenden Politiker der Vereinigten Staaten und die 'Appeasement-Politik'. Diss. Marburg.

Diner, Dan (1985). Imperialismus, Universalismus, Hegemonie. Zum Verhältnis von Politik und Ökonomie in der Weltgesellschaft. In: **Fetscher/Münkler** (Hg.) 1985: 326-360.

Diner, Dan (1989). Rassistisches Völkerrecht. Elemente einer nationalsozialistischen Weltordnung. In: *VfZ*, 37, 1, 23-56.

Divine, Robert A. (1979). The Reluctant Belligerent: American Entry into World War II. 2. Aufl. New York.

Doering, Dörte (1969). Deutsche Außenwirtschaftspolitik 1933-35. Die Gleichschaltung der Außenwirtschaft in der Frühphase des nationalsozialistischen Regimes. Diss. Berlin.

Döscher, Hans-Jürgen (1987). Das Auswärtige Amt im Dritten Reich. Diplomatie im Schatten der 'Endlösung'. Berlin.

Dowd, Douglas F. (1977). The Twisted Dream. Capitalist Development in the United States Since 1776. 2. Aufl. Cambridge, Mass.

Doyle, Michael W. (1986). Liberalism and World Politics. In: *APSR*, 80, 4, 1151-1169.

DuBois, Josiah E. (1952). The Devil's Chemists. 24 Conspirators of the International Farben Cartel Who Manufacture Wars. Boston.

Dülffer, Jost (1973). Weimar, Hitler und die Marine. Reichspolitik und Flottenbau 1920-1939. Düsseldorf.

Dülffer, Jost (1976). Zum 'decision-making process' in der deutschen Außenpolitik 1933-1939. In: **Funke** (Hg.) 1976: 186-204.

Ebel, Arnold (1971). Das Dritte Reich und Argentinien. Die diplomatischen Beziehungen unter besonderer Berücksichtigung der Handelspolitik (1933-1939). Köln – Wien.

Efinger, Manfred/**Rittberger**, Volker/**Zürn**, Michael (1988). Internationale Regime in den Ost-West-Beziehungen. Ein Beitrag zur Erforschung der friedlichen Behandlung internationaler Konflikte. Frankfurt/M.

Efinger, Manfred et.al. (1990). Internationale Regime und internationale Politik. In: **Rittberger** (Hg.) 1990: 263-285.

Ehrhardt, Max (1950). Deutschlands Beziehungen zu Großbritannien, den Vereinigten Staaten und Frankreich vom Mai 1930 bis zum Juni 1932. Untersuchungen zur Außen- und Innenpolitik des Kabinetts Brüning an Hand der angelsächsischen diplomatischen Korrespondenzen. Diss. Hamburg.

Eichengreen, Barry (1990). Elusive Stability. Essays in the History of International Finance, 1919-1939. Cambridge, Mass.

Eichholtz, Dietrich (1969). Zum Anteil des IG-Farben-Konzerns an der Vorbereitung des zweiten Weltkrieges. In: *JfW*, II, 83-105.

Elfstrom, Gerard (1991). Moral Issues and Multinational Corporations. Basingstoke – London.

Erdmann, Karl Dietrich (1964). Die Zukunft als Kategorie der Geschichte. In: *HZ*, 198, 1, 44-61.

Esenwein-Rothe, Ingeborg (1965). Die Wirtschaftsverbände von 1933 bis 1945. Berlin.

Etzioni, Amitai (1963). The Epigenesis of Political Communities at the International Level. In: *AJS*, 68, 4, 407-421.

Falk, Richard A. (1987). The Promise of World Order. Essays in Normative International Relations. Philadelphia.

Feis, Herbert (1950). The Diplomacy of the Dollar. First Era 1919-1932. Baltimore.

Feldenkirchen, Wilfried (1987). Big Business in Interwar Germany: Organizational Innovation at Ver-einigte Stahlwerke, IG Farben, and Siemens. In: *BHR*, 61, 3, 417-451.

Feldenkirchen, Wilfried (1988). Zur Unternehmenspolitik des Hauses Siemens in der Zwischenkriegszeit. In: *ZfU*, 33, 22-57.

Feldenkirchen, Wilfried (1995a). Die Anfänge des Siemensgeschäfts in Amerika. In: **Feldenkirchen/Schönert-Röhlk/Schulz** (Hg.) 1995: 891-900.

Feldenkirchen, Wilfried (1995b). Siemens 1918-1945. München – Zürich.

Feldenkirchen, Wilfried/**Schönert-Röhlk**, Frauke/**Schulz**, Günther (Hg.) (1995). Wirtschaft, Gesellschaft, Unternehmen. Festschrift für Hans Pohl zum 60. Geburtstag. 2 Bde. Bd. 2. Stuttgart.

Feldman, Gerald D. (1969). The Social and Economic Policies of German Big Business 1918-1929. In: *AHR*, 75, 1, 47-55.

Feldman, Gerald D. (1978). Aspekte deutscher Industriepolitik am Ende der Weimarer Republik 1930-1932. In: **Holl** (Hg.) 1978: 103-125.

Feldmann, Gerald D. (Hg.) (1985). Die Nachwirkungen der Inflation in der deutschen Geschichte. München.

Feldman, Gerald D. et.al. (Hg.) (1982). Die deutsche Inflation. Eine Zwischenbilanz 1982. Berlin – New York.

Fest, Joachim C. (1973). Hitler. Eine Biographie. Frankfurt/M. u.a.

Fest, Joachim C. (1978). Anmerkungen zu Hitler. München.

Fetscher, Iring/**Münkler**, Herfried (Hg.) (1985). Politikwissenschaft. Begriffe– Analysen–Theorien. Ein Grundkurs. Reinbek bei Hamburg.

Fine, Sidney (1969). Sit-down. The General Motors Strike of 1936-1937. Ann Arbor.

Fischer, Alexander/**Moltmann**, Günter/**Schwabe**, Klaus (Hg.) (1978). Rußland-Deutschland-Amerika. Russia-Germany-America. Festschrift für Fritz T. Epstein zum 80. Geburtstag. Wiesbaden.

Fischer, Wolfram (1968). Deutsche Wirtschaftspolitik 1918-1945. 3. verb. Aufl. Opladen.

Fischer, Wolfram (1977). Die Weimarer Republik unter den weltwirtschaftlichen Bedingungen der Zwischenkriegszeit. In: **Mommsen/Petzina/Weisbrod** (Hg.) 1977, I: 26-50.

Foreman-Peck, James (1982). The American Challenge of the Twenties: Multinationals and the European Motor Industry. In: *JEH*, 42, 4, 865-881.

Forndran, Erhard (1977). Zur Theorie der internationalen Beziehungen – Das Verhältnis von Innen-, Außen- und internationaler Politik und die historischen Beispiele der 30er Jahre. In: **Forndran/Golczewski/Riesenberger** (Hg.) 1977: 315-361.

Forndran, Erhard/**Golczewski**, Frank/**Riesenberger**, Dieter (Hg.) (1977). Innen- und Außenpolitik unter nationalsozialistischer Bedrohung. Determinanten internationaler Beziehungen in historischen Fallstudien. Opladen.

Forstmeier, Friedrich/**Volkmann**, Hans-Erich (Hg.) (1975). Wirtschaft und Rüstung am Vorabend des Zweiten Weltkrieges. Düsseldorf.

Forstmeier, Friedrich/**Volkmann**, Hans-Erich (Hg.) (1977). Kriegswirtschaft und Rüstung 1939-1945. Düsseldorf.

Fraenkel, Ernst (1974). Der Doppelstaat. Frankfurt/M. – Köln.

Franz, Otmar (Hg.) (1976). Vom Sinn der Geschichte. Stuttgart.

Franz, Otmar (Hg.) (1981). Am Wendepunkt der europäischen Geschichte. Göttingen – Zürich.

Frei, Daniel (1977). Sicherheit. Grundfragen der Weltpolitik. Stuttgart – Berlin – Köln – Mainz.

Frei, Daniel (1985). Feindbilder und Abrüstung. Die gegenseitige Einschätzung der UdSSR und der USA. Eine Studie des Instituts der Vereinten Nationen für Abrüstungsforschung (UNIDIR). München.

Frieden, Jeffrey A./**Lake**, David A. (1991). International Political Economy. Perspectives on Global Power and Wealth. 2. Aufl. London.

Friedländer, Saul (1965). Auftakt zum Untergang. Hitler und die Vereinigten Staaten von Amerika 1939-1941. Stuttgart – Berlin – Köln – Mainz.

Frisch, Harald (1967). Das Deutsche Rooseveltbild (1933-1941). Diss. Berlin.

Fröhlich, Friedrich W. (1974). Multinationale Unternehmen. Entstehung, Organisation und Management. Baden-Baden.

Frye, Alton (1967). Nazi Germany and the American Hemisphere 1933-1941. New Haven – London.

Funke, Manfred (1976a). Die deutsch-italienischen Beziehungen. Antibolschewismus und außenpolitische Interessenkongruenz als Strukturprinzip der 'Achse'. In: **Funke** (Hg.) 1976: 823-846.

Funke, Manfred (1989). Starker oder schwacher Diktator? Hitlers Herrschaft und die Deutschen. Ein Essay. Düsseldorf.

Funke, Manfred (Hg.) (1976). Hitler, Deutschland und die Mächte. Materialien zur Außenpolitik des Dritten Reiches. Düsseldorf.

Galbraith, John K. (1989). Der große Crash 1929. Ursachen – Verlauf – Folgen. München.

Gallup, George H. (1972). The Gallup Poll. Public Opinion 1935-1971. Bd. 1: 1935-1948. New York.

Gantzel, Klaus-Jürgen (Hg.) (1973). Internationale Beziehungen als System. PVS-Sonderheft 5. Opladen.

Gardner, Lloyd C. (1964). Economic Aspects of New Deal Diplomacy. Madison.

Garraty, John A. (1987). The Great Depression. Garden City, N.Y.

Gatzke, Hans W. (1980). Germany and the United States. A 'Special Relationship'?. Cambridge, Mass. – London.

Gessner, Dieter (1977). Agrardepression und Präsidialregierungen in Deutschland 1930 bis 1933. Pro-bleme des Agrarprotektionismus am Ende der Weimarer Republik. Düsseldorf.

Geyer, Michael (1980). Aufrüstung oder Sicherheit. Die Reichswehr in der Krise der Machtpolitik 1924-1936. Wiesbaden.

Gibb, George S./**Knowlton**, Evelyn H. (1956). The Resurgent Years 1911-1927. History of Standard Oil Company (New Jersey) Vol. 2.

Gillingham, John (1985). Industry and Politics in the Third Reich. Ruhr Coal, Hitler and Europe. Stuttgart.

Gillingham, John (1989). Coal and Steel Diplomacy in Interwar Europe. In: **Wurm** (Hg.) 1989: 83-101.

Gilpin, Robert G. (1975a). Three Models of the Future. In: **Bergsten/Krause** (Hg.) 1975: 37-60.

Gilpin, Robert G. (1975b). U.S. Power and the Multinational Corporation. The Political Economy of Foreign Direct Investment. New York.

Gilpin, Robert G. (1986). The Richness of the Tradition of Political Realism. In: **Keohane** (Hg.) 1986: 301-321.

Gilpin, Robert G. (1987a). The Political Economy of International Relations. Princeton, N.J.

Gilpin, Robert G. (1987b). War and Change in World Politics. Cambridge – New York – New Rochelle – Melbourne – Sydney.

Glashagen, Winfried (1980). Die Reparationspolitik Heinrich Brünings 1930-1931. Studien zum wirtschafts- und außenpolitischen Entscheidungsprozeß in der Auflösungsphase der Weimarer Republik. 2 Bde. Diss. Bonn.

Glucksmann, André (1991). Am Ende des Tunnels. Das falsche Denken ging dem katastrophalen Handeln voraus. Eine Bilanz des 20. Jahrhunderts. Berlin.

Gottlieb, Moshe R. (1982). American Anti-Nazi Resistance, 1933-1941. A Historical Analysis. New York.

Gottwald, Robert (1965). Die deutsch-amerikanischen Beziehungen in der Ära Stresemann. Berlin – Dahlem.

Gourevitch, Peter (1978). The Second Image Reversed: The International Sources of Domestic Politics. In: *IO*, 32, 4, 881-912.

Gourevitch, Peter A. (1986). Politics in Hard Times. Comparative Responses to International Economic Crisis. Ithaca London.

Graebner, Norman A. (1986). America as a World Power. A Realist Appraisal from Wilson to Reagan. Essays. 2. Aufl. Wilmington, Delaware.

Graml, Hermann (1973). Präsidialsystem und Außenpolitik. In: *VfZ*, 21, 2, 134-145.

Graml, Hermann (1990). Europas Weg in den Krieg. Hitler und die Mächte. München.

Greenwood, Ronald G. (1982). Managerial Decentralization. A Study of the General Electric Philosophy. 2., erw. Aufl. Easton.

Grenzebach, William S., Jr. (1988). Germany's Informal Empire in East-Central Europe. German Economic Policy Toward Yugoslavia and Rumania, 1933-1939. Stuttgart.

Gruchmann, Lothar (1962). Nationalsozialistische Großraumordnung. Die Konstruktion einer 'deutschen Monroe-Doktrin'. Stuttgart.

Grunberg, Isabelle (1990). Exploring the 'Myth' of Hegemonic Stability. In: *IO*, 44,4, 431-477.

Guinsburg, Thomas N. (1982). The Pursuit of Isolationism in the United States Senate from Versailles to Pearl Harbor. New York – London.

Haber, Ludwig F. (1971). The Chemical Industry 1900-1930. International Growth and Technological Change. Oxford.

Haberler, Gottfried (1976). Die Weltwirtschaft und das internationale Währungssystem in der Zeit zwischen den beiden Weltkriegen. In: **Deutsche Bundesbank** (Hg.) 1976: 205-248.

Hänel, Wolfgang (1984). Hermann Rauschnings 'Gespräche mit Hitler'–eine Geschichtsfälschung. Ingolstadt.

Hall, John A. (Hg.) (1987). States in History. Oxford – New York.

Hardach, Gerd (1977). Deutschland in der Weltwirtschaft 1870-1970. Eine Einführung in die Sozial- und Wirtschaftsgeschichte. Frankfurt/M. – New York.

Hardach, Karl (1976). Wirtschaftsgeschichte Deutschlands im 20. Jahrhundert. Göttingen.

Harper, Glenn T. (1967). German Economic Policy in Spain During the Spanish Civil War, 1936-1939. The Hague – Paris.

Hass, Gerhart (1965). Von München bis Pearl Harbor. Zur Geschichte der deutsch-amerikanischen Beziehungen 1938-1941. Berlin.

Hauner, Milan (1978). Did Hitler Want a World Dominion?. In: *JCH*, 13, 1, 15-32.

Hauser, Oswald (Hg.) (1973). Weltpolitik 1933-1939. 13 Vorträge. Göttingen – Frankfurt/M. – Zürich.

Hauser, Oswald (Hg.) (1975). Weltpolitik II 1939-1945. 14 Vorträge. Göttingen – Frankfurt/M. – Zürich.

Hayes, Peter (1987). Industry and Ideology. IG Farben in the Nazi Era. Cambridge – New York – Melbourne.

Haynes, William (1948). American Chemical Industry. A History. Bd. 4: 1923-1929. The Merger Era. Toronto – New York – London.

Haynes, William (1954). American Chemical Industry. A History. Bd. 5: 1930-1939. Decade of New Products. Toronto – New York – London.

Hearden, Patrick J. (1987). Roosvelt Confronts Hitler. America's Entry into World War II. DeKalb, Ill.

Heindl, Josef E. (1964). Die diplomatischen Beziehungen zwischen Deutschland und den Vereinigten Staaten von Amerika von 1933 bis 1939. Diss. Würzburg.

Heinrichs, Waldo (1988). Threshold of War. Franklin D. Roosevelt and American Entry into World War II. New York – Oxford.

Heintzen, Markus (1989). Private Außenpolitik. Baden-Baden.

Helbich, Wolfgang J. (1962). Die Reparationen in der Ära Brüning. Zur Bedeutung des Young-Plans für die deutsche Politik 1930 bis 1932. Berlin.

Helbich, Wolfgang J. (1971). Franklin D. Roosevelt. Berlin.

Henning, Friedrich-Wilhelm (1975). Das industrialisierte Deutschland 1914 bis 1972. 2. Aufl. Paderborn.

Henning, Hansjoachim (1978). Kraftfahrzeugindustrie und Autobahnbau in der Wirtschaftspolitik des Nationalsozialismus 1933-1936. In: *VSWG*, 65, 2, 217-242.

Herbst, Ludolf (1979). Die Mobilmachung der Wirtschaft 1938/39 als Problem des nationalsozialistischen Herrschaftssystems. In: **Benz/Graml** (Hg.) 1979: 62-106.

Herbst, Ludolf (1989). Der Krieg und die Unternehmensstrategie deutscher Industrie-Konzerne in der Zwischenkriegszeit. In: **Broszat/Schwabe** (Hg.) 1989: 72-134.

Hertner, Peter (1989): Financial Strategies and Adaptation to Foreign Markets: The German Electro-Technical Industry and Its Multinational Activities: 1890s to 1939. In: **Teichova/Lévy-Leboyer/Nussbaum** (Hg.) 1989: 145-159.

Herz, Dietmar (1987). Frieden durch Handel. Zur Außen- und Außenwirtschaftspolitik der Roosevelt-Administration in der ersten Hälfte der dreißiger Jahre. Frankfurt/M. – Bern – New York – Paris.

Herz, John H. (1974a). Aufstieg und Niedergang des Territorialstaates. In: **Herz** 1974: 63-81.

Herz, John H. (1974b). Auswirkungen des wissenschaftlich-technischen Prozesses auf die internationalen Beziehungen. In: **Herz** 1974: 103-121.

Herz, John H. (1974c). Gedanken über Legitimität, Gewalt und die Zukunft des Staates. In: **Herz** 1974: 183-197.

Herz, John H. (1974d). Rückblick auf den Territorialstaat. Betrachtungen über die Zukunft des Nationalstaates. In: **Herz** 1974: 123-142.

Herz, John H. (1974). Staatenwelt und Weltpolitik. Aufsätze zur internationalen Politik im Nuklearzeit-alter. Hamburg.

Herzstein, Robert E. (1989). Roosevelt and Hitler. Prelude to War. 2. Aufl. New York.

Hesse, Helmut (1987). Außenwirtschaftspolitik. In: **Beyme et.al.** (Hg.) 1987: 158-179.

Heyl, John D. (1973). Hitler's Economic Thought: A Reappraisal. In: *CEH*, 6, 1, 83-96.

Higham, Charles (1983). Trading with the Enemy: An Exposé of the Nazi-American Money Plot 1933-1949. New York.

Hildebrand, Klaus (1973). Deutsche Außenpolitik 1933-1945. Kalkül oder Dogma? 2. überarb. Aufl. Stuttgart – Berlin – Köln – Mainz.

Hildebrand, Klaus (1974). Die innenpolitischen Antriebskräfte der nationalsozialistischen Außenpolitik. In: **Wehler** (Hg.) (1974): 635-651.

Hildebrand, Klaus (1975). Weltmacht oder Untergang: Hitlers Deutschland 1941-1945. In: **Hauser** (Hg.) 1975: 286-322.

Hildebrand, Klaus (1976a). Hitlers 'Programm' und seine Realisierung 1939-1942. In: **Funke** (Hg.) 1976: 63-93.

Hildebrand, Klaus (1976b). Innenpolitische Antriebskräfte der nationalsozialistischen Außenpolitik. In: **Funke** (Hg.) 1976: 223-238.

Hildebrand, Klaus (1979). Das Dritte Reich. München – Wien.

Hildebrand, Klaus (1981). Monokratie oder Polykratie? Hitlers Herrschaft und das Dritte Reich. In: **Hirschfeld/Kettenacker** (Hg.) 1981: 73-97.

Hildebrand, Klaus/**Pommerin**, Reiner (Hg.) (1985). Deutsche Frage und europäisches Gleichgewicht. Festschrift für Andreas Hillgruber zum 60. Geburtstag. Köln – Wien.

Hildebrand, Klaus/**Schmädeke**, Jürgen/**Zernack**, Klaus (Hg.). 1939. An der Schwelle zum Krieg. Die Entfesselung des Zweiten Weltkrieges und das internationale System. Berlin – New York.

Hillgruber, Andreas (1976). Die 'Endlösung' und das deutsche Ostimperium als Kernstück des rassen-ideologischen Programms des Nationalsozialismus. In: **Funke** (Hg.) 1976: 94-114.

Hillgruber, Andreas (1979a). Der Faktor Amerika in Hitlers Strategie 1938-1941. In: **Hillgruber** 1979: 197-222.

Hillgruber, Andreas (1979). Deutsche Großmacht- und Weltpolitik im 19. und 20. Jahrhundert. 2. Aufl. Düsseldorf.

Hillgruber, Andreas (1989a). Politische Geschichte in moderner Sicht. In: **Hillgruber** 1989: 13-31.

Hillgruber, Andreas (1989). Die Zerstörung Europas. Beiträge zur Weltkriegsepoche 1914-1945. 2. Aufl. Frankfurt/M. – Berlin.

Hilton, Stanley E. (1975). Brazil and the Great Powers, 1930-1939. The Politics of Trade Rivalry. Austin – London.

Hirschfeld, Gerhard/**Kettenacker**, Lothar (Hg.) (1981). Der 'Führerstaat': Mythos und Realität. Studien zur Struktur und Politik des Dritten Reiches. Stuttgart.

Höpfner, Hans-Paul (1983). Deutsche Südosteuropapolitik in der Weimarer Republik. Frankfurt/M. – Bern.

Hoffmann, Stanley (1966). Obstinate or Obsolete? The Fate of the Nation-State and the Case of Western Europe. In: *Daedalus*, 95, 3, 862-915.

Hoffmann, Walter G. (1965). Das Wachstum der deutschen Wirtschaft seit der Mitte des 19. Jahrhunderts. Berlin.

Holl, Karl (Hg.) (1978). Wirtschaftskrise und liberale Demokratie. Das Ende der Weimarer Republik und die gegenwärtige Situation. Göttingen.

Holsti, Kalevi J. (1978). A New International Politics? Diplomacy in Complex Interdependence. In: *IO*, 32, 2, 513-530.

Holsti, Kalevi J. (1989). Mirror, Mirror on the Wall, Which Are the Fairest Theories of All? In: *ISQ*, 33, 3, 255-261.

Holsti, Kalevi J. (1991a). Change in the International System: Interdependence, Integration, and Fragmentation. In: **Holsti** 1991: 23-54.

Holsti, Kalevi J. (1991b). The Necrologists of International Relations. In: **Holsti** 1991: 203-220.

Holsti, Kalevi J. (1991c). Politics in Command: Foreign Trade as National Security Policy. In: **Holsti** 1991: 101-130.

Holsti, Kalevi J. (1991). Change in the International System. Essays on the Theory and Practice of International Relations. Aldershot – Brookfield, Vermont.

Holtfrerich, Carl-Ludwig (1980). Amerikanischer Kapitalexport und Wiederaufbau der deutschen Wirtschaft 1919-1923 im Vergleich zu 1924-1929. In: **Stürmer** (Hg.) 1980: 131-157.

Holtfrerich, Carl-Ludwig (1982a). Alternativen zu Brünings Wirtschaftspolitik in der Weltwirtschaftskrise?. In: *HZ*, 235, 3, 605-631.

Holtfrerich, Carl-Ludwig (1982b). Die konjunkturanregenden Wirkungen der deutschen Inflation auf die US-Wirtschaft in der Weltwirtschaftskrise 1920/21. In: **Feldmann et.al.** (Hg.) 1982: 207-234.

Holtfrerich, Carl-Ludwig (1984). Zu hohe Löhne in der Weimarer Republik? Bemerkungen zur Borchardt-These. In: *GG*, 10, 1, 122-141.

Homburg, Heidrun (1985). Die Neuordnung des Marktes nach der Inflation. Probleme und Widerstände am Beispiel der Zusammenschlußprojekte von AEG und Siemens 1924-1933 oder: 'Wer hat den längeren Atem?'. In: **Feldmann** (Hg.) 1985: 117-156.

Hopkins, Terence K./**Wallerstein**, Immanuel (1979). Grundzüge der Entwicklung des modernen Weltsystems. Entwurf für ein Forschungsvorhaben. In: **Senghaas** (Hg.) 1979: 151-200.

Hoppe, Hans-Joachim (1976). Deutschland und Bulgarien 1918-1945. In: **Funke** (Hg.) 1976: 604-611.

Hounshell, David A./**Smith**, John K., Jr. (1988). Science and Corporate Strategy. Du Pont R&D, 1902-1980. Cambridge – New York.

Howard, Frank A. (1947). Buna Rubber. The Birth of an Industry. 2. Aufl. New York.

Howard, Michael (1981). Der Krieg in der europäischen Geschichte. Vom Ritterheer zur Atomstreitmacht. München.

Hüttenberger, Peter (1976). Nationalsozialistische Polykratie. In: *GG*, 2, 4, 417-442.

Hütter, Joachim (1976). Einführung in die internationale Politik. Stuttgart – Berlin – Köln – Mainz.

Hughes, Thomas P. (1991). Die Erfindung Amerikas. Der technologische Aufstieg der USA seit 1870. München.

Huntington, Samuel P. (1973). Transnational Organizations in World Politics. In: *WP*, 25, 3, 333-368.

Huntington, Samuel P./**Nye**, Joseph S., Jr. (Hg.) (1985). Global Dilemmas. Boston – London.

Ikenberry, G. John/**Kupchan**, Charles A. (1990). Socialization and Hegemonic Power. in: *IO*, 44, 3, 283-315.

Jacobsen, Hans-Adolf (1968). Nationalsozialistische Außenpolitik 1933-1938. Frankfurt/M. – Berlin.

Jacobsen, Hans-Adolf (1973). Die Rolle Deutschlands in der Weltpolitik 1933-1935. In: **Hauser** (Hg.) 1973: 255-269.

Jacobsen, Hans-Adolf (1976). Zur Struktur der NS-Außenpolitik 1933-1945. In: **Funke** (Hg.) 1976: 137-185.

Jacobsen, Hans-Adolf (1982). Zur Rolle der Diplomatie im Dritten Reich. In: **Schwabe** (Hg.) 1982: 171-199.

Jäckel, Eberhard (1981). Hitlers Weltanschauung. Entwurf einer Herrschaft. erw. und überarb. Neu-aufl. Stuttgart.

Jäckel, Eberhard (1986). Hitlers Herrschaft. Vollzug einer Weltanschauung. Stuttgart.

Jäger, Jörg-Johannes (1969). Die wirtschaftliche Abhängigkeit des Dritten Reiches vom Ausland dargestellt am Beispiel der Stahlindustrie. Berlin.

Jäger, Thomas/**Kümmel**, Gerhard (1994.). Isolation und Dissoziation in der internationalen Politik. In: **Bredow/Jäger** (Hg.) 1994: 151-170.

James, Alan (1986). Sovereign Statehood: The Basis of International Society. London.

James, Harold (1988). Deutschland in der Weltwirtschaftskrise 1924-1936. Stuttgart.

Jervis, Robert (1976). Perception and Misperception in International Politics. Princeton, N.J.

Jonas, Manfred (1965). Prophet without Honor: Hans Heinrich Dieckhoff's Reports from Washington. In: *MA*, 47, 222-233.

Jonas, Manfred (1966). Isolationism in America 1935-1941. Ithaca – New York.

Jonas, Manfred (1984). The United States and Germany. A Diplomatic History. Ithaca – London.

Jones, Kenneth P. (Hg.) (1983). U.S. Diplomats in Europe, 1919-1941. Reprint. Santa Barbara – Oxford.

Jones, Robert/**Marriott**, Oliver (1970). Anatomy of a Merger. A History of G.E.C., A.E.I. and English Electric. London.

Jones, Walter S. (1991). The Logic of International Relations, 7. Aufl. New York.

Junker, Detlef (1975a). Der unteilbare Weltmarkt. Das ökonomische Interesse in der Außenpolitik der USA 1933-1941. Stuttgart.

Junker, Detlef (1975b). Nationalstaat und Weltmacht. Die globale Bestimmung des nationalen Interesses der USA durch die Internationalisten 1938-1941. In: **Hauser** (Hg.) 1975: 17-36.

Junker, Detlef (1979). Franklin D. Roosevelt. Macht und Vision: Präsident in Krisenzeiten. Göttingen – Zürich – Frankfurt.

Junker, Detlef (1981). Die Außenpolitik der USA 1920-1941. In: **Franz** (Hg.) 1981: 200-217.

Junker, Detlef (1986). Franklin D. Roosevelt und die nationalsozialistische Bedrohung der USA. In: **Trommler** (Hg.) 1986: 379-392.

Junker, Detlef (1988). Kampf um die Weltmacht. Die USA und das Dritte Reich 1933-1945. Düsseldorf.

Junker, Detlef (1989). Deutschland im politischen Kalkül der Vereinigten Staaten 1933-1945. In: **Michalka** (Hg.) 1989: 57-73.

Junker, Detlef (1992). Hitler's Perception of Franklin D. Roosevelt and the United States of America. In: **Minnen/Sears** (Hg.) 1992: 145-156.

Kaiser, David E. (1980). Economic Diplomacy and the Origins of the Second World War. Germany, Britain, France, and Eastern Europe, 1930-1939. Princeton, N.J.

Kaiser, Karl (1969). Transnationale Politik. Zu einer Theorie der multinationalen Politik. In: **Czempiel** (Hg.) 1969: 80-109.

Kaiser, Karl/**Schwarz**, Hans-Peter (Hg.) (1985). Weltpolitik. Strukturen, Akteure, Perspektiven. Bonn.

Kant, Immanuel (1984). Zum ewigen Frieden. Ein philosophischer Entwurf. Hrsg. von Rudolf Malter. Stuttgart.

Kapoor, A./**Grub**, Phillip D. (Hg.) (1973). The Multinational Enterprise in Transition. Selected Readings and Essays. 2. Aufl. Princeton, N.J.

Kaser, M.C./**Radice**, E.A. (Hg.) (1985). The Economic History of Eastern Europe 1919-1975. Bd. 1: Economic Structure and Performance Between the Two Wars. Oxford.

Keck, Otto (1991). Der neue Institutionalismus in der Theorie der Internationalen Politik. In: *PVS*, 32, 4, 635-653.

Keese, Dietmar (1967). Die volkswirtschaftlichen Gesamtgrößen für das Deutsche Reich in den Jahren 1925-1936. In: **Conze/Raupach** (Hg.) 1967: 35-81.

Kellenbenz, Hermann (1981). Deutsche Wirtschaftsgeschichte. Bd. 2: Vom Ausgang des 18. Jahrhunderts bis zum Ende des Zweiten Weltkrieges. München.

Keohane, Robert O. (1984). After Hegemony. Cooperation and Discord in the World Political Economy. Princeton, N.J.

Keohane, Robert O. (1986a). Theory of World Politics: Structural Realism and Beyond. In: **Keohane** (Hg.) (1986): 158-203.

Keohane, Robert O. (1989a). International Institutions: Two Approaches. In: **Keohane** 1989: 158-179.

Keohane, Robert O. (1989b). Neoliberal Institutionalism: A Perspective on World Politics. In: **Keohane** 1989: 1-20.

Keohane, Robert O. (1989c). The Demand for International Regimes. In: **Keohane** 1989: 101-131.

Keohane, Robert O. (1989). International Institutions and State Power. Essays in International Relations Theory. Boulder – San Francisco – London.

Keohane, Robert O. (Hg.) (1986). Neorealism and Its Critics. New York.

Keohane, Robert O./**Nye**, Joseph S. (1977). Power and Interdependence. World Politics in Transition. Boston – Toronto.

Keohane, Robert O./**Nye**, Joseph S. (1985). Macht und Interdependenz. In: **Kaiser/ Schwarz** (Hg.) 1985: 74-88.

Keohane, Robert O./**Nye**, Joseph S. (1987). Power and Interdependence Revisited. In: *IO*, 41, 4, 725-753.

Kershaw, Ian (1980). Der Hitler-Mythos. Volksmeinung und Propaganda im Dritten Reich. Stuttgart.

Kershaw, Ian (1981). The Führer Image and Political Integration: The Popular Conception of Hitler in Bavaria during the Third Reich. In: **Hirschfeld/Kettenacker** (Hg.) 1981: 133-163.

Kerz, Heinz (1947). Die Handelspolitik der Vereinigten Staten von Hamilton bis zum Ausbruch des Zweiten Weltkrieges unter besonderer Berücksichtigung ihrer Wirtschaftsbeziehungen zu Deutschland. Diss. Köln.

Kettenacker, Lothar (1981). Sozialpsychologische Aspekte der Führer-Herrschaft. In: **Hirschfeld/Kettenacker** (Hg.). 1981: 98-132.

Kiesewetter, Hubert (1992). Beasts or Beagles? Amerikanische Unternehmen in Deutschland. In: **Pohl** (Hg.) 1992: 165-196.

Kindermann, Gottfried-Karl (1981a). Zur Methodik der Internationalen Konstellationsanalyse. In: Kindermann (Hg.) 1981: 68-106.

Kindermann, Gottfried-Karl (Hg.) (1981). Grundelemente der Weltpolitik. 2. Aufl. München.

Kindleberger, Charles P. (1977). America in the World Economy (Headline Series 237). New York.

Kindleberger, Charles P. (1981). Dominance and Leadership in the International Economy. Exploitation, Public Goods, and Free Rides. In: *ISQ*, 25, 2, 242-254.

Kindleberger, Charles P. (1984). Die Weltwirtschaftskrise 1929-1939. 3. Aufl. München.

Kindleberger, Charles P. (Hg.) (1971). The International Corporation. A Symposium. 2. Aufl. Cam-bridge, Mass. -. London.

Kinsella, William E., Jr. (1987). The Prescience of a Statesman: FDR's Assessment of Adolf Hitler before the World War, 1933-1941. In: **Rosenbaum/Bartelme** (Hg.) 1987: 73-84.

Kluke, Paul (1955). Nationalsozialistische Europaideologie. In: *VfZ*, 3, 3, 240-275.

Knapp, Manfred et.al. (1978). Die USA und Deutschland 1918-1975. Deutsch-amerikanische Beziehungen zwischen Realität und Partnerschaft. München.

Knieper, Rolf (1991). Nationale Souveränität. Versuch über Ende und Anfang einer Weltordnung. Frankfurt/M.

Knipping, Franz (1976). Frankreich in Hitlers Außenpolitik 1933-1939. In: **Funke** (Hg.) 1976: 612-627.

Knipping, Franz/**Müller**, Klaus-Jürgen (Hg.) (1984). Machtbewußtsein in Deutschland am Vorabend des Zweiten Weltkrieges. Paderborn.

Knorr, Klaus (1973). Power and Wealth. The Political Economy of International Power. New York.

Knorr, Klaus/**Verba**, Sidney (Hg.) (1961). The International System. Theoretical Essays. Princeton, N.J.

Köhler, Henning (Hg.) (1984). Deutschland und der Westen. Vorträge und Diskussionsbeiträge des Symposiums zu Ehren von Gordon A. Craig. Berlin.

Kohler-Koch, Beate (1989a). Zur Empirie und Theorie internationaler Regime. In: **Kohler-Koch** (Hg.) 1989: 17-85.

Kohler-Koch, Beate (Hg.) (1989). Regime in den internationalen Beziehungen. Baden-Baden.

Kolko, Gabriel (1962). American Business and Germany, 1930-1941. In: *WPQ*, 15, 713-728.

Kossmann, Joachim (1989). Nationale und internationale Technologie-Kartelle als Aspekt der amerikanischen Politik am Ende des 'New Deal': Die Renaissance der Antitrust-Bewegung und das Problem der Patent- und Lizenzgemeinschaften 1937-1939. In: **Wurm** (Hg.) 1989: 151-179.

Kossmann, Joachim (1991). Nationale Sicherheitspolitik und transnationaler Technologie-Transfer. Das 'Nye-Committee' und die deutsche Luftrüstung, 1934-1936. In: **Schröter/Wurm** (Hg.) 1991: 97-116.

Kottmann, Richard N. (1968). Reciprocity and the North Atlantic Triangle 1932-1938. Ithaca – New York.

Krasner, Stephen D. (1975). State Power and the Structure of International Trade. In: *WP*, 24, 3, 317-347.

Krasner, Stephen D. (1982a). Structural Causes and Regime Consequences: Regimes as Intervening Variables. In: **Krasner** (Hg.) 1982: 185-205.

Krasner, Stephen D. (1982b). Regimes and the Limits of Realism: Regimes as Autonomous Variables. In: **Krasner** (Hg.) 1982: 497-510.

Krasner, Stephen D. (Hg.) (1982). International Regimes. A Special Issue of *International Organization*, 36, 2, Spring 1982. Cambridge, Mass.

Kreikamp, Hans-Dieter (1977). Die Entflechtung der I.G. Farbenindustrie AG und die Gründung der Nachfolgegesellschaften. In: *VfZ*, 25, 2, 220-251.

Krippendorff, Ekkehart (1963). Ist Außenpolitik *Außen*politik? Ein Beitrag zur Theorie und der Versuch, eine unhaltbare Unterscheidung aufzugeben. In: *PVS*, 4, 3, 243-266.

Krippendorff, Ekkehart (1986). Internationale Politik. Geschichte und Theorie. Frankfurt/M. – New York.

Krosigk, Lutz Graf Schwerin von (1958). Die große Zeit des Feuers. Der Weg der deutschen Industrie. Bd. 2. Tübingen.

Krüger, Peter (1980). Zu Hitlers 'nationalsozialistischen Wirtschaftserkenntnissen'. In: *GG*, 6, 2, 263-282.

Krüger, Peter (1982). Struktur, Organisation und außenpolitische Wirkungsmöglichkeiten der leitenden Beamten des Auswärtigen Dienstes 1921-1933. In: **Schwabe** (Hg.) 1982: 101-169.

Krüger, Peter (1985). Die Außenpolitik der Republik von Weimar. Darmstadt.

Krüger, Peter (1989). „Man läßt sein Land nicht im Stich, weil es eine schlechte Regierung hat". Die Diplomaten und die Eskalation der Gewalt. In: **Broszat/Schwabe** (Hg.) 1989: 180-225.

Kümmel, Gerhard (1992a). Der Triumph der 'Gesellschaftswelt'? Das internationale System im Umbruch. In: *liberal*, 34, 3, 95-98.

Kümmel, Gerhard (1992b). Die Suche nach dem neuen Nomos der Erde für das 21. Jahrhundert im Widerstreit der Theorien. Unveröff. Manuskript. Marburg.

Kümmel, Gerhard (1994). UN Overstretch: A German Perspective. In: *IP*, 1, 2, 160-178.

Kümmel, Gerhard (i.E.). States and Markets. A Tentative Assessment of the Effects of External Factors on Conditions of Authoritarianism, Fascism and Democracy in Europe in the Inter-War Period. In: **Berg-Schlosser/Mitchell** (Hg.) (i.E.b).

Kuhn, Arthur J. (1986). GM Passes Ford, 1918-1938. Designing the General Motors Performance-Control System. University Park – London.

Kuhn, Axel (1970). Hitlers außenpolitisches Programm. Entstehung und Entwicklung 1919-1939. Stuttgart.

Lake, David A. (1984). Beneath the Commerce of Nations: A Theory of International Economic Structures. In: *ISQ*, 28, 2, 143-170.

Lake, David A. (1988). Power, Protection, and Free Trade. International Sources of U.S. Commercial Strategy, 1887-1939. Ithaca – London.

Langer, William L./**Gleason**, S. Everett (1964). The Challenge to Isolation. The World Crisis of 1937-1940 and American Foreign Policy. Bd. 1. New York – Evanston – London.

Langworth, Richard M./**Norbye**, Jan P. (1985). The Complete History of Chrysler Corporation 1924-1985. Skokie, Ill.

Langworth, Richard M./**Norbye**, Jan P. (1986). The Complete History of General Motors 1908-1986. New York.

Larson, Henrietta M./**Knowlton**, Evelyn H./**Popple**, Charles S. (1971): New Horizons 1927-1950. History of Standard Oil Company (New Jersey) Vol. 3. New York – Evanston – San Francisco – London.

Lee, Marshall M./Michalka, Wolfgang (1987). German Foreign Policy 1917-1933. Continuity or Break? Leamington – Spa – Hamburg – New York.

Leffler, Melvyn P. (1974). Political Isolationism, Economic Expansionism, or Diplomatic Realism: American Policy toward Western Europe 1921-1933. In: *PAH*, VIII, 413-461.

Leffler, Melvyn P. (1979). The Elusive Quest America's Pursuit of European Stability and French Security, 1919-1933. Chapel Hill, NC.

Leffler, Melvyn P. (1984). 1921-1932. Expansionist Impulses and Domestic Constraints. In: **Becker/Wells** (Hg.) 1984: 225-275.

Lemper, Alfons (1974). Handel in einer dynamischen Weltwirtschaft. Ansatzpunkte für eine Neuorientierung der Außenhandelstheorie. München.

Lewis, William A. (1963). Economic Survey 1919-1939. 6. Aufl. London.

Link, Werner (1970). Die amerikanische Stabilisierungspolitik in Deutschland 1921-32. Düsseldorf.

Link, Werner (1973). Das nationalsozialistische Deutschland und die USA 1933-1941. In: *NPL*, 18, 2, 225-233.

Link, Werner (1978). Die Beziehungen zwischen der Weimarer Republik und den USA. In: **Knapp et.al.** 1978: 62-106.

Link, Werner (1988). Der Ost-West-Konflikt. Die Organisation der internationalen Beziehungen im 20. Jahrhundert. 2. überarb. und erw. Aufl. Stuttgart – Berlin – Köln – Mainz.

Link, Werner (1989). Reflections on Paradigmatic Complementarity in the Study of International Relations. In: **Czempiel/Rosenau** (Hg.) 1989: 99-116.

List, Martin (1992). Weltgesellschaft, Staatengemeinschaft und umfassende Sicherheit im Rahmen ökologischer Verträglichkeit. Gedanken zu einigen Grundbegriffen der internationalen Beziehungen am Ende des 20. Jahrhunderts. In: *polis*, 21, 2-28.

Lowenthal, Mark M. (1981). Roosevelt and the Coming of the War: The Search for United States Policy 1937-42. In: *JCH*, 16, 3, 413-440.

Luhmann, Niklas (1975a). Die Weltgesellschaft. In: **Luhmann** 1975: 51-71.

Luhmann, Niklas (1975). Soziologische Aufklärung 2. Aufsätze zur Theorie der Gesellschaft. Opladen.

Luhmann, Niklas (1985). Die Autopoiesis des Bewußtseins. In: *SW*, 36, 4, 402-446.

Luhmann, Niklas (1989). Politische Steuerung: Ein Diskussionsbeitrag. In: *PVS*, 30, 1, 4-9.

Lurie, Samuel (1947). Private Investment in a Controlled Economy. Germany, 1933-1939. New York.

MacDonald, Callum A. (1981). The United States, Britain and Appeasement, 1936-1939. New York.

Maddox, Robert J. (1971). Another Look at the Legend of Isolationism in the 1920's. In: *MA*, 53, 35-43.

Mann, Golo (1950). Der Fortschrittsglaube Amerikas. In: *Universitas*, 5, 10, 1153-1161.

Mann, Golo (1955). Vom Geist Amerikas. Eine Einführung in amerikanisches Denken und Handeln im zwanzigsten Jahrhundert. 2. Aufl. Stuttgart.

Mansbach, Richard W./**Ferguson**, Yale H./**Lampert**, Donald E. (1976). The Web of World Politics. Nonstate Actors in the Global System. Englewood Cliffs, N.J.

Martin, Bernd (1974). Friedensinitiativen und Machtpolitik im Zweiten Weltkrieg, 1939-1942. Düsseldorf.

Martin, Bernd (1976). Friedens-Planungen der multinationalen Großindustrie (1932-1940) als politische Krisenstrategie. In: *GG*, 2, 1, 66-88.

Martin, Bernd (1981). Amerikas Durchbruch zur politischen Weltmacht. Die interventionistische Globalstrategie der Regierung Roosevelt 1933-1941. In: *MGM*, 2, 57-98.

Martin, Bernd (1989). Weltmacht oder Untergang? Deutsche Großmachtpolitik im 20. Jahrhundert. Darmstadt.

Martinelli, Alberto/**Somaini**, Eugenio (1974). Multinationale Konzerne und Nationalstaaten. In: **Tudyka** (Hg.) 1974: 64-78.

Mason, Timothy W. (1966). Der Primat der Politik – Politik und Wirtschaft im Nationalsozialismus. In: *Argument*, 8, 6, 473-494.

Mason, Timothy W. (1975). Innere Krise und Angriffskrieg 1938/1939. In: **Forstmeier/Volkmann** (Hg.) 1975: 158-188.

Mason, Timothy W. (1981). Intention and Explanation: A Current Controversy about the Interpretation of National Socialism. In: **Hirschfeld/Kettenacker** (Hg.) 1981: 23-42.

Mastanduno, Michael/**Lake**, David A./**Ikenberry**, G. John (1989). Toward a Realist Theory of State Action. In: *ISQ*, 33, 4, 457-474.

Mathiopoulos, Margarita (1987). Amerika: Das Experiment des Fortschritts. Ein Vergleich des politischen Denkens in den USA und Europa. Paderborn – München – Wien – Zürich.

McGrew, Anthony G. et.al. (1992). Global Politics. Globalization and the Nation-State. Cambridge – Oxford.

McKale, Donald M. (1977). The Swastika Outside Germany. Kent, Ohio.

McQuaid, Kim (1977a). Young, Swope and General Electric's 'New Capitalism': A Study in Corporate Liberalism, 1920-33. In: *AJES*, 36, 3, 323-334.

McQuaid, Kim (1977b). Competition, Cartellization and the Corporate Ethic: General Electric's Leadership During the New Deal Era, 1933-40. In: *AJES*, 36, 4, 417-428.

Megerle, Klaus (1979). Weltwirtschaftskrise und Außenpolitik. Zum Problem der Kontinuität der deutschen Politik in der Endphase der Weimarer Republik. In: **Bergmann et.al.** (Hg.) 1979: 116-140.

Meier, Manfred (1953). Deutsche Außenhandelsregulierung von 1933 bis 1939. Diss. Basel.

Melnikow, J.M. (1959). Die Rolle der amerikanisch-deutschen Gegensätze bei der Entstehung des zweiten Weltkrieges. In: *Sowjetwissenschaft*, 1, 617-643.

Meyer, August (1986). Das Syndikat. Reichswerke 'Hermann Göring'. Braunschweig.

Meyer, Gerd (1991). Die deutsche Reparationspolitik von der Annahme des Young-Plans im Reichstag (12. März 1930) bis zum Reparationsabkommen auf der Lausanner Konferenz (9. Juli 1932). Diss. Bonn.

Meyers, Reinhard (1976). Britische Sicherheitspolitik 1934-1938. Studien zum außen- und sicherheitspolitischen Entscheidungsprozeß. Düsseldorf.

Meyers, Reinhard (1979). Weltpolitik in Grundbegriffen. Bd. 1: Ein lehr- und ideengeschichtlicher Grundriß. Düsseldorf.

Meyers, Reinhard (1981). Die Lehre von den Internationalen Beziehungen. Ein entwicklungsgeschichtlicher Überblick. Korrigierter und erw. Nachdruck. Königstein/Ts.

Meyers, Reinhard (1989). Wie viele Schwalben machen einen Sommer? (Re-)Naissance der Internationalen Politischen Ökonomie?. In: *NPL*, 34, 1, 5-40.

Michalka, Wolfgang (1976). Die nationalsozialistische Außenpolitik im Zeichen eines 'Konzeptionen-Pluralismus'. Fragestellungen und Forschungsaufgaben. In: **Funke** (Hg.) 1976: 46-62.

Michalka, Wolfgang (1989a). 'Vom Motor zum Getriebe'. Das Auswärtige Amt und die Degradierung einer traditionsreichen Behörde 1933 bis 1945. In: **Michalka** (Hg.) 1989: 249-259.

Michalka, Wolfgang (Hg.) (1989). Der Zweite Weltkrieg. Analysen, Grundzüge, Forschungsbilanz. München – Zürich.

Mikesell, Raymond F. (Hg.) (1962). U.S. Private and Government Investment Abroad. Eugene, Oregon.

Miller, Lynn (1990). Global Order. Values and Power in International Politics. 2. erw. Aufl. Boulder – San Francisco – London.

Milward, Alan S. (1981). The Reichsmark Bloc and the International Economy. In: **Hirschfeld/Ketten-acker** (Hg.) 1981: 377-413.

Minnen, Cornelis A. van/**Sears**, John F. (Hg.) (1992). FDR and His Contemporaries. Foreign Perceptions of an American President. New York.

Mirow, Kurt R./**Maurer**, Harry (1982). Webs of Power. International Cartels and the World Economy, Boston, Mass.

Modelski, George (1976). The Long Cycle of Global Politics and the Nation-State. In: *CSSH*, 20, 2, 214-235.

Modelski, George (1987). Long Cycles in World Politics. Seattle.

Modelski, George (1990). Is World Politics Evolutionary Learning?. In: *IO*, 44, 1, 1-24.

Mollin, Gerhard Th. (1988). Montankonzerne und 'Drittes Reich'. Der Gegensatz zwischen Monopol-industrie und Befehlswirtschaft in der deutschen Rüstung und Expansion 1936-1944. Göttingen.

Moltmann, Günter (1961). Weltherrschaftsideen Hitlers. In: **Brunner/Gerhard** (Hg.) 1961: 197-240.

Moltmann, Günter (1969). Isolation oder Intervention. Ein Prinzipienkonflikt amerikanischer Europapolitik im 19. Jahrhundert. In: *HZ*, 208, 1, 24-51.

Moltmann, Günter (1973). Die weltpolitische Lage 1936-1939: Die USA. In: **Hauser** (Hg.) 1973: 146-166.

Moltmann, Günter (1976). Deutscher Anti-Amerikanismus heute und früher. In: **Franz** (Hg.) 1976: 85-105.

Mommsen, Hans (1981). Hitlers Stellung im natinalsozialistischen Herrschafts-system. In: **Hirschfeld/Kettenacker** (Hg.) 1981: 43-72.

Mommsen, Hans/**Petzina**, Dietmar/**Weisbrod**, Bernd (Hg.) (1977). Industrielles System und politische Entwicklung in der Weimarer Republik. 2 Bde. 2. Aufl. Düsseldorf.

Monsen, R. Joseph, Jr./**Downs**, Anthony (1968). A Theory of Large Managerial Firms. In: **Russett** (Hg.) 1968: 343-362.

Morin, Edgar et.al. (1992). Einen neuen Anfang wagen. Überlegungen für das 21. Jahrhundert. Hamburg.

Morris, Peter J.T. (1982). The Development of Acetylene Chemistry and Synthetic Rubber by I.G. Farbenindustrie Aktiengesellschaft: 1926-1945. Diss. Oxford.

Mosley, Leonard (1980). Blood Relations. The Rise and Fall of the du Ponts of Delaware. New York.

Mueller, John (1989). Retreat from Doomsday. The Obsolescence of Major War. New York.

Müller, Harald (1993). Die Chance der Kooperation. Regime in den internationalen Beziehungen. Darmstadt.

Müller, Klaus-Jürgen (1987). Armee und Drittes Reich 1933-1939. Darstellung und Dokumentation. Paderborn.

Murray, Williamson (1984). The Change in the European Balance of Power, 1938-1939. The Path to Ruin. Princeton, N.J.

Nadolny, Sten (1978). Abrüstungsdiplomatie 1932/33. Deutschland auf der Genfer Konferenz im Übergang von Weimar zu Hitler. München.

Neal, Larry (1979). The Economics and Finance of Bilateral Clearing Agreements: Germany, 1934-38. In: *EHR*, 32, 3, 391-404.

Neuendorf, Gerhard (1976). Das Eindringen der IG-Farbenindustrie AG in Lateinamerika 1932-45. Diss. Halle.

Neumann, Franz L. (1986a). Ökonomie und Politik im zwanzigsten Jahrhundert. In: **Neumann** 1986: 248-260.

Neumann, Franz L. (1986). Demokratischer und autoritärer Staat. Studien zur politischen Theorie. Hrsg. von Herbert Marcuse. Frankfurt/M.

Nevins, Allan/**Hill**, Frank E. (1957). Ford. Expansion and Challenge 1915-1933. New York.

Nevins, Allan/**Hill**, Frank E. (1963). Ford. Decline and Rebirth 1933-1962. New York.

Niedhart, Gottfried (1978). Appeasement. In: *HZ*, 226, 1, 67-88.

Niedhart, Gottfried (1989). Internationale Beziehungen 1917-1947. Paderborn – München – Wien – Zürich.

Nipperdey, Thomas (1978). 1933 und Kontinuität der deutschen Geschichte. In: *HZ*, 227, 1, 86-111.

Nussbaum, Helga (1989). International Cartels and Multinational Enterprise. In **Teichova/Lévy-Leboyer/Nussbaum** (Hg.) 1989: 131-144.

Nye, Joseph S., Jr. (1990). The Changing Nature of World Power. In: *PSQ*, 105, 2, 177-192.

Offner, Arnold A. (1969). American Appeasement. United States Foreign Policy and Germany, 1933-1938. Cambridge, Mass.

Offner, Arnold A. (1986a). Forschungen zum deutsch-amerikanischen Verhältnis. Eine kritische Stellungnahme. In: **Trommler** (Hg.) 1986: 514-527.

Offner, Arnold A. (1986b). The Origins of the Second World War. American Foreign Policy and World Politics, 1917-1941. Reprint Malabor, Florida.

OMGUS (1986). Ermittlungen gegen die I.G. Farbenindustrie AG September 1945. Nördlingen.

Overy, Richard J. (1982). Hitler's War and the German Economy: A Reinterpretation. In: *EHR*, 35, 2, 272-291.

Oye, Kenneth A. (1985). The Sterling-Dollar-Franc Triangle: Monetary Diplomacy 1929-1937. In: *WP*, 38, 1, 173-199.

Pal, Leslie A. (1991). The State in Mind: The Future of the Nation-State. In: **Pal/Schultze** (Hg.) 1991: 361-377.

Pal, Leslie A./**Schultze**, Rainer-Olaf (Hg.) (1991). The Nation State versus Continental Integration: Canada in North America – Germany in Europe. Bochum.

Pastor, Robert A. (1980). Congress and the Politics of U.S. Foreign Economic Policy 1929-1976. Berkeley – Los Angeles – London.

Perlmutter, Howard V. (1973). The Tortuous Evolution of the Multinational Corporation. In: **Kapoor/Grub** (Hg.) 1973: 53-66.

Petzina, Dieter (1968a). Autarkiepolitik im Dritten Reich. Der nationalsozialistische Vierjahresplan. Stuttgart.

Petzina, Dieter (1968b). IG-Farben und nationalsozialistische Autarkiepolitik. In: *Tradition*, 13, 2, 250-254.

Petzina, Dietmar (1975). Vierjahresplan und Rüstungspolitik. In: **Forstmeier/Volkmann** (Hg.) 1975: 65-80.

Petzina, Dietmar/**Abelshauser**, Werner/**Faust**, Anselm (Hg.) (1978): Sozialgeschichtliches Arbeits-buch. Bd. III: Materialien zur Statistik des Deutschen Reiches 1914-1945. München.

Plumpe, Gottfried (1990). Die I.G. Farbenindustrie AG. Wirtschaft, Technik und Politik 1904-1945. Berlin.

Pohl, Hans (1983). Commentary. In: **Teichova/Cottrell** (Hg.) 1983: 203-206.

Pohl, Hans (Hg.) (1989). Wilhelm Treue. Unternehmens- und Unternehmergeschichte aus fünf Jahrzehnten. Stuttgart.

Pohl, Hans (Hg.) (1992). Der Einfluß ausländischer Unternehmen auf die deutsche Wirtschaft vom Spätmittelalter bis zur Gegenwart. *Zeitschrift für Unternehmensgeschichte*, Beiheft 65. Stuttgart.

Pommerin, Reiner (1977). Das Dritte Reich und Lateinamerika. Die deutsche Politik gegenüber Süd- und Mittelamerika 1939-1942. Düsseldorf.

Popple, Charles Sterling (1952). Standard Oil Company (New Jersey) in World War II. New York.

Possin, H. (1965). Die ökonomischen, militärischen und politischen Ergebnisse aus Monopolvereinbarungen der IG-Farbenindustrie AG mit amerikanischen Monopolen und deren Bedeutung für die Vorbereitung und Durchführung des II. Weltkrieges. Diss. Halle.

Predöhl, Andreas (1953). Die Epochenbedeutung der Weltwirtschaftskrise von 1929 bis 1931. In: *VfZ*, 1, 1, 97-118.

Prinz, Michael/**Zitelmann**, Rainer (Hg.) (1991). Nationalsozialismus und Modernisierung. Darmstadt.

Radkau, Joachim (1976). Entscheidungsprozesse und Entscheidungsdefizite in der deutschen Außenwirtschaftspolitik 1933-1940. In: *GG*, 2, 1, 33-65.

Randall, Stephen J. (1972). Colombia, the United States, and Interamerican Aviation Rivalry, 1927-1940. In: *JISWA*, 14, 3, 297-324.

Range, Willard (1959). Franklin D. Roosevelt's World Order. Athens.

Reader, William J. (1975). Imperial Chemical Industries. A History. Vol. 2: The First Quarter-Century 1926-1952. London – New York – Toronto.

Recker, Marie-Luise (1990). Die Außenpolitik des Dritten Reiches. München.

Reich, Robert B. (1992). The Work of Nations. Preparing Ourselves for 21st-Century Capitalism. New York.

Reid, Procter Page (1989). Private and Public Regimes: International Cartelization of the Electrical Equipment Industry in an Era of Hegemonic Change, 1919-1939. Diss. Washington D.C.

Remak, Joachim (1955). Hitlers Amerikapolitik. Das Auswärtige Amt dachte anders. In: *AP*, 6, 11, 706-714.

Renouvin, Pierre/**Duroselle**, Jean-Baptiste (1968). Introduction to the History of International Relations. Oxford.

Rich, Norman (1973). Hitler's War Aims. Ideology, the Nazi State, and the Course of Expansion. New York.

Riemenschneider, Michael (1987). Die deutsche Wirtschaftspolitik gegenüber Ungarn 1933-1944. Ein Beitrag zur Interdependenz von Wirtschaft und Politik unter dem Nationalsozialismus. Frankfurt/M. – Bern – New York – Paris.

Rieselbach, Leroy N. (1966). The Roots of Isolationism. Congressional Voting and Presidential Leadership in Foreign Policy. Indianapolis – New York – Kansas City.

Riesser, Hans E. (1969). Haben die deutschen Diplomaten versagt? Eine Kritik an der Kritik von Bismarck bis heute. Bonn.

Ritschl, Albrecht (1990). Zum Verhältnis von Markt und Staat in Hitlers Weltbild. Überlegungen zu einer Forschungskontroverse. In: **Backes/Jesse/Zitelmann** (Hg.) 1990: 243-264.

Ritschl, Albrecht (1991). Die NS-Wirtschaftsideologie – Modernisierungsprogramm oder reaktionäre Utopie. In: **Prinz/Zitelmann** (Hg.) 1991: 48-70.

Ritschl, Albrecht (1992). Wirtschaftspolitik im Dritten Reich – Ein Überblick. In: **Bracher/Funke/Jacobsen** (Hg.) 1992: 118-134.

Rittberger, Volker (Hg.) (1990). Theorien der Internationalen Beziehungen. Bestandsaufnahme und Forschungsperspektiven. Opladen.

Rose, Klaus (Hg.) (1966). Theorie der internationalen Wirtschaftsbeziehungen. 2. Aufl. Köln – Berlin.

Rosecrance, Richard (1987). Der neue Handelsstaat. Herausforderungen für Politik und Wirtschaft. Frankfurt/M.

Rosellen, Hanns-Peter (1986). '... und trotzdem vorwärts'. Die dramatische Entwicklung von Ford in Deutschland 1903 bis 1945. Frankfurt/M.

Rosenau, James N. (1990). Turbulence in World Politics. A Theory of Change and Continuity. Princeton, N.J.

Rosenbaum, Herbert D./**Bartelme**, Elizabeth (Hg.) (1987). Franklin D. Roosevelt. The Man, the Myth, the Era, 1882-1945. New York – Westport, Conn. – London.

Ruggie, John G. (1975). International Responses to Technology: Concepts and Trends. In: *IO*, 29, 3, 557-583.

Ruggie, John G. (1986). Continuity and Transformation in the World Polity: Toward a Neorealist Synthesis. In: **Keohane** (Hg.) 1986: 131-157.

Ruloff, Dieter (1988). Weltstaat oder Staatenwelt? Über die Chancen globaler Zusammenarbeit. München.

Rummel, Rudolph (1983). Libertarianism and International Violence. In: *JCR*, 27, 1, 27-71.

Rupieper, Hermann-Josef (1984). Das amerikanische Deutschlandbild der Zwischenkriegszeit. In: **Köhler** (Hg.) 1984: 131-139.

Russet, Bruce M. (Hg.) (1968). Economic Theories of International Politics. Chicago.

Ryan, Halford R. (1988). Franklin D. Roosevelt's Rhetorical Presidency. New York – Westport, Conn. – London.

Sagladin, Vadim (1990). Und jetzt Weltinnenpolitik. Rosenheim.

Sampson, Anthony (1973). The Sovereign State of ITT. New York.

Schäfer, Peter (1960). Die Beziehungen zwischen Deutschland und den Vereinigten Staaten 1933-1939. Diss. Berlin (Ost).

Scharpf, Fritz W. (1991). Die Handlungsfähigkeit des Staates am Ende des zwanzigsten Jahrhunderts. In: *PVS*, 32, 4, 621-634.

Schausberger, Norbert (1970). Wirtschaftliche Aspekte des Anschlusses Österreichs an das Deutsche Reich. In: *MGM*, 2, 133-165.

Schausberger, Norbert (1976). Österreich und die nationalsozialistische Außenpolitik. In: **Funke** (Hg.) 1976: 728-756.

Schiemann, Jürgen (1980). Die deutsche Währung in der Weltwirtschaftskrise 1929-1933. Währungspolitik und Abwertungskontroverse unter den Bedingungen der Reparationen. Bern – Stuttgart.

Schmidt, Gustav (1981). England in der Krise. Grundzüge und Grundlagen der britischen Appeasement-Politik 1930-1937. Wiesbaden.

Schmiederer, Ursula (1973). Systemkonkurrenz als Strukturprinzip der internationalen Politik. In: **Gantzel** (Hg.) 1973: 309-346.

Schoenbaum, David (1980). Die braune Revolution. Eine Sozialgeschichte des Dritten Reiches. München.

Schoenthal, Klaus F. (1959). American Attitudes toward Germany, 1918-1932. Diss. Ohio State University.

Schreiber, Gerhard (1984). Hitler. Interpretationen 1923-1983. Ergebnisse, Methoden und Probleme der Forschung. Darmstadt.

Schreier, Anna Elizabeth/**Wex**, Manuela (1990). Chronik der Hoechst Aktiengesellschaft 1863-1988. Frankfurt/M.

Schröder, Hans-Jürgen (1969). Die 'neue deutsche Südamerikapolitik'. Dokumente zur nationalsozialistischen Wirtschaftspolitik in Lateinamerika von 1934 bis 1936. In: *JfG*, 6, 337-451.

Schröder, Hans-Jürgen (1970a). Deutschland und die Vereinigten Staaten von Amerika 1933-1939. Wirtschaft und Politik in der Entwicklung des deutsch-amerikanischen Gegensatzes. Wiesbaden.

Schröder, Hans-Jürgen (1970b). Die Vereinigten Staaten und die nationalsozialistische Handelspolitik gegenüber Lateinamerika 1937/38. In: *JfG*, 7, 309-371.

Schröder, Hans-Jürgen (1976a). Das Dritte Reich, die USA und Lateinamerika 1933-1941. In: **Funke** (Hg.) 1976: 339-364.

Schröder, Hans-Jürgen (1976b). Der Aufbau der deutschen Hegemonialstellung in Südosteuropa 1933-1936. In: **Funke** (Hg.) 1976: 757-773.

Schröder, Hans-Jürgen (1976c). Deutsche Südosteuropapolitik 1929-1936. Zur Kontinuität deutscher Außenpolitik in der Weltwirtschaftskrise. In: *GG*, 2, 1, 5-32.

Schröder, Hans-Jürgen (1978). Das Dritte Reich und die USA. In: **Knapp et.al.** 1978: 107-152.

Schröder, Hans-Jürgen (1982). Economic Appeasement. Zur britischen und amerikanischen Deutschlandpolitik vor dem Zweiten Weltkrieg. In: *VfZ*, 30, 1, 82-97.

Schröder, Hans-Jürgen (1984). Machtpolitik und Ökonomie. Zur nationalsozialistischen Außenpolitik im Jahre 1938. In: **Knipping/Müller** (Hg.) 1984: 211-222.

Schröder, Hans-Jürgen (1986). Deutsch-amerikanische Beziehungen im 20. Jahrhundert. Geschichtsschreibung und Forschungsperspektiven. In: **Trommler** (Hg.) 1986: 491-513.

Schröter, Harm G. (1983a). Außenpolitik und Wirtschaftsinteresse. Skandinavien im außenwirtschaftlichen Kalkül Deutschlands und Großbritanniens 1918-1939. Frankfurt/M. – Bern – New York.

Schröter, Harm G. (1983b). Siemens and Central and South-East Europe between the two World Wars. In: **Teichova/Cottrell** (Hg.) 1983: 173-192.

Schröter, Harm G. (1987). Kartelle als Form industrieller Konzentration: Das Beispiel des internationalen Farbstoffkartells von 1927 bis 1939. In: *VSWG*, 74, 4, 479-513.

Schröter, Harm G. (1989). A Typical Factor of German International Market Strategy: Agreements Between the US and German Electrotechnical Industries up to 1939. In: **Teichova/Lévy-Leboyer/Nussbaum** (Hg.) 1989: 160-170.

Schröter, Harm G./**Wurm**, Clemens A. (Hg.) (1991). Politik, Wirtschaft und Internationale Beziehungen. Studien zu ihrem Verhältnis in der Zeit zwischen den Weltkriegen. Mainz.

Schröter, Verena (1983). The IG Farbenindustrie AG in Central and South-East Europe, 1926-38. In: **Teichova/Cottrell** (Hg.) 1983: 173-192.

Schröter, Verena (1984). Die deutsche Industrie auf dem Weltmarkt 1929-1932. Außenwirtschaftliche Strategien unter dem Druck der Weltwirtschaftskrise. Frankfurt/M. – Bern – New York – Nancy.

Schröter, Verena (1989). Participation in Market Control through Foreign Investment: IG Farbenindustrie AG in the United States: 1920-1938. In: **Teichova/ Lévy-Leboyer/Nussbaum** (Hg.) 1989: 171-184.

Schüler, Andreas (1990). Erfindergeist und Technikkritik. Der Beitrag Amerikas zur Modernisierung und die Technikdebatte seit 1900. Stuttgart.

Schuker, Stephen A. (1985). American 'Reparations' to Germany, 1919-1933. In: **Feldman** (Hg.) 1985: 335-384.

Schulz, Gerhard (1980). Reparationen und Krisenprobleme nach dem Wahlsieg der NSDAP 1930. Betrachtungen zur Regierung Brüning. In: *VSWG*, 67, 2, 200-222.

Schulz, Gerhard (Hg.) (1985). Die Große Krise der dreißiger Jahre. Vom Niedergang der Weltwirtschaft zum Zweiten Weltkrieg. Göttingen.

Schwabe, Klaus (1971). Deutsche Revolution und Wilson-Frieden. Die amerikanische und deutsche Friedensstrategie zwischen Ideologie und Machtpolitik 1918/19. Düsseldorf.

Schwabe, Klaus (1975). Der amerikanische Isolationismus im 20. Jahrhundert. Legende und Wirklichkeit. Wiesbaden.

Schwabe, Klaus (1976). Anti-Americanism within the German Right 1917-1933. In: *AmSt*, 21, 1, 89-107.

Schwabe, Klaus (1977). Die entfernteren Staaten am Beispiel der Vereinigten Staaten von Amerika – Weltpolitische Verantwortung gegen nationale Isolation. In: **Forndran/Golczewski/Riesenberger** (Hg.) 1977: 277-294.

Schwabe, Klaus (1982). Die Regierung Roosevelt und die Expansionspolitik Hitlers vor dem Zweiten Weltkrieg. Appeasement als Folge eines 'Primats der Innenpolitik'?. In: **Rohe** (Hg.) 1982: 103-132.

Schwabe, Klaus (1985). Die Ära Roosevelt in der Geschichte der Vereinigten Staaten und ihr Einfluß auf die Weltpolitik. In: **Schulz** (Hg.) 1985: 200-214.

Schwabe, Klaus (1986). Die Vereinigten Staaten und die Weimarer Republik. Das Scheitern einer 'besonderen Beziehung'. In: **Trommler** (Hg.) 1986: 367-378.

Schwabe, Klaus (Hg.) (1982). Das diplomatische Korps 1871-1945. Boppard am Rhein.

Schweitzer, Arthur (1962). Der organisierte Kapitalismus. Die Wirtschaftsordnung in der ersten Phase der nationalsozialistischen Herrschaft. In: *HJWG*, 7, 32-47.

Scott, Andrew M. (1977). The Logic of International Interaction. In: *ISQ*, 21,3, 429-460.

Seabury, Paul (1956). Die Wilhelmstraße. Die Geschichte der deutschen Diplomatie 1930-1945. Frankfurt/M.

Seherr-Thoss, H.C. Graf von (1974). Die deutsche Automobilindustrie. Eine Dokumentation von 1886 bis heute. Stuttgart.

Seitz, Konrad (1991). Die japanisch-amerikanische Herausforderung. Deutschlands Hochtechnologie-Industrien kämpfen ums Überleben. 2. Aufl. München.

Senghaas, Dieter (1992). Weltinnenpolitik – Ansätze für ein Konzept. In: *EA*, 47, 22, 643-652.

Senghaas, Dieter (1994). Wohin driftet die Welt? Über die Zukunft friedlicher Koexistenz. Frankfurt/M.

Senghaas, Dieter (Hg.) (1979). Kapitalistische Weltökonomie. Kontroversen über ihren Ursprung und ihre Entwicklungsdynamik. Frankfurt/M.

Siebert, Horst (1989). Außenwirtschaft. 4. völlig neubearb. und erw. Aufl. Stuttgart.

Siemens, Georg (1960). Carl Friedrich von Siemens. Ein großer Unternehmer. Freiburg – München.

Siemens, Georg (1961a). Der Weg der Elektrotechnik. Geschichte des Hauses Siemens. Bd. 1: Die Zeit der freien Unternehmung 1847-1910. Freiburg – München.

Siemens, Georg (1961b). Der Weg der Elektrotechnik. Geschichte des Hauses Siemens. Bd. 2: Das Zeitalter der Weltkriege 1910-1945. Freiburg – München.

Singer, J. David (1961). The Level-of-Analysis Problem in International Relations. In: **Knorr/Verba** (Hg.) 1961: 77-92.

Sloan, Alfred P. (1965). Meine Jahre mit General Motors. München.

Smith, Adam (1974). Der Wohlstand der Nationen. Eine Untersuchung seiner Natur und seiner Ursachen. München.

Snell, Bradford C. (1974). American Ground Transport. A Proposal for Restructuring the Automobile, Truck, Bus, and Rail Industries. Submitted to the Subcommittee on Antitrust and Monopoly of the Committee on the Judiciary United States Senate, 93. Congress. Washington.

Snidal, Duncan (1985). The Limits of Hegemonic Stability Theory. In: *IO*, 39, 4, 579-614.

Sohn-Rethel, Alfred (1981). Ökonomie und Klassenstruktur des deutschen Faschismus. Aufzeichnungen und Analysen. Hrsg. von Johannes Agnoli et.al. 3. Aufl. Frankfurt/M.

Solom, Rudolf (1949). Die Handelsbeziehungen zwischen Deutschland und den Vereinigten Staaten von Amerika von 1871-1937. Diss. Köln.

Sprout, Harold/**Sprout**, Margaret. (1974). Multiple Vulnerabilities. The Context of Environmental Repair and Protection. Princeton, N.J.

Stead, William T. (1972). The Americanization of the World or The Trend of the Twentieth Century. Reprint (1902). New York – London.

Stein, Arthur A. (1982). Coordination and Collaboration: Regimes in an Anarchic World. In: **Krasner** (Hg.) 1982: 299-324.

Stelzner, Jürgen (1976). Arbeitsbeschaffung und Wiederaufrüstung 1933-1936. Nationalsozialistische Beschäftigungspolitik und Aufbau der Wehr- und Rüstungswirtschaft. Diss. Tübingen.

Stiller, Jesse H. (1987). George S. Messersmith. Diplomat of Democracy. Chapel Hill – London.

Stocking, George W./**Watkins**, Myron W. (1946). Cartels in Action. Case Studies in International Business Diplomacy. New York.

Stokes, Raymond G. (1985). The Oil Industry in Nazi Germany, 1936-1945. In: *BHR*, 59, 2, 254-277.

Stopford, John M./**Strange**, Susan/**Henley**, John S. (1993). Rival States, Rival Firms. Competition for World Market Shares. Cambridge.

Strange, Susan (1970). International Economics and International Relations. A Case of Mutual Neglect. In: *IA*, 46, 2, 304-315.

Strange, Susan (1982). Cave! Hic Dragones: A Critique of Regime Analysis. In: **Krasner** (Hg.) 1982: 479-496.

Strange, Susan (1985). Protectionism and World Politics. In: *IO*, 39, 2, 233-259.

Strange, Susan (1987). Supranationals and the State. In: **Hall** (Hg.) 1987: 289-305.

Strange, Susan (1988). States and Markets. An Introduction to International Political Economy. London.

Strange, Susan (1992). States, Firms and Diplomacy. In: *IA*, 68, 1, 1-15.

Strasser, Otto (1969). Mein Kampf. Eine politische Autobiographie. Frankfurt/M.

Stratmann, Friedrich (1985). Chemische Industrie unter Zwang? Staatliche Einflußnahme am Beispiel der chemischen Industrie Deutschlands 1933-1949. Stuttgart.

Stromberg, Roland N. (1953). American Business and the Approach of War 1935-1941. In: *JEH*, 13, 1, 58-78.

Stürmer, Michael (Hg.) (1980). Die Weimarer Republik. Belagerte Civitas. Königstein/Ts.

Sundhaussen, Holm (1976a). Die Weltwirtschaftskrise im Donau-Balkan-Raum und ihre Bedeutung für den Wandel der deutschen Außenpolitik unter Brüning. In: **Benz/Graml** (Hg.) 1976: 121-164.

Sundhaussen, Holm (1976b). Politisches und wirtschaftliches Kalkül in den Auseinandersetzungen über die deutsch-rumänischen Präferenzvereinbarungen von 1931. Ein Beitrag zur Vorgeschichte des deutschen 'Informal Empire' in Südosteuropa. In: *RESE*, XIV, 3, 405-424.

Swatek, Dieter (1972). Unternehmenskonzentration als Ergebnis und Mittel nationalsozialistischer Wirtschaftspolitik. Berlin.

Tammen, Helmut (1978). Die IG Farbenindustrie Aktiengesellschaft 1925-1933. Ein Chemiekonzern in der Weimarer Republik. Berlin.

Taylor, Graham D./**Sudnik**, Patricia E. (1984). Du Pont and the International Chemical Industry. Boston.

Teichert, Eckart (1984). Autarkie und Großraumwirtschaft in Deutschland 1930-1939. Außenwirtschaftliche Konzeptionen zwischen Wirtschaftskrise und Zweitem Weltkrieg. München.

Teichova, Alice (1974). An Economic Background to Munich. International Business and Czechoslovakia 1918-1939. London – New York.

Teichova, Alice/**Cottrell**, P.L. (Hg.) (1983). International Business and Central Europe, 1918-1939. New York.

Teichova, Alice/**Lévy-Leboyer**, Maurice/**Nussbaum**, Helga (Hg.) (1989). Multinational Enterprise in Historical Perspective. Reprint. Cambridge – Paris.

Teltschik, Walter (1992). Geschichte der deutschen Großchemie. Entwicklung und Einfluß in Staat und Gesellschaft. Weinheim – New York – Basel – Cambridge.

Ter Meer, Fritz (1953). Die I.G. Farben Industrie Aktiengesellschaft. Ihre Entstehung, Entwicklung und Bedeutung. Düsseldorf.

Tetsuo, Abo (1991). ITT's International Business Activities, 1920-1940: The Remarkable Advance and Setback of a „Pure International Utility Company". In: **Wilkins** (Hg.) 1991: 512-536.

Thielenhaus, Marion (1985). Zwischen Anpassung und Widerstand: Deutsche Diplomaten 1938-1941. Die politischen Aktivitäten der Beamtengruppe um Ernst von Weizsäcker im Auswärtigen Amt. 2. durchgesehene Aufl. Paderborn.

Thies, Jochen (1980). Architekt der Weltherrschaft. Die 'Endziele' Hitlers. Reprint. Düsseldorf.

Thies, Jochen (1983). Hitlers 'Endziele': Zielloser Aktionismus, Kontinentalimperium oder Weltherrschaft? In: **Bracher/Funke/Jacobsen** (Hg.) 1983: 390-406.

Thomas, Georg (1966). Geschichte der deutschen Wehr- und Rüstungswirtschaft (1918-1943/45). Hrsg. von Wolfgang Birkenfeld. Boppard am Rhein.

Thomson, Janice E. (1992). Explaining the Regulation of Transnational Practices: A State-Building Approach. In: **Czempiel/Rosenau** (Hg.) 1992: 195-218.

Thomson, Janice E./**Krasner**, Stephen D. (1989). Global Transactions and the Consolidation of Sovereignty. In: **Czempiel/Rosenau** (Hg.) 1989: 195-219.

Thorp, Willard L. (1960). Trade Barriers and National Security. In: *AER*, 50, 2, 433-442.

Thurow, Lester C. (1992). Head to Head. The Coming Economic Battle Among Japan, Europe, and America. New York.

Treue, Wilhelm (1953). Das Dritte Reich und die Westmächte auf dem Balkan. Zur Struktur der Außenhandelspolitik Deutschlands, Großbritanniens und Frankreichs 1933-1939. In: *VfZ*, 1, 1, 45-64.

Treue, Wilhelm (1955). Hitlers Denkschrift zum Vierjahresplan 1936. In: *VfZ*, 3, 2, 184-210.

Treue, Wilhelm (1989). Das Verhältnis des Unternehmers zur Politik und zum Staat. In: **Pohl** (Hg.) 1989: 54-81.

Trommler, Frank (Hg.) (1986). Amerika und die Deutschen. Bestandsaufnahme einer 300jährigen Geschichte. Opladen.

Trute, Hellmut (1968). 50 Jahre Wirtschaftsverband der Elektroindustrie. In: **Zentralverband** (Hg.) 1968: 43-68.

Tucker, Robert W. (1977). The Inequality of Nations. New York.

Tudyka, Kurt P. (1984). Transnationale Konzerne. In: **Boeckh** (Hg.) 1984: 482-486.

Tudyka, Kurt P. (1990). Politische Ökonomie der internationalen Beziehungen. In: **Rittberger** (Hg.) 1990: 130-150.

Tudyka, Kurt P. (Hg.) (1974). Multinationale Unternehmen und Gewerkschaftsstrategie. Hamburg.

Tussing, Werner (1970). Die internationalen Eisen- und Stahlkartelle. Ihre Entstehung, Entwicklung und Bedeutung zwischen den beiden Weltkriegen. Diss. Köln.

United Nations. Department of Economic Affairs (1949). International Capital Movements During the Inter-War Period. Lake Success, New York.

Verba, Sidney (1961). Assumptions of Rationality and Non-Rationality in Models of the International System. In: **Knorr/Verba** (Hg.) 1961: 93-117.

Verg, Erik (1988). Meilensteine. 125 Jahre Bayer 1863-1988. Die Geschichte von Bayer in 130 Kapiteln. Leverkusen.

Vernon, Raymond (1971). Sovereignty at Bay. The Multinational Spread of U.S. Enterprises. London.

Vogel, Detlef (1989). Deutschland und Südosteuropa. Von politisch-wirtschaftlicher Einflußnahme zur offenen Gewaltanwendung und Unterdrückung. In: **Michalka** (Hg.) 1989: 532-550.

Volkmann, Hans-Erich (1975). Außenhandel und Aufrüstung in Deutschland 1933 bis 1939. In: **Forstmeier/Volkmann** (Hg.) 1975: 81-113.

Volkmann, Hans-Erich (1976a). Ökonomie und Machtpolitik. Lettland und Estland im politisch-ökonomischen Kalkül des Dritten Reiches (1933-1940). In: *GG*, 2, 4, 471-500.

Volkmann, Hans-Erich (1976b). Politik, Wirtschaft und Aufrüstung unter dem Nationalsozialismus. In: **Funke** (Hg.) 1976: 269-291.

Volkmann, Hans-Erich (1989). Polen im politisch-wirtschaftlichen Kalkül des Dritten Reiches 1933-1939. In: **Michalka** (Hg.) 1989: 74-92.

Waldmann, Peter (1975). Zeit und Wandel als Grundbestandteile sozialer Systeme. In: **Bühl** (Hg.) 1975: 132-150.

Wall, Bennett H./**Gibb**, George S. (1974). Teagle of Jersey Standard. New Orleans.

Wallerstein, Immanuel (1979). Aufstieg und künftiger Niedergang des kapitalistischen Weltsystems. Zur Grundlegung vergleichender Analyse. In: **Senghaas** (Hg.) 1979: 31-67.

Waltz, Kenneth N. (1968). Man, the State and War. A Theoretical Analysis. 6. Aufl. New York – London.

Waltz, Kenneth N. (1971). The Myth of National Interdependence. In: **Kindleberger** (Hg.). 1971: 205-223.

Waltz, Kenneth N. (1979). Theory of International Politics. Reading, Mass.

Waltz, Kenneth N. (1986). Reflections on 'Theory of International Politics': A Response to My Critics. In: **Keohane** (Hg.) 1986: 322-345.

Wandel, Eckhard (1971). Die Bedeutung der Vereinigten Staaten von Amerika für das deutsche Reparationsproblem 1924-1929. Tübingen.

Wandschneider, Hermann (1970). Pläne der deutschen Elektrokonzerne zur 'Neuordnung der europäischen Wirtschaft' im zweiten Weltkrieg. In: *JfW*, IV, 219-243.

Weber, Eckhard (1971). Stadien der Außenhandelsverflechtung Ostmittel- und Südosteuropas. Stuttgart.

Weede, Erich (1989). Der ökonomische Erklärungsansatz in der Internationalen Politik. In: *PVS*, 30, 2, 254-272.

Wegner, Bernd (1982). Hitlers Politische Soldaten: Die Waffen-SS 1933-1945. Studien zu Leitbild, Struktur und Funktion einer nationalsozialistischen Elite. Paderborn.

Wehler, Hans-Ulrich (1970). Krisenherde des Kaiserreichs 1871-1918. Studien zur deutschen Sozial- und Verfassungsgeschichte. Göttingen.

Wehler, Hans-Ulrich (Hg.) (1974). Sozialgeschichte heute. Festschrift für Hans Rosenberg zum 70. Geburtstag. Göttingen.

Weigelt, Klaus (Hg.) (1986). Das Deutschland- und Amerikabild. Beiträge zum gegenseitigen Verständnis beider Völker. Melle.

Weiher, Sigfrid von/**Goetzeler**, Herbert (1981). Weg und Wirken der Siemens-Werke im Fortschritt der Elektrotechnik 1847-1980. Ein Beitrag zur Geschichte der Elektroindustrie. 3. neubearb. und erw. Aufl. Wiesbaden.

Weinberg, Gerhard L. (1986). Von der Konfrontation zur Kooperation. Deutschland und die Vereinigten Staaten 1933-1949. In: **Trommler** (Hg.) 1986: 393-405.

Weinberg, Gerhard L. (1963). Schachts Besuch in den USA im Jahre 1933. In: *VfZ*, 11, 2, 166-180.

Weinberg, Gerhard L. (1964). Hitler's Image of the United States. In: *AHR*, 69, 4, 1006-1021.

Weinberg, Gerhard L. (1970). The Foreign Policy of Hitler's Germany. Vol. 1: Diplomatic Revolution in Europe 1933-36. Chicago – London.

Weinberg, Gerhard L. (1980). The Foreign Policy of Hitler's Germany. Vol. 2: Starting World War II 1937-1939. Chicago – London.

Weinberg, Gerhard L. (1983). Deutschlands Wille zum Krieg. Die internationalen Beziehungen 1937-1939. In: **Bracher/Funke/Jacobsen** (Hg.) 1983: 407-426.

Weinberg, Gerhard L. (1986). Deutschland und Amerika 1917 bis 1949. In: **Weigelt** (Hg.) 1986: 21-28.

Weizsäcker, Ernst U. von (1992). Erdpolitik. Ökologische Realpolitik an der Schwelle zum Jahrhundert der Umwelt. 3. aktual. Aufl. Darmstadt.

Wendt, Alexander E. (1987). The Agent-Structure Problem in International Relations Theory. In: *IO*, 41, 3, 335-370.

Wendt, Bernd-Jürgen (1971). Economic Appeasement. Handel und Finanz in der britischen Deutschlandpolitik 1933-1939. Düsseldorf.

Wendt, Bernd-Jürgen (1981). Südosteuropa in der nationalsozialistischen Großraumwirtschaft. Eine Antwort auf Alan S. Milward. In: **Hirschfeld/Kettenacker** (Hg.) 1981: 414-428.

Wendt, Bernd-Jürgen (1983). Commentary. In: **Teichova/Cottrell** (Hg.) 1983: 196-203.

Wendt, Bernd-Jürgen (1984). Nationalsozialistische Großraumwirtschaft zwischen Utopie und Wirklichkeit – Zum Scheitern einer Konzeption 1938/39. In: **Knipping/Müller** (Hg.) 1984: 223-245.

Wendt, Bernd-Jürgen (1987). Großdeutschland. Außenpolitik und Kriegs-vorbereitung des Hitler-Regimes. München.

Wendt, Bernd-Jürgen (1990). Durch das 'strategische Fenster' in den Zweiten Welt-krieg. Die Motive Hitlers. In: **Backes/Jesse/Zitelmann** (Hg.) 1990: 344-374.

Wilkins, Mira (1974). The Maturing of Multinational Enterprise. American Business Abroad from 1914 to 1970. Cambridge.

Wilkins, Mira (Hg.) (1991). The Growth of Multinationals. Aldershot – Brookfield, VT.

Wilkins, Mira/**Hill**, Frank E. (1964). American Business Abroad. Ford on Six Conti-nents. Detroit.

Williams, William A. (1954). The Legend of Isolationism in the 1920's. In: *SaS*, 18, 1-20.

Williamson, Oliver E. (1968). A Dynamic Theory of Interfirm Behavior. In: **Russett** (Hg.) 1968: 209-228.

Wilson, Joan Hoff (1971). American Business and Foreign Policy 1920-1933. Lexington, KY.

Winnacker, Karl (1971). Nie den Mut verlieren. Erinnerungen an Schicksalsjahre der deutschen Chemie. Düsseldorf – Wien.

Wippermann, Wolfgang (1989). Der konsequente Wahn. Ideologie und Politik Adolf Hitlers. Gütersloh – München.

Wise, George (1985). Willis R. Whitney, General Electric, and the Origins of U.S. Industrial Research. New York.

Wolf, Gerhart (1970). Die BASF. Vom Werden eines Weltunternehmens. Lever-kusen.

Wolfers, Arnold (1962). Discord and Collaboration. Essays on International Politics. Baltimore.

Wollstein, Günter (1973). Vom Weimarer Revisionismus zu Hitler. Das Deutsche Reich und die Großmächte in der Anfangsphase der nationalsozialistischen Herrschaft in Deutschland. Bonn – Bad Godesberg.

Wollstein, Günter (1976). Die Politik des nationalsozialistischen Deutschlands gegenüber Polen 1933-1939/45. In: **Funke** (Hg.) 1976: 795-810.

Wriston, Walter B. (1991). Agents of Change Are Rarely Welcome. In: **Frieden/ Lake** (Hg.) 1991: 161-170.

Wulf, Jürgen (1968). Der deutsche Außenhandel seit 1850. Entwicklung, Struktur-wandlungen und Beziehungen zum Wirtschaftswachstum. Basel.

Wurm, Clemens A. (1988). Industrielle Interessenpolitik und Staat. Internationale Kartelle in der britischen Außen- und Wirtschaftspolitik während der Zwischenkriegszeit. Berlin – New York.

Wurm, Clemens A. (1989a). Handelsdiplomatie in der Weltwirtschaftskrise. Inter-nationale Kartelle, Stahl und Baumwolltextilien in der Außenpolitik Groß-britanniens 1924-1939. In: **Wurm** (Hg.) 1989: 103-150.

Wurm, Clemens A. (1989b). Politik und Wirtschaft in den Internationalen Beziehungen. Internationalen Kartelle, Außenpolitik und weltwirtschaftliche Beziehungen 1919-1939: Einführung. In: **Wurm** (Hg.) 1989: 1-31.

Wurm, Clemens A. (Hg.) (1989). Internationale Kartelle und Außenpolitik. Beiträge zur Zwischenkriegszeit. Stuttgart.

Young, Oran R. (1969). Interdependencies in World Politics. In: *IJ*, 24, Autumn, 726-750.

Young, Oran R. (1982). Regime Dynamics: The Rise and Fall of International Regimes. In: **Krasner** (Hg.) 1982: 277-297.

Zentralverband der Elektrotechnischen Industrie e.V. (Hg.) (1968). Elektrotechnik im Wandel der Zeit. 50 Jahre ZVEI. Mindelheim.

Ziebura, Gilbert (1984). Weltwirtschaft und Weltpolitik 1922/24-1931. Zwischen Rekonstruktion und Zusammenbruch. Frankfurt/M.

Zilg, Gerard Colby (1974). Du Pont Behind the Nylon Curtain. Englewood Cliffs, N.J.

Zilg, Gerard Colby (1984). Du Pont Dynasty. Secaucus, N.J.

Zitelmann, Rainer (1987). Hitler. Selbstverständnis eines Revolutionärs. Hamburg – Leamington – Spa – New York.

Zitelmann, Rainer (1989). Zur Begründung des 'Lebensraum'-Motivs in Hitlers Weltanschauung. In: **Michalka** (Hg.) 1989: 551-567.

Zürn, Michael (1992). Interessen und Institutionen in der internationalen Politik. Grundlegung und Anwendungen des situationsstrukturellen Ansatzes. Opladen.